Ab(

T.J. Coles is the author of *Your Brain in Quarantine: The Neuroscience of Human Isolation and Confinement*. A postdoctoral researcher at Plymouth University's Cognition Institute in the UK, where he studies blindness and visual impairment, his doctoral thesis *The Knotweed Factor* can be read online.

Coles also writes about politics and human rights for a number of publications including *CounterPunch*, *The London Economic*, *Newsweek*, *The New Statesman* and *Truthout*. His books include *The War on You* and *Capitalism and Coronavirus*.

By the same author

Britain's Secret Wars

The Great Brexit Swindle

President Trump, Inc.

Voices for Peace (ed.)

Human Wrongs

Fire and Fury

Real Fake News

Union Jackboot (with Matthew Alford)

Manufacturing Terrorism

Privatized Planet

Your Brain in Quarantine

The War on You

Capitalism and Coronavirus

WE'LL
TELL
YOU
WHAT
TO
THINK

Wikipedia, Propaganda
and the Making of Liberal Consensus

By

T.J. Coles

URSA MAJOR

Contents

Part I Structural Analysis

Part II Content Analyses

Acknowledgements

Thanks to Richard Keeble for his peer-review and to John Pilger for helpful comments about readability. Errors and shortcomings are entirely my own.

Glossary

BBC British Broadcasting Corporation
BBG Broadcasting Board of Governors
BDFL Benevolent Dictator for Life
BMEWS Ballistic Missile Early Warning System
BMJ *British Medical Journal*
CCTV Closed-circuit television
CFR Council on Foreign Relations
CGO Center for Grassroots Oversight
CIA Central Intelligence Agency
CIPR Chartered Institute of Public Relations
COVID-19 Coronavirus disease 2019
CREWE Corporate Representatives for Ethical
Wikipedia Engagement
DOE Department of Energy
EFF Electronic Frontier Foundation
EU European Union
FAO Food and Agriculture Organization of the
United Nations
FBI Federal Bureau of Investigation
FOIA Freedom of Information Act
GDP Gross domestic product
GNI Gross national income
HRW Human Rights Watch
IBC Iraq Body Count
ICAN International Campaign to Abolish Nuclear
Weapons
ICBM Intercontinental ballistic missile
ICJ International Court of Justice
ID Iraqi dinars

IMF International Monetary Fund
IPCC Intergovernmental Panel on Climate Change
IST International Studies Team
ISO International Organisation for Standardisation
KEI Knowledge Economy Index
LGBTQ+ Lesbian, Gay, Bisexual,
Transgender/Transsexual, Queer, Plus
MI6 Military Intelligence, Section Six
MAK Maktab al-Khidamat
MAD Mutual/mutually-assured destruction
MSM Mainstream media
NAFTA North American Free Trade Agreement
NASA National Aeronautics and Space
Administration
NATO North American Treaty Organization
NHS National Health Service
NHTSA National Highways and Traffic Safety
Administration
NPOV Neutral Point of View
NREL National Renewable Energy Laboratory
NSA National Security Agency
NSC National Security Council
OAS Organization of American States
OECD Organisation for Economic Co-operation and
Development
OSTP Office of Science and Technology Policy
PDPA People's Democratic Party of Afghanistan
PET Potential evapotranspiration
PLO Palestine Liberation Organization
RoK Republic of Korea (South Korea)
SAC Strategic Air Command
SAS Special Air Service
SOPA Stop Online Piracy Act

SSA Sub-Saharan Africa(n)
STEM Science, technology, engineering and mathematics
UN United Nations
UNICEF UN Children's Fund
UNSC UN Security Council
UNSCR UN Security Council Resolution
URL Uniform Resource Locator
USAID United States Agency for International Development
USSR Union of Soviet Socialist Republics
WEF World Information Forum
WMD Weapons of Mass Destruction
WMO World Meteorological Organization
WPC World Peace Council
WWII World War II
YES Yalta European Strategy
YGL Young Global Leader

Introduction
Normalizing Conflict of Interest

Wikipedia can be a useful tool for learning about celebrities, sports stars and science. But when it comes to politics, Wikipedia is a propaganda platform for corporations, politicians and public relations specialists to push agendas, shape narratives, ruin reputations, marginalize opponents, and build a consensus to support policies that most human beings oppose, such as big power rivalries, multilateral nuclear armaments and climate change.

Wikipedia is a major influencer. A few years ago, polling suggested that in the UK, more people trust Wikipedia than the BBC (64 percent to 61).[1] Indicative of its power, pages on the website caution users not to rely on it as a source of information, yet it is widely considered by the general public to be credible:

> Wikipedia is not a reliable source. Wikipedia can be edited by anyone at any time. This means that any information it contains at any particular time could be vandalism, a work in progress, or just plain wrong. Biographies of living persons, subjects that happen to be in the news, and politically or culturally contentious topics are especially vulnerable to these issues.

Edits on Wikipedia that are in error may eventually be fixed. However, because Wikipedia is a volunteer-run project, it cannot monitor every contribution all the time. There are many errors that remain unnoticed for days, weeks, months, or even years. Therefore, Wikipedia should *not* be considered a definitive source in and of itself. (Emphasis in original)[2]

Wikipedia is also an exercise in Orwellian doublethink. Despite being admittedly unreliable, it is seeking to shape the narrative around COVID-19. In 2020, escalation of coronavirus contagion was met with the following response from Wikipedia, a direct contradiction of the above quote: "With the uncertainty surrounding the outbreak of the [COVID-19] pandemic, we want to reassure our readers across the globe that our volunteers are working to bring you a trusted source of unbiased information." The message concludes: "Throughout these challenging times, knowledge must and will remain open for all."[3]

It was reported in November 2020 that the UK government's Scientific Advisory Group for Emergencies consulted Wikipedia.[4]

AGENDAS

When it comes to politics, Wikipedia serves power while convincingly presenting itself as the opposite of power: a non-hierarchical, egalitarian public service provider. Historian Daniel O'Sullivan argues that "Wikipedia has the potential to proliferate voices and dissent—and yet the increasingly bureaucratic 'policing' of its content ... means it is in danger of mirroring the typical knowledge economy of the West."[5] Funded by a politically-connected Foundation, maintained by an army of bots, filtered by an Arbitration Committee and constrained by editorial codes of conduct, the political entries on the free encyclopedia are typically biased in favor of Western interests and at times littered with errors.

This book documents cases of politically-motivated hacks vandalizing entries, the use of corporate-funded editors to boost the profile of big companies and denigrate opponents, the ruination of individuals' reputations via the creation of unjust biographies and the regular interference by intelligence agencies.

But a deeper problem is the fact that, unlike the broader public, the dedicated editors are educated, have the time to edit entries and are tech-savvy. Co-founder Larry Sanger said of the biases of editors: "the skills to marshal an argument, and represent the facts correctly are all skills encouraged by a solid liberal arts education. It's a problem associated more with a lack of training in the liberal arts."[6] This means that undereducated, employed and non-tech-savvy individuals, i.e., the broader population, haven't the time, skills or inclination to participate in editing Wikipedia. This has implications for the quality and slant of Wikipedia's content.

Sydow and the team found that diversity increases product quality. Their results "indicate that 'new' and 'old' editors in an article through exchanging their experience create articles of better quality."[7] But, as we shall see in Chapter 2, the old Wikipedian guard typically chases away the newbies, partly because of elitism and cliquishness and partly due to infiltration by paid public relations editors who foment mistrust. The underlying economic system of neoliberalism that creates class, wealth, education and opportunity divisions on all levels of society also influences the form and content of Wikipedia entries.

A scholarly study of Wikipedia finds that the average editor is "a young, well-educated, and affluent Western male with time and resources to invest in this voluntary activity."[8] Given their typical class backgrounds, it is probable that Wikipedia's editors will have a politically liberal bias. But this bias will likely be at the expense of any ideology, event, movement or individual considered to be a danger to "liberal" interests; be that enemy too far left or too far right. Surveys suggest that the overwhelming majority of Wikipedians are motivated by a desire for public service.[9]

However, well-meaning people operating within and refusing to challenge the structures of a global superpower, in this case the United States, are likely to reflect the interests of that superpower's elite. Co-founder Jimmy Wales says: "We're really interested in all the issues of the digital divide, poverty worldwide, empowering people everywhere to have the information that they need to make good decisions."[10] But when we learn that Wales is a "free marketeer," we should also try to understand what he means by "empowering people"; empowering them to work in a so-called market economy, for example?

Wikipedia's "entries" are often less like typical, concise encyclopedic articles and more akin to short books or pamphlets in length. For example, at the time of writing, the entry for "Hillary Clinton" is around 30,000 words.[11] By comparison, the entry for the online *Encyclopædia Britannica* is less than 3,000.[12] Dr. Feng Zhu says that "some studies show [*Wikipedia*] is just as good as the experts, others show [that] *Wikipedia* is not accurate at all." To learn more, Zhu and Greenstein paired 4,000 *Encyclopædia Britannica* entries to the same number of Wikipedia articles. The authors found that 73% of Wikipedia entries compared to 34% of *Encyclopædia Britannica*'s contained biased words.[13]

HILLARY CLINTON: A CASE-STUDY IN "LIBERAL" BIAS

In "locking" its entry for US President Barack Obama's Secretary of State and future Presidential candidate, Hillary Clinton, Wikipedia decrees that only senior editors can change her page. This ensures Clinton's digital canonization. In the section *Overall themes*, Clinton's Wikipedia entry gushes: "[S]he became the first secretary of state to methodically implement the smart power approach" (but the source also talks about Middle East perceptions of "the American bully").[14] Pioneering the State Department's use of social media, Clinton "help[ed] empower citizens of foreign countries vis-à-vis their governments" (actually, one of the sources talks about how Clinton used social media to stoke civil war in

Libya).[15] "[I]n the Mideast turmoil, Clinton particularly saw an opportunity to advance one of the central themes of her tenure, the empowerment and welfare of women and girls worldwide" (the source actually quotes Clinton's self-interest: "where women are disempowered and dehumanized, you are more likely to see not just antidemocratic forces, but extremism that leads to security challenges for us").[16]

Perhaps most toe-curling of all: "there was a trend of women around the world finding more opportunities, and in some cases feeling safer, as the result of [Clinton's] actions and visibility" (citing genuine feminists, like CODEPINK, the source actually goes on to say: "Some have ... seen in the Hillary Doctrine echoes of the imperial feminism they so criticized during the Bush administration").[17]

Wikipedia's co-founder Jimmy Wales spoken at Clinton Global Initiative events. There are links between the Wikimedia Foundation (worth $97 million by 2018)[18] and the Clinton Foundation. Wikimedia's external contractors and volunteers include associates of Minassian Media: Jove Oliver, Dasha Burns and Helen Platt. In 2014, these individuals trained Wikimedia's so-called c-level directors and managers in 24-hour PR response times to counter "emerging threats" (i.e., criticism of Wikipedia) and in preparation for major media appearances, such as *60 Minutes*.[19] Minassian Media's founder, Craig Minassian, worked at HBO and as a consultant for ABC. He also worked as President Bill Clinton's press secretary, director of TV news and his presidential campaigner. Minassian also worked on Hillary Clinton's 2008 campaign. He then took a job as Chief Communications and Marketing Officer at the Clinton Foundation.[20]

These are just a couple of examples of Wikipedia's conflicts of interest. During the 2016 Presidential election campaign, the editors authored a guideline. *The Washington Post* reports: "In the Clinton editing camp, editors discussed including information about campaign-related emails leaked from WikiLeaks," which is not related to Wikipedia. There was a debate about whether to include them in the Clinton entry. "One editor said the group couldn't assume the emails were authentic, saying their other sources claimed Russia might have manipulated the emails for 'political gains'."[21]

GOOGLE-WIKIPEDIA-YOUTUBE AXIS

In the West, the seemingly endless repository of information varying in quality, known as the internet, is largely filtered through half a dozen giant corporations: Google (owned by Alphabet), YouTube (owned by Google), Facebook, Twitter and Wikipedia. In many non-Western countries, notably China, the state wields tight control over the internet. The site-ranking companies Alexa (owned by Amazon) and SimilarWeb put Wikipedia in the top 20 and top 10 most viewed Western websites, respectively.[22]

For many, these and a few other digital conglomerates have become the internet. They are a monopoly directing users to each other's sites.[23] In doing so, they trap users in a web of mutual corporate interest. Wikipedia has gone from being an entity whose founders claim that they wanted to free knowledge to being an organization that partly dominates knowledge.

For billions of people, Google is the go-to search engine.[24] Its status gives it enough power to direct the user to the Google elite's preferred information; be it news, forums or businesses. Google CEOs, developers, owners, programmers and ideological shapers anonymously employ algorithms. As its parent Alphabet diversifies its stock portfolio, buying shares in big pharma, for instance,[25] we can expect to see a change in search results, such as the promotion of sites with pro-drug as opposed to natural health solutions.

If one Googles a political search term, one is typically directed to corporate and/or state media: CNN, the *New York Times*, the BBC, the *Daily Mail*, and so on; though Wikipedia decided a few years ago to stop using the latter as a source, ironically because its editors deemed it unreliable.[26] Google's algorithms direct users away from independent media, such as AlterNet, CounterPunch, and Truthout.[27] Close behind MSM on Google search result rankings is Wikipedia. Indeed, if one wishes to learn something about a particular political or historical event, Wikipedia is often the first place they look: apparently unbiased, ranked high by Google and above all, ad- and subscription-free. Researchers Lee and the team note: "Wikipedia articles are a constituent part of 95% of all Google searches. Even poor quality pages in Wikipedia get millions of hits because they benefit from the popularity of the site."[28] There are power conflicts, such as the vandalism of the Republican Party's Wikipedia entry during the 2016 Presidential election campaign, which likened the California Republican Party to Nazis. Google apologized for continuing to promote the article via its knowledge panels, even though the vandalism had not yet been fixed.[29]

Despite the occasional disputes, the platform given to Wikipedia by Google has made Wikipedia a potentially powerful political weapon. Biased content or not, any organization that has the power to shape the public perception of individuals and entities, be they governmental departments or corporations, is not only an influential body, it is one that will inevitably influence and be influenced by those seeking and indeed paying to better their public image. An insightful *New York Times Magazine* profile of Wikipedia's co-founder Jimmy Wales notes: "Powerful people like to be around Wales … [and he] likes to be around them, too … [S]ome famous people treat Wales a little bit like their own personal editor." The reporter notes that the "proximity to famous people doesn't sit well with some members of the Wikipedia community who assert that Wales's new life is, in some ways, contradictory to the egalitarian online world he created."[30] For example, in 2014 Wales was a guest of honor at the Sultan Qaboos Cultural Centre in a country known for its authoritarianism, namely the close British ally, Oman. Wales delivered a speech organized by Oman's Commerce and Industry Minister, Dr. Ali bin Masoud Al Sunaidy.[31] On a more positive note, Wales worked with the *Guardian* to oppose the extradition to the US of Richard O'Dwyer, a young British internet developer, on spurious charges of copyright infringement.[32] Wales also opposed the UK's draft surveillance bill, known as the "snooper's charter" (2012).[33] These progressive examples, regardless of the self-interest that might lay behind them, are some of the more benevolent instances of Wales's otherwise toxic brand of "libertarianism," to which we shall return.

Wikipedia works in tandem with other big websites. Most online videos are watched on YouTube, which like Wikipedia is one of the world's most visited websites. But for the last couple of years, YouTube has incorporated Google-style knowledge panels beneath certain videos and beneath its search field, both as a disclaimer and as a way of directing the thoughts of the YouTube user back to the elite view of reality, which, via dissemination across social media and search engine results, they hope will maintain or become the consensus view of any particular subject. Most of the knowledge panels are Wikipedia, though more recently the *Encyclopædia Britannica* has been used to describe some subjects.

When one looks for a YouTube video on "the Holocaust," for instance, a Wikipedia knowledge panel appears, stating: "The Holocaust, also known as the Shoah, was the World War II genocide of the European Jews. Between 1941 and 1945, across German-occupied Europe, Nazi Germany and its collaborators systematically murdered some six million Jews, around two-thirds of Europe's Jewish population."[34] Actually, the Holocaust was the extermination of 11 million people, including six million Jews, by the Nazis: Gypsy-Roma, disabled people, homosexuals, political dissidents, and many others.[35] In an attempt to counter anti-Semitic Holocaust-denial, which permeates YouTube and the internet,[36] the Google-YouTube-Wiki alliance has engaged in its own form of Holocaust denial by omitting from the embedded knowledge panels the suffering of non-Jews. Given that certain Zionist groups attempt to make the Holocaust exclusively about Jewish suffering in an attempt to justify Israel's continued annexation of Palestine,[37] Wikipedia's action also has the unintended effect of bolstering Israeli foreign policy: The knowledge panel subliminally tells YouTube users that only Jews died in the Holocaust and by implication Israel, the self-professed Jewish State, can do as its elites choose, supposedly in order to prevent another Holocaust. As we shall see, Wikipedia's entry on the Israel-Palestine conflict is biased toward Israeli foreign policy because Israel is an ally of the US and Wikipedia is largely a US invention.

Consider bias in YouTube-Wikipedia's treatment of domestic vs. foreign media. According to the Google-YouTube-Wiki alliance, Russia's state broadcaster RT is "funded in whole or in part by the Russian government." Whenever one watches any RT video on YouTube (at least the English language version), this knowledge panel appears. The accompanying link is to the Wikipedia entry on RT. This inclusion of Wikipedia by YouTube legitimizes Wikipedia and creates an unconscious notion that it is a reliable source: otherwise, why would YouTube or indeed any organization use it? However, according to YouTube's knowledge panel that appears beneath all BBC uploads, Britain's state broadcaster "is a British public broadcast service." The link is also to Wikipedia's entry on the BBC. From this, we learn that Russian state media are bad and British state media are good, and by implication that Russia is bad and Britain is good. A truly neutral organization would include statements that both RT and the BBC are state-funded propaganda machines. But Wikipedia is primarily a US entity and Russia is the enemy of the US. It follows that Wikipedia's US-based, English-language contributors would be culturally biased against the Russian state or indeed any country that doesn't mirror US "values." As we shall see, many of Wikipedia's top shapers are ideologically anti-Russian and anti-"communist." Hube and the team find that the Neutral Point of View (NPOV) is violated in Wikipedia due to: "(i) Wikipedia contributors not being aware of NPOV policies or (ii) intentional push towards specific points of views."[38]

In addition to the reputational protection afforded by anonymity, consider the exclusion of self-proclaimed Marxist editors. In September 2008, a Wikipedia administrator sent out a request for colleagues to back their nomination in support of a new administrator, "Lorry"; a skilled Wikipedia editor who later became a member of the Polish branch of the organization's Arbitration Committee. Because Lorry failed to reach the required 85 percent votes, her nomination fell. One of the administrators who blocked Lorry's nomination was "Prot," a Wikipedian reportedly known for their divisive tactics and right-wing views. Prot's objection was that Lorry was an open Trotskyite. During the debate on the vote, Prot asked colleagues: "How many users would vote for a candidate, who, just one day before ..., on their own userpage would declare 'This user loves Adolf Hitler'?". Having made the comparison between Hitler and Trotsky, Prot then went on to call Trotsky "one of the biggest murderers and criminals in world history [sic]." True or not, colleagues raised the point that political beliefs should not influence editorial appointments as long as the appointee's work follows the neutrality principle. In the end, a Lorry defender, Dariusz Jemielniak, ended up getting a 24-hour ban by the Arbitration Committee for hurting Prot's feelings during a discussion on the topic. Jemielniak's treatment by people he considered friends left him feeling wronged and "with no recourse."[39]

More important than the petty internal bureaucracy of Wikipedia is the question of how a supposedly free-to-use encyclopedia, that allegedly anyone can edit, can be truly neutral and representative when ideologues working within its structures can so easily influence content and create an atmosphere of conformity. Given the omnipresence of Wikipedia, this has wide-ranging implications for politics and those at the bottom of power systems in general.

THE FOUNDATION

The fact that an encyclopedia takes money from wealthy individuals and organizations presents a *prima facie* conflict of interest issue. But not only does the Wikimedia Foundation take money from anonymous donors, it proudly publishes a list of those who do not wish to remain anonymous, meaning that conflict of interest is normal in the world of Wikipedia and indeed forms its very basis. The donors are essentially the individuals and corporations that make up America's plutocracy.

In 2011, the Wikipedian "rfaulk" accidentally published a list of donors to the Wikimedia Foundation, which at the time was using on average just 46.2 cents in every donated dollar, allegedly putting the rest in savings accounts and paying its CEOs' quarter-of-a-million-dollar annual salaries.[40] The alleged, anonymous donors included people on both the political left and the political right: Jeff Bezos (multibillionaire, founder of Amazon); Warren Buffett (multibillionaire investor who once said that the mega-rich were fighting a class war against everyone else);[41] Jimmy Carter (former US President); Anurag Dikshit (billionaire gambling software writer); Arianna Huffington (co-founder of *The Huffington Post*); David Koch (multibillionaire energy investor); Pierre Omidyar (multibillionaire founder of eBay); George Soros (multibillionaire investor); Mark Zuckerberg (multibillionaire Facebook founder); and Larry Page and Sergey Brin (billionaire Google founders). Anti-establishment organizations have also donated to the Wikimedia Foundation, including the right-wing "libertarian" Newsmax[42] website and the Republican "libertarian" multimillionaire, Ron Unz.

The Wikimedia Foundation has a list of three-tier donors, who are bracketed according to the value of their donations, which start at $1,000 and go as high as just under $50,000:[43] Adobe (software); AIG (multibillion dollar insurance and finance); American Express (multibillion dollar financial services); Apple (the world's first trillion dollar company); Astex (multimillion dollar drug company); AT&T (multibillion dollar communications company which owns CNN, HBO and others); BAE Systems (multibillion dollar aerospace and weapons); Bank of America (worth tens of billions of dollars); BlackRock (multibillion dollar asset management and hedge fund, managing over $6 trillion); *Bloomberg* (business journal); Boeing (multibillion dollar aerospace and weapons company); BP (multibillion dollar oil company); Bristol Myers Squibb (multibillion dollar drug company); Chevron (multibillion dollar energy company); the Coca-Cola Company; ConocoPhillips (multibillion dollar energy company); Deutsche Bank Americas; the eBay Foundation; ExxonMobil (multibillion dollar oil company); Goldman Sachs (multibillion dollar financial institution); the Google Foundation; the International Monetary Fund (a body described by one of its economic reviewers and later advisor to George Soros as "the credit community's enforcer");[44] JPMorgan Chase (multibillion dollar financial institution); Merck (multibillion dollar drug company); Microsoft; Netflix; Nike (multibillion dollar apparel company); Oracle (multibillion dollar computer corporation); PayPal (worth tens of billions); Pfizer (multibillion dollar drug company); Prudential Finance (insurance firm managing trillions of dollars of assets); UnitedHealthcare (multibillion dollar insurance provider with a reputation for cutting costs at patients' expenses); Verizon (multibillion dollar communications company which owns AOL, Yahoo! and others); and Walt Disney (which owns ABC, the History Channel, Vice Media and others).

Given that Wikipedia has the power to harm reputations via its content and given its popularity and usability, it is arguable that these and other companies donate to the Wikimedia Foundation as part of their "reputation management" operations. From this, we can reasonably assume that Wikipedia's content will reflect the interests of its donors. Featuring an image of a smiling, avuncular David Koch, the Wikipedia entry for the late investor does not accurately describe him as helping endanger the planet by promoting fossil fuel industries and climate-change denial, as he did, but rather as: "An American businessman, philanthropist, political activist, and chemical engineer."[45] Like Hillary Clinton's entry, it gushes: "Koch supported policies that promote individual liberty and free market principles, and supported reducing government spending"; "David and Charles Koch were commended by both President Obama and activist Anthony Van Jones for their bipartisan efforts to reform the prison system in the United States"; "the Chronicle of Philanthropy listed Koch as one of the world's top 50 philanthropists"; "Koch pledged $100 million over 10 years to renovate the New York State Theater"; and so on. The subsection on the Koch brothers' funding of climate change-denial amounts to a pitiful two sentences and nowhere near approaches expansion on their malign influence over media and education.[46] Interestingly, Wikipedia is out of step with its usual MSM echo chambers on this issue, with Google returning critical articles on David Koch in its search results.

Returning to Donors and their influence: As we shall see, at least one high-level BP public relations employee edited the company's Wikipedia entry, while Verizon paid Wiki-PR (a reputation-management firm not related to the company) to fix its image on the site. There is nuance, however. It is obvious that the number of drug companies funding the Wikimedia Foundation means that alternative health practitioners are met with defamatory entries, e.g., referring to them as "quacks," etc. Yet, the Foundation has taken money from Wellness Acupuncture and Natural Medicine Inc.[47] Another Wikimedia Foundation "benefactor" is the medical supply company, Medtronic. In 2013, one Kim Schelble tried to edit an entry on kyphoplasties (a treatment for spinal fractures), despite his being employed by Medtronic, which sells the equipment. Kyphoplasties are little different from vertebroplasties, except in that they are more expensive. A radiologist named Douglas Beall was a consultant for Medtronic who tried to bolster the entry for kyphoplasties with peer-reviewed articles most likely funded by Medtronic.[48]

WIKIPEDIA IN THE CLASSROOM...AND WHITE HOUSE

To cement its nascent academic credentials, Wikipedia and the various arms that support it have been working with schools, universities and even the White House to promote itself and various fields including science, technology, engineering and mathematics (STEM), which is a notoriously underfunded and deskilled field in the US.

Di Lauro and Johinke argue that "omissions, along with inaccuracies and failures to comply with Wikipedia rules, yield rich teaching and learning opportunities for higher education teachers"[49] in that entries teach kids how not to research and write and how to improve that which already exists. The economy of large-scale collaboration creates what Yochai Benchler described as a Commons-Based Peer Production. This philosophy can be applied to the Wiki Education Foundation, established in 2010 to give Wikipedia more credibility among academics. It soon established a presence in universities, supporting 24 higher-learning institutions within a year via its Public Policy Initiative. By 2016, 6,000 US students were enrolled on Wiki-funded courses. A survey indicates that students can successfully be absorbed into the Wiki culture, with 30 percent being initially negative about the idea of taking a course on Wikipedia and 30 percent being neutral, but ending with clear majorities--in the high-70 percentiles and even 90 percentiles for some questions--enjoying their experience in writing "clearly" for general readers, learning about using Wikipedia instead of other digital literacy programs and learning about the reliability of Wikipedia as a source. After the course, 63 percent of students came to believe that Wikipedia can be a reliable source. The Wiki Education Foundation offers college courses in writing and composition.[50]

As part of its *We The Geeks* series, in 2015 "[r]esearchers, students, and expert Wikipedia editors [...] convene[d] in the Eisenhower Executive Office Building" of the White House "for a two-hour editing sprint to research and crowd-source the stories of

African American STEM all-stars – past and present – and share those stories online through social media." Wikipedia editors, supposedly neutral, in the White House? Even though they were not told what to write and how to write it, the enculturation of Wikipedia editors into the upper echelons of US power surely had the effect of biasing their opinions and thus articles relating to the Obama administration?[51] In 2015, the Obama website posted: "the Wiki Education Foundation launched a Year of Science initiative that aims to not only improve the quality of science articles on Wikipedia, but also expand Wikipedia's representation of women scientists … [. The Office of Science and Technology] OSTP held an 'Edit-A-Thon' during Black History Month to help source and share inspiring stories of African Americans who made important contributions in STEM."[52]

Here, we see Wikipedia's transformation from knowledge provider to knowledge shaper.

ABOUT THIS BOOK

This book is a critique of US power, both state and corporate, and a critique of those who support it, including the UK and Israel. The book uses Wikipedia content as a framework in which to analyze US power.

The first couple of chapters ask who founded Wikipedia, who runs it, how it is used in the interests of powerful groups (including state and corporate) and whose interests it serves. The remaining chapters are an entry-by-entry content analysis of several Wikipedia English entries. For example, an important research article by Dr. Matt Bridgewater examines different languages for the Wikipedia entry for "The Atomic Bombings of Hiroshima and Nagasaki." Wikipedia entries tend to be specific to each language. Translation errors or ambiguities aside, the English-language version of the entry is different from the Chinese-language version because they were written by different contributors. That particular entry was selected for analysis by Bridgewater for a number of reasons: it is a "contentious" event (from an elite, Western perspective); its presence continues to be felt, particularly as a warning to the world about the reality of nuclear weapons; the author was well acquainted with the topic; and the entry is well-developed in terms of length in several languages, making a comparative analysis possible.[53]

There are 6 million entries on the English-language version of Wikipedia alone.[54] At least tens of thousands of them are political. Picking random examples for analysis is not an instructive approach, unless the sample size is huge. But a huge sample size would prevent in-depth content-analysis. The method employed here, therefore, is the use of universal political themes. Regardless of political ideology, affiliation or identity, each one of us is affected by the prospect of nuclear war/accident, the power struggles of the nations that possess nuclear weapons, anthropogenic climate change and the prospect of terrorists coming into possession of nuclear weapons, which while causing regional damage could also trigger the nuclear involvement of state powers.

The COVID pandemic is not included here because unlike the other entries, it is a live page and being too frequently updated to make an analysis useful.

In addition to these practical concerns, there are moral issues. By death toll and preventability, one of the worst moral crimes of the 20th and 21st centuries (i.e., within most of our times) was the US-British embargo on Iraq (1990-2003), which killed a million people, reduced the living standards of the country from a middle-income one like Greece to a destitute one like Burundi, and made the infrastructures of the country vulnerable to the US-British invasion in March 2003, which killed another million people over five years. Another moral issue is the death of the prospects for a Palestinian state, as the occupation by Israel becomes full-scale annexation. The same moral question arises with regards to other colonial hangovers, including India's annexation of Kashmir and Ethiopia's annexation of Somalia's Ogaden.[55] Unlike Ethiopia-Somalia, but like Kashmir, the Israel-Palestine crisis also takes place against the backdrop of nuclear weapons. Like the nuclear-armed India and Pakistan, which periodically fight over Kashmir,[56] Israel also has nuclear weapons in a region which includes two allies of the nuclear-armed Russia, namely Iran and Syria. Israel-Palestine is selected for discussion here because the US does not enable India's annexation of Kashmir or Ethiopia's occupation of Ogaden the way it does with Israel's annexation of Palestine. The US supports Israel's actions with its record levels of foreign "aid" (investment in reality) and arms exports.[57]

The entries analyzed here were viewed by the author in late-2018/early-2019. Having checked the edit histories, there were deemed by the author to change little substantively over time. Many are now "protected," meaning that only senior editors can make changes and in the context of notable events taking place.

Chapters 1 and 2 constitute a structural analysis of Wikipedia: who founded it and what interests they have; who funds the Wikimedia Foundation and their interests; who edits and re-edits Wikipedia; the relationship dynamics of the contributors vs. senior editors/bots; and the relationship between Wikipedia, US governmental departments, and US-based transnational corporations. It argues that Wikipedia's content reflects its structures. The second part of the book is a content analysis.

Chapter 3 is a comparative analysis of Wikipedia's entries for the foreign relations of the US and Russia. This topic was selected because the United States is the global superpower, so any military or economic policy enacted by the US has geopolitical repercussions on a scale that those of other nations do not have. Given the balance of power in favor of the US, we would expect any objective encyclopedia entry to be more critical of US power (assuming we follow the principle that power is linked to responsibility). But this is not the case. As anticipated from Wikipedia's structural limitations noted above, the entries are more critical of the less powerful Russia.

Chapter 4 is about nuclear warfare. This topic was selected on the basis that a nuclear war and/or accident between two major powers (including the US and

Russia) would either wipe out most of the human species and make life unliveable across the global for a century or more, or at the very least release enough radioactive and carbon materials into the atmosphere to radically change our societies for the worse. The chapter argues that the Wikipedia entry minimizes the impact of potential nuclear war, makes US possession of nuclear weapons seem like an accident of history and omits any reference to the international laws and contemporary peace activists that might undermine US nuclear weapons systems.

Chapter 5 explores climate change, which along with nuclear war/accident is a major obstacle to decent, long-term survival. The entry borders on climate change denial. While it does not outright deny the human contribution to CO_2 emissions and their influence on global warming and thus climate change, the article over-emphasizes the role of the Sun and volcanoes in climate variation and uses equivocal language, all the while omitting references to fossil fuel companies and the anticipated social consequences of climate change.

Chapter 6 considers the history of the most notorious terrorist group, Al-Qaeda. This topic was chosen because many people, rightly or wrongly, believe that terrorism remains a serious threat. While Daesh (a.k.a., Islamic State) has replaced Al-Qaeda in mainstream media coverage, it is worth considering the history of these *jihadi* organizations. The Wikipedia entry makes it seem as if the US-British war against the Soviets (1979-89), which was fought in Afghanistan and made use of *jihadis*, had little to do with creating Al-Qaeda. Rather, the blame is shifted onto Osama bin Laden's comparatively inconsequential group, which others later dubbed "Al-Qaeda."

Chapter 7 analyzes the embargo imposed by the US and Britain on Iraq (1990-2003), which amounted to one of the worst economic crimes of the latter-half of the 20th century. It resulted in the deaths of over half a million infants. This Wikipedia entry was selected for analysis, given the gravity of the topic and its acting as a measure of Wikipedia's moral credibility. The book argues that the entry gives a platform to revisionists who invent "evidence" and suppress real evidence. Here, Wikipedia is complicit in giving ideological support to near-genocidal levels of denial in an effort to make the US and its allies look good.

Chapter 8 concerns the so-called Israel-Palestine conflict, which in reality is the Israeli occupation/annexation of Palestine and the Palestinian struggle for self-determination. The occupation/annexation is important, hence its inclusion here, because it not only affects Palestinians, it has wider regional implications, discussed in the chapter. Wikipedia's introduction to the occupation/annexation is analyzed and found to ignore entirely the core issue: that every Palestinian act of terrorism and Israeli military "response" is taking place in the context of illegal Israeli occupation/annexation, meaning that Palestinian terror is a response to Israeli occupation/annexation. The US role in enabling Israel is omitted, Israel's legal obligations are not discussed and many of the sources either don't actually say what is attributed to them or they also say other, more important things that are ignored.

In conclusion, Wikipedia is not an open encyclopedia, balanced by the wisdom of crowds. It is a tool of US state-military-corporate propaganda, albeit with competing and conflicting interests which seeks to minimize US malevolence and maximize the horrors of US enemies. This seems to be a reflection of the culture in which its founders, editors and contributors were raised more than of a conspiracy. It is therefore a much harder problem to overcome.

Part I
Structural Analysis

Chapter 1
Manufacturing Consensus

Wikipedia is supposed to run on the "wisdom of crowds" philosophy, first proposed by Aristotle (384-22 BCE)[58] and refined for the information age by James Surowiecki.[59] Anarchist theories posit that when freed from the arbitrary constraints of dominant power, humans, like other group-organisms, develop functioning and self-correcting systems.[60] That may or may not be true, but we certainly won't be able to find out by using Wikipedia as a test-case. The erroneous idea that many people have about Wikipedia is that there is no hierarchy and little quality control because the system is self-correcting. In reality, Wikipedia runs on fairly rigid structures and has been likened by scholars (cited below) to a federalized state more than an anarchist collective. All totalitarian systems seek to manufacture consensus, to get the "masses" following the orders of the rulers and to do so by getting the "masses" to internalize the rulers' values; e.g., the admonition of individualistic concepts in the Soviet Union (1922-91).[61] In so-called capitalist societies, like the US and Britain, technological power systems seek the same (in this case, individualism over collectivism).

In the 1950s, Bertrand Russell warned that individuals living in such societies would be convinced by technofascist rulers that black is white and white is black;[62] just like in Orwell's *Nineteen Eighty-four*. In other words, to be free of control, consensus has to be challenged because when consensus is built from above by a small number of controllers it is not necessarily in the interests of the governed. Indeed, rigid consensus is a rejection of the Marxist principle, that everything should be questioned.[63] The rigid adherence to the kind of consensus built by the English-language version of Wikipedia on political issues is that which the Enlightenment (17th-19th centuries) tried to destroy by demanding that the period's religious dogmas, that had prevented scientific inquiry and thus advancement, be rejected. The Wikimedia Foundation's CEO Katherine Maher said: "Even when you have contested facts or contested information, Wikipedia tries to provide you some sort of consensus amidst all that complexity."[64] But the people building the "consensus" are the privileged editors and donors. In other words, we'll tell you how to think and what to think about.

This chapter explores who runs Wikipedia and how the system works internally. As we shall see, the co-founder Jimmy Wales is a self-made stock trader who believes in Ayn Rand's brand of so-called "free market" economics, but with a culturally-liberal twist. It is not, therefore, surprising to see that Wales married into the British political aristocracy, supports the Clinton Global Initiative, hobnobs with stars like Bono and speaks at the World Economic Forum. The Wikimedia Foundation represents corporate, not working-class interests. Its CEO, Katherine Maher, is a Fellow of the Truman Project, which seeks to instil US imperial "values" under the guise of democracy promotion. Wikipedia's top editor (by number of contributions), Steven Pruitt, is the son of military parents, one of whom left Soviet Russia to live in the USA. As we shall see, the National Security Agency has its own Wikipedia mirror site and the Central Intelligence Agency offers guidance on how its information officers should edit entries sensitive to the Agency's interests, as does the private Stratfor intelligence corporation. We shall also see that, inspired by Wikipedia, the US Army sought to develop a similar interactive, updatable system for its field manuals.

Far from being "the free encyclopedia that anyone can edit,"[65] as its subtitle claims, Wikipedia runs along a series of guidelines. The Five Pillars of content standards as well as other practices include: the adoption of neutrality; the principle that entries should be "notable" (no articles about obscure community organizers, for instance); and that research should not be original (i.e., information that reflects the system).[66] The Arbitration Committee (a panel consisting of editors) settles disputes,[67] including by temporarily and permanently banning editors who have been judged to have violated standards and practices.[68] Entries on particularly controversial subjects are granted "protection" status, meaning that only senior administrators can alter them.[69] As we shall see, one of the dirty little secrets is that most of the site's major editors rely on algorithms ("bots") to do the vast amount of editing work including checking for vandalism. So much for the "wisdom of crowds."

Despite giving the impression to many that Wikipedia's supposed egalitarianism and inclusivity made it anarchistic,[70] the logic is that only relatively privileged individuals, paying corporations or intelligence agencies will have the time, energy, skills and commitment to shape the organization's content. The kind of ordinary people whom Wikipedia was supposed to include (if we believe the self-serving image) are too busy and exhausted making a living to fully commit to editing and maintaining their work online.[71] So, one may attempt to create an entry for a subject, only to find that the administrators or top editors reject the entry. One can register, log in and edit an entry, but one will likely find that senior editors object, particularly when the entry is political. Also contradicting the egalitarian ethos is the fact that most editors have a college-level or higher education, tend to be white (the majority of non-English language entries are created or edited by bots) and they tend to be male. This chapter also documents a bullying and sexist culture, which means that despite the culturally liberal veneer, the percentage of women participating in content creation is small compared to men.

Given that this is the structure of Wikipedia, it follows that the content of Wikipedia's English-language entries will reflect the interests of the political, social and economic climate in the US. They will reflect the interests of the US state, US corporations and relatively privileged, liberal, middle-class men.

WHO IS JIMMY WALES?

Wales has been a fan of Ayn Rand since reading her novels as an undergraduate at the University of Alabama in the 1980s. Rand was a politically useful tool for American "capitalists"; the living embodiment of the American Dream: a Russian who rejected "communism" and who made it big in "the land of the free." Not only did Rand rightly reject the wretched Bolshevik dictatorship that masqueraded as communism,[72] she and her US-capitalist counterparts also rejected the genuine elements of communism, such as solidarity and mutual reciprocity. Rand's family lost their wealth in Bolshevik Russia, forcing Rand to emigrate to the US, where she became a best-selling novelist and the inspiration for US-style "libertarianism" and "free market" economics.[73] This brand of "libertarianism" has helped to lead to enormous concentrations of wealth and power, the financialization of the economy at the expense of manufacturing and production, wage stagnation, periodic crises, the weakening of the middle-classes and the assault on basic humane principles, like social security and free healthcare. It has also meant mega-profits for the top earners.

Rand's supposed theory of "objectivism" inspired Wikipedia in that Wales wanted to create an encyclopedia containing "truth free from bias," in the words of Wales's biographer, Susan Meyer.[74] Wales's objectivism is such that he named his daughter after Kira, the protagonist in Rand's novel, *We the Living* (1936). Kira is a thinly-veiled autobiographical version of Rand; the daughter of a textiles factory-owner whose assets are nationalized by the Bolsheviks. Indeed, anti-Russian themes run throughout Wikipedia's structures and, as we shall see, the content of its English-language version. In addition to hosting a website about Rand entitled *Freedom's Nest*, a Rand biographer Jenifer Burns reports that she and Wales co-authored a paper on objectivism.[75] Michael J. Wolf, the Managing Director of the consultancy firm Activate and a board-member of Yahoo!, says that Wikipedia is a "paradox" because "what makes Wikipedia so valuable for users is what gets in its way of becoming a valuable, for-profit enterprise."[76] But it is only a "paradox" if we accept the fallacy that all Americans are pathologically motivated to make money. Wales is more of an ideological promoter of "libertarianism" than a direct beneficiary of it via Wikipedia, though he does appear to profit from speaking engagements.[77]

At the World Economic Forum (WEF), to which he was first invited by Bono in 2005 and subsequently managed by the Boston Consulting Group,[78] Wales said: "As an entrepreneur, I want everyone to get out of my way. Government should just establish the simplest business framework." The WEF report quoting Wales also says: "Another way to eliminate red tape and encourage entrepreneurs is to legalize microfinance. (However, it must be regulated to some degree to ensure poor people are not exploited.)" Notice the WEF's blatant parenthetical disclaimer about non-exploitation.[79] But there is nuance in Wales's worldview. The Atlas Society (named after another of Rand's novels) published a video of Wales on YouTube in which he says: "I think it's really fine, it's really great" for people to make "lots of money."[80] This was said in response to the fact that he's "only" worth \$1m, as *The Atlantic* puts it.[81] Invoking the side of Rand's "objectivism" that puts self-fulfillment above profit, Wales said that he prefers artistic freedom to profit-driven compromise.

Returning to the more profit-oriented side of "objectivism": Prior to facing personal financial commitments, Wales thought he was set for life after successfully working as a stock trader at Chicago Options Associates in the 1990s. Wales married the steel trader, Christine Rohan. He co-founded a service website, Bomis, which sold among other things "adult content" (not pornography, he assures us).[82] Wales later edited the Wikipedia entry for Bomis to change the description of "soft-core pornography" to "adult content." He says that this was solely to correct a factual error and that he regrets editing his own Wikipedia biography, which is why he reportedly edited it 18 times.[83] Wikipedia started life as Nupedia, a nonprofit website formed by Wales and Larry Sanger, whom Wales met at university. The aim was to provide free, peer-reviewed information to the broader public; one of the more genuine strands of Wales's notion of "libertarianism." Sanger left Nupedia (rebranded as the Wikipedia we know today) in 2002, a year after its founding. Sanger says that one of the "hurdle[s] was to figure out how to rein in the bad actors so that they did not ruin the project for everyone else. Unfortunately, we never did come up with a good solution for that one." Sanger doesn't define "bad actors," but as we shall see, they include corporate shills, politicians and intelligence agencies.

"Wikipedia is a broken system as a result."[84] Wales later scrubbed all reference to Sanger being the co-founder of Wikipedia.[85]

Richard Branson is a British billionaire whose Virgin corporation and its subsidiaries owns an airline and trains and provides healthcare "services" for Britain's supposedly public-owned National Health Service (NHS). Virgin Care later sued the NHS, meaning the British taxpayer, for alleged breach of contract. The NHS settled out of court for £2m.[86] In 2008, Wales jetted off to Branson's private Caribbean investment, Necker Island, where he met up with Google's Larry Page (who married on the island) and Britain's former PM and war criminal, Tony Blair,[87] who was then "advising" JPMorgan. The men discussed ways of profiting from the bourgeoning green technology revolution. Wales's wife Kaye Garvey was Blair's diary secretary. She then worked as director of Freud Communications, a PR firm run by the famous psychoanalyst Sigmund's great-grandson, Matthew. Matthew Freud is also the media tycoon Rupert Murdoch's son-in-law. Wedding attendees included the Blairs, Blair's propagandist and fellow war criminal Alastair Campbell and Steven Hilton, former aide to British PM and war criminal David Cameron.[88] After leaving office, Tony Blair received a cool $13m for "advising" Kazakhstan's dictator, Nursultan Nazarbayev. In 2011, the Kazakh autocracy established the WikiBilim foundation to produce material for the Kazakh Wikipedia. The foundation is funded by grants from the Wikimedia Foundation and from the country's sovereign oil-wealth fund. It is run by former government official, Rauan

Kenzhekhanuly, whom Wales named "Wikipedian of the Year." Telling *The Telegraph* that he believes in "free speech," Wales shut down his Talk page on Wikipedia when the Wikipedian and critic, Andreas Kolbe, raised the link between Wales and Blair and Blair and Nazarbayev. Wales dismissed any influence on Wikipedia's entries as "totally weird and irrelevant" accusations made by "deranged conspiracy theorists."[89] A comprehensive *New York Times Magazine* profile said that Wales was referred to by colleagues and ran Wikipedia, the supposedly free-to-use and anarchistic knowledge source, as the BDFL: the Benevolent Dictator for Life. Examples include direct influence on whether or not personal details about Dr. Lynette Nusbacher be included in the military historian's biographical entry (Wales said they should) and whether homeopathy merits description by Wikipedia as "quackery"[90] (Wales said it should. We shall later explore Wikipedia's links to big pharma).

These paragraphs only scratch the surface of what Wales's connections might mean for Wikipedia's content, but the intention is not to crucify Wales, who is a cog in a machine. Rather the examples illustrate the kind of thinking that we can expect from Wikipedia's managers and content.

A MILITARY-INTELLIGENCE PRODUCT

Some of the individuals involved at the top of Wikipedia's hierarchy, be they CEOs or reputable editors, either champion US global imperialism or at least come from anti-Soviet/Russian, pro-US military backgrounds.

A Truman National Security Project Fellow and author of the book *State Power 2.0*, the Wikimedia Foundation's CEO, Katherine Maher, is a specialist in Middle East studies and CEO and Executive Director of the Leadership Team. Before joining the Wikimedia Foundation in 2014, she worked at the World Bank.[91] According to the Truman National Security Project: "America is at its best when we use all the tools in our toolbox: diplomacy, defense, development, and democracy promotion. [The] Truman National Security Project, along with our sister organization Truman Center, identifies, trains, and positions leaders across America who share this worldview."[92] It follows that Wikipedia is part of the propaganda network backing the implementation of this agenda. The Project republished an article by Maher in which she writes: "Information has always been power, and governments have long sought to control it. So for countries where power is a tightly controlled narrative, parsed by state television and radio stations, the Internet has been catastrophic." The implication is that enemy states can be undermined by US-led, online propaganda. Maher attacks a number of US enemies: "The Great Firewall of China is almost as old as the Internet itself"; "Iran's proposed halal Internet seeks to impose Islamic virtue on the browsing masses"; "In Russia, the state agency Roskomnadzor enforces an Internet block list that has filtered the blogs of government critics."[93] With the exception of Saudi Arabia, whose society elements of the US establishment want to liberalize in order to boost US investments, notice Maher's lack of criticism of the internet policies of brutal US allies. Maher is also World Economic Young Global Leader (YGL).[94] The YGL role was established in 2004 with funding from the Israel-based Dan David Foundation.[95] In 2015, Jimmy Wales received a $1m prize from the Foundation.[96] Wales says that he got involved in a YGL meeting in Dailan, China, where there was "a healthy mix of non-profits, academics, media and government people."[97]

Consider Wikipedia's top editor, Steven Pruitt. Alla Pruitt (maiden name not known) was born in Soviet Russia and emigrated to the US in 1979, following an agreement between the Soviet leader Leonid Brezhnev and US President Jimmy Carter to allow Soviet Jews to reunite with relatives, most of whom were in Israel, says Alla. Donald Pruitt, a multilingual Army veteran, met Alla in the 1980s (i.e., during the Cold War) while the pair were teaching languages at the Lackland Air Force Base Defense Language Institute's Russian Department, San Antonio, Texas. The Pruitts moved to Virginia with their son, Steven. Steven Pruitt works at US Customs and Border Protection in Washington, D.C. He describes his job as involving "everything from discussing policy to making recommendations to actually processing movement of records" to the National Archives.[98] In his spare time and using AutoWikiBrowser, a semiautonomous tool, Pruitt edits Wikipedia, becoming its No. 1 editor with 2.5 million edits to his (and his robot's) name.[99] Corporate media promoted Pruitt's achievements, with *TIME* magazine naming him one of the most influential internet users in 2017 and CBS's This Morning profiling him.[100] But there are discrepancies in the profile. The film says that he lives with Alla and Donald "in the home he grew up in," which is likely to be in Virginia (he was born in Texas), yet Pruitt works an hour's flying time away, in Washington, DC. Does he really jet into work each morning or did the CBS report get it wrong?

Wikipedia is part of the internet system that was developed by the military with public money in the 1950s-60s as the ARPANET.[101] Corporations hope that the systems developed in the military sector that evolve in the public-corporate realm will in turn inspire military-intelligence innovations.

In 2003, the CIA's Director of Central Intelligence established the Galileo Awards Program to inspire intelligence community officers to submit unclassified papers to shape the CIA's adaptive capacities in the information age. One partly-declassified report from 2004 states that times have changed and that CIA now exists in a real-time information environment.[102] Just as Woodrow Wilson said that most nations don't need direct rule, merely the inculcation of US elite "values" where possible,[103] the officer who contributed to the Galileo report includes an anecdote about the Mayor of Nauvoo, Illinois, who said that he kept the massive frontier city in order because he taught the inhabitants the "correct principles and they govern themselves." The Mayor was Joseph Smith (1805-44), founder of Mormonism. This principle applies to Wikipedia: set the overarching "values" and contributors will reflect those "values." It also applies to the CIA's "complexity theory": "a simple tradecraft regime will emerge an Intelligence Community that continuously and dynamically reinvents itself" (tradecraft means having the skills of spying, disrupting, etc.). The changes that require the intelligence community to adapt are unpredictable.[104]

Consequently, the CIA is given five prescriptions: 1) Just as consumers are supposedly autonomous in market systems, officers must be free to act when necessary. 2) Just as cities are governed by property rules, officers must be "hardwired" with the techniques of tradecraft. 3) Officers must share more information to help the CIA thrive, just as consumers share information about niche products to help markets. 4) Officers need more feedback from the National Security environment. 5) Intelligence managers must be persuasive in their objectives, such as via communication with officers. Technology makes the five "prescriptions" more realistic. The author cites Wikipedia as an interesting "tradecraft ... or a rule set to which contributors and editors must abide." The self-initiation is analogous to one of the five prescriptions. Wikipedia inspired the author's advocacy of fostering a "healthy market of debatable ideas emerges from the sharing of points of view." But Wikipedia does not exist in isolation: "The occasional brilliant blog comment will shape the Wiki." These principles, says the author, should be incorporated into the Defense Information Systems Agency's SIPRNet.[105]

The document in question was signed by CIA Director Porter Goss. Just a few years later, software had traced Wikipedia edits on Goss's entry to the CIA. Other CIA edits included vandalism of the biographical entry for Iran's President, Mahmoud Ahmadinejad.[106] At the time, the CIA, Britain's MI6 and Israel's Mossad were attacking Iran in various ways, including via the funding of anti-regime terrorists, such as the Jundullah, a Balochi Sunni group. Interestingly, the Wikipedia entry for Jundullah dismisses claims that the CIA had been working with the group. It does so by citing what it says is an "investigation" that debunked the claims. But in reality, the debunking source is merely a Reuters article that rejects the claim of CIA involvement, but provides no counterevidence.[107] Some of the information concerning anti-Iranian CIA activity came from Fred Burton. Between 2012-13, WikiLeaks published emails from Burton's employer, Stratfor; the private intelligence agency/global risks analyst. Not only do the leaked Stratfor emails confirm that edits had been made to Burton's Wikipedia entry, they confirm that Stratfor wanted to use Wikipedia to boost its own company profile. Brian Genchur, Stratfor's PR Manager, told colleagues: "I COULD alter part of Fred Burton's Wikipedia entry (done a few days ago) because it contained a factual error that he was part of a gov. department that he really was never a part of because 1) it's false and 2) it did not have sourcing attached" (emphasis in original).[108] On an unrelated matter, Larry Sanger told WikiLeaks: "Speaking as Wikipedia's co-founder, I consider you enemies of the U.S.—not just the government, but the people."[109]

By 2006, the Intelligence Community had developed its own Intellipedia. A Top Secret report released under a FOIA request instructed intelligence officers how to edit Wikipedia's entry on MK-

ULTRA, the CIA's mind control program (1953-circa 1970s), for Intellipedia. MK-ULTRA led to deaths and involved the exploitation of prisoners, mental patients and foreign POWs. The CIA document reveals that the NSA has a mirror-site of Wikipedia. It states: "Be bold in modifying this Wikipedia import ... Correct mistakes; remove bias; categorize; ... when assimilation into Intellipedia is complete, remove this template and add {{From Wikipedia}}."[110]

During the Obama Years (2008-2016), the US Army sought the creation of Wikipedia-style Army Manuals. "Using the same free software behind Wikipedia, the Army's 'wikified' field manuals invite military personnel – from the privates to the generals - to collaboratively update the Army Tactics, Techniques, and Procedures in real time."[111] Similarly, the US Department of Energy (DOE), which has partial control over the development of nuclear weapons (along with the Pentagon) sought to develop its Open Energy Information (OpenEI), "an open source web platform—similar to the one used by Wikipedia—developed by DOE and the National Renewable Energy Laboratory (NREL) to make the large amounts of energy-related data and information more easily searched, accessed, and used both by people and automated machine processes."[112]

There are cases of Wikipedia opposing the military-intelligence-complex. An article posted on the US Council on Foreign Relations website notes that "Wikimedia, the non-profit organization that runs Wikipedia, and the American Civil Liberties Union are suing the NSA over its 'upstream' intelligence collection capabilities." The report notes that the lawsuit alleged that the National Security Agency's "ability to access information from the Internet's backbone as it transits through the United States amounts to a violation of the First and Fourth amendments of the U.S. constitution, which protect free speech and prohibit unreasonable search and seizure respectively."[113] Often, self-proclaimed libertarians like Wales are constitutionalists. Another pro is that Wikimedia is not as bad as some other companies for betraying user data, such as spying and selling it to other companies. In 2015, it was given top marks by the Electronic Frontier Foundation. But this doesn't say much because the report also gave top marks to Yahoo!, which it turns out was being used by the NSA and the British Ministry of Defence as part of their Optic Nerve program, which took pictures of unsuspecting users through the cameras on their laptops, particularly when they were in sexually-compromising positions.[114] The Electronic Frontier Foundation (EFF) writes: "Nine Companies Receive All Available Stars: Adobe, Apple, CREDO, Dropbox, Sonic, Wickr, Wikimedia, Wordpress.com, and Yahoo." The EFF says that Wikimedia requires a warrant before passing user data to law enforcement and it also publishes a transparency report. Together with Twitter, it signed a letter written by the Open Technology Institute opposing so-called back-door technologies that give intelligence agencies open access to user data; most of which Wikimedia says it deletes after 90 days.[115]

A NOTE ON UKRAINE

Since the breakup of the Soviet Union in the late-1980s/early-90s, Ukraine has been a proxy battleground for US-Russian influence. Ukraine declared independence from the Soviet Union in 1991. Within 12 month, the US-led North Atlantic Treaty Organization (NATO) had been offering Ukraine alliance, though not full membership, including the conducting of joint, NATO-Ukraine war games.[116] Russia's geostrategic interests in Ukraine include the ethnic-majority Russian presence in Donbas,[117] the Russian military base in Sevastopol (Crimea, which Russia annexed in 2014,)[118] and the use of Ukraine as a strategic route for Russia's lucrative and politically-important energy export pipelines to Europe.[119] As NATO and the European Union (EU) both discretely absorb Ukraine's neighbors into their respective spheres of influence, either through EU members or through military basing and war gaming,[120] Russia increases its defensive capacities. For years, the US State Department, with the help of various agencies, including the US Agency for International Development (USAID), has sponsored anti-Russia activity in Ukraine, supporting the Orange Revolution 2004, which helped to oust the pro-Russia President, Viktor Yanukovych.[121] In 2014, four years after Yanukovych regained power, the US sponsored the so-called Euromaidan (Europe Square) protests that ended with the election of the pro-US-EU President, Petro Poroshenko.[122]

YES, the Yalta European Strategy, supports Ukraine's integration into the EU system. Its board includes the former President of Poland and NATO Secretary-general, Aleksander Kwaśniewski, the former Swedish Foreign Minister, Carl Bildt, former President of the European Parliament, Patrick Cox, and so on.[123] In September 2014, Jimmy Wales attended YES's workshop in Kyiv, *Media and Digital Communications as a Tool in Revolutions and Wars: Information/Disinformation, Media and Digital Communications as a Tool in Revolutions and Wars: Information/Disinformation.* Wales said: "We call upon Ukrainian Wikipedia writers to target both on-line and in physical environment the Russian speaking Wikipedia community in order to enable cooperation...so that Wikipedia remains the way of alternative views, alternative statements." Wales also revealed that far from being an encyclopedia, Wikipedia's role is counter-propaganda; counter-Russian propaganda, of course, not counter-US-EU propaganda. "We can see the weakness of the Russian model," he said. "There is very potent impact and control on the part of Russian government, they have stopped many mouths including the good journalists and independent mass media sources. The propaganda...goes top-down and is more efficient than we expected" (ellipsis in original).[124]

Roozenbeek and Terentieva note that the English language version of the entries for the Ukraine conflicts 2014 are the most read of all language versions of the subject. "Ukrainian as well as Russian editors have an incentive to contribute to global Wikipedia to share unique knowledge or make sure their preferred narrative becomes dominant." Their statistical analysis shows that between December 2013 and February 2014, more than twice as many English and Ukrainian edits were made for the various topics of the period, including Euromaidan and the war in Donbas, than Russian edits.[125] Using their Wikiwhere, Körner and colleagues found a way of tracing the location of Wikipedia editors using different language versions of the site. Using the article on Russia's annexation of Ukraine as a baseline, the authors found that the majority of pro-Russian edits appeared in the German as opposed to English language edition of Wikipedia.[126]

At the time of writing, the Vice Chair of the Wikimedia Foundation is the Ukrainian, Nataliia Tymkiv. In addition to Vice Chairing the Wikimedia Foundation, Tymkiv is "Financial Director of the Centre for Democracy and Rule of Law, a Ukrainian media policy and human rights nonprofit." Tymkiv became an administrator for the Ukrainian Wikipedia.[127] Tymik's Centre for Democracy and Rule of Law describes itself as "a think-and-act tank, which has been working in the civil society sector of Ukraine since 2005 channelling its efforts for the development of independent media, support of civic platforms and movements, and building a legal state in Ukraine."[128] Its partners include USAID, Radio Liberty and the European Commission.[129] As noted, USAID has been involved in subverting Ukraine's domestic politics under the guise of democracy promotion. Radio Liberty began as a CIA-funded counter-Soviet broadcast in the 1950s.[130]

THE COMPANY THEY KEEP

Until 2020, the Wikimedia Foundation website was a single page with links to other Wiki ventures, including Wikipedia, WikiData, WikiNews, WikiSpecies, WikiVersity, WikiVoyage, and so on. More recently, the site has flaunted its progressive credentials, with illustrations of the Reverend Martin Luther King, Jnr. addressing crowds, as well as LGBTQ+ people holding rainbow flags.[131] But the Wikimedia Foundation's Trustees and leading figures do not represent unemployed people, working-class, unions, environmental campaigners, community organizers, grassroots political leaders or other people considered by the neoliberal system to be social failures. Rather, figures from large- and medium-sized domestic and US-based multinational corporations are overrepresented. Their corporate enculturation and resultant world view influences their actions, including the shape of the Wikimedia Foundation. It follows that the corporate worldview will influence, to a lesser or greater extent, Wikipedia's editorial policy.

Wikimedia Trustee Dr. Raju Narisetti majored in journalism, co-founded *Mint*, one of India's largest newspapers, worked at the *Wall Street Journal* and *Washington Post*, and served as Senior Vice President of Strategy at Murdoch's News Corp.[132] Trustee Dr. Dariusz Jemielniak "studies open collaboration communities, the phenomenon of organized sharing (including piracy), and anti-scientific movements," hence Wikipedia's regular assault on alternative health practitioners and independent scientific researchers. "He was a scientific advisor to the Ministry of Science in Poland from 2015-2016, and currently serves on the steering committee of Internet Governance Forum in Poland ... Dariusz has held a variety of different roles on Wikipedia, including administrator, bureaucrat, checkuser, steward, and ombudsman."[133] Another Trustee, Shani Evenstein Sigalov, is an EdTech Innovation Strategist at Tel Aviv University and former Wikimedia Israel board member. She is a Fellow at the Azrieli Foundation.[134] The Azrieli Foundation has a program in Holocaust studies and presents the Shoah as being exclusively a Jewish tragedy: "Six million Jews, more than two thirds of Europe's Jewish population, were murdered between 1933 and 1945 in the Holocaust. These lives must never be forgotten. Through a commitment to expanding our collective knowledge of all that was lost and of the experiences of those who survived, the Azrieli Foundation strives to cultivate a better understanding of the enormity of this tragedy."[135] Evenstein Sigalov teaches Wikidata at Tel Aviv University and edits under the name Esh77.[136]

Tanya Capuano is another Wikimedia Trustee. She worked at Intuit, Hewlett-Packard and APM Management Consultants/CSC Healthcare.[137] Her current position is with the G5 property marketing company, where she is described as "a veteran Silicon Valley financial executive." The G5 bio gives some clues as to what Capuano did at Hewlett-Packard, namely "leading acquisitions and divestitures."[138]

Trustee Lisa Lewin[139] worked at NPD marketing and BCG consulting before establishing The Ready, a public benefit corporation partnered with Johnson & Johnson, Microsoft, Fidelity Investments and others.[140]

Another Trustee, Valerie D'Costa, is a former information and communications technology advisor to the Singaporean government who worked at the World Bank, "where she was charged with leading international initiatives to support communities of entrepreneurs in emerging markets around the world."[141] Lisa Seitz-Gruwell, Wikimedia's Chief Advancement Officer, "previously worked as a Political Consultant and Campaign Manager for Democratic candidates in California, Montana, Michigan, Connecticut and Oregon" and has a Bachelor's in PR.[142] Lila Tretikov is CEO of Terrawatt, a company that blends eco concerns with big money. A former Chief Executive at Wikimedia, she is described by the World Economic Forum as: "launch[ing] her first company, Grok, while attending college at UC Berkeley creating intelligent data mapping of the Human Genome Project. She founded and scaled several pre-[initial public offering] companies, as well as accelerated 10-100% [year-on-year] growth of strategic projects within multi-billion USD corporations."[143]

The World Economic Forum (WEF) is an annual meeting of the super-rich held in Davos, Switzerland. Harvard's late Professor Samuel P. Huntington described Davos people as sharing "beliefs in individualism, market economies, and political democracy ... Davos people control virtually all international institutions, many of the world's governments, and the bulk of the world's economic and military capabilities."[144] Several Wikimedia Foundation bigwigs became Davos people or moved from Davos to Wikimedia. Former Wikimedia

Foundation Advisor, Trevor Neilson, founder and CEO of i(x) investments, worked for the White House Travel Office, Council on Foreign Relations, World Economic Forum, the Bill & Melinda Gates Foundation and the Clinton Global Initiative.[145] In 2008, the Wikimedia Foundation was listed as one of the top tech pioneers by the WEF. Then chaired by the geneticist and recipient of the French Order of Merit, Florence Devouard, the Foundation was described by the WEF as "a nonprofit charitable organization dedicated to encouraging the growth, development and distribution of free, multilingual content, and to providing the full content of these wiki-based projects to the public free of charge."[146]

In 2017, Wikimedia's Katherine Maher spoke at WEF's Annual Meeting of the Global Future Council's Globalization of Knowledge session. Her talk *The web of lies (and how not to get caught in it)* was described by the WEF as advocating "the need to give people access to free, trustworthy information on an internet besieged and beset by 'alternative facts'."[147] The summary links to an interview in which Maher decries fake news and promotes Wikimedia as a possible antidote, omitting Wikipedia's own distortions of reality, of course; some of which are analyzed in the following chapters. Maher said: "With great respect for the press, for a very long time now there has been an assumption of trust." So, the issue is not the production and dissemination of technologies carrying objectively factual information, but rather, one of trust. The public has to "trust" the information it receives from the kind of organizations supporting and supported by Wikimedia. Maher continues: "What I'm really seeing from many outlets is a conversation that they're having with their readers around what do we need to do in order to regain your trust?" Maher concludes: "The types of sources we want to have in Wikipedia are publications and outlets that engage in fact checking and issue corrections when they get things wrong."[148]

WEF's Technology Pioneer community notes that "[p]ast selected companies include: Airbnb, Bluebird Bio, Bloom Energy, Cyberdyne, Editas, Foundation Medicine, Google, Kaggle, Kickstarter, Mozilla, Palantir Technologies, Proteus Digital Health, Rethink Robotics, Scribd, Solazyme, Spotify, [and] Twitter."[149] Wikipedia finds itself in dubious company. Airbnb has developed a reputation for using algorithms that discriminate on a class basis by showing poorer consumers low-grade accommodation, advertising illegal properties that fail to meet health and safety requirements, suggesting properties that use CCTV in private rooms and putting local businesses out of work.[150] The pro-Trump investor, Peter Thiel, founded Palantir with money from the CIA's In-Q-Tel venture capital firm. The company developed profiling software for use in Iraq and Afghanistan, as well as in the US against black people in New Orleans and against immigrants and refugees trying to get into the US.[151] Twitter allowed the spread of fake news during the US Presidential Election 2016, the UK Brexit Referendum 2016 and the UK general election 2019.[152]

Consider also the connections between Wikipedia's top developers and US institutions that shape state-power. At the Council on Foreign Relations' symposium Moderating Online Content with the Help of Artificial Intelligence (2018), Tiffany Li of the

Wikimedia/Yale Law School Initiative on Intermediaries and Information spoke with Robert Caplan of Data & Society. Caplan described the system as being "community-reliant, so this is Reddit and Wikimedia, where there is basically kind of federal model." How to manage freedom vs. social control? Li says: "You can have regulations from the U.S., for example, which very much protect free speech and free expression. You have regulations in the EU that have very strong laws on things like hate speech or extremist speech that require very quick or fast content takedowns." Li went on to note that "the most important thing ... is that the promise of the internet was to allow for online speech." She added that her colleague, Professor Jack Balkin of Yale Law School, proposed "a triangle model of speech regulation, so three types of regulation of speech." The three types are: government regulation, corporate regulation, and speech regulation, such as agencies asking corporations to remove content. Li concludes that "on issues like extremist content, there's a lot of collaboration inside a sector, as well as with the public sector. So there's a lot of very close collaboration with law enforcement, with national security, and on international security issues."[153]

Like the US government, Wikipedia resents sovereign states exercising executive control over their internets and thus the limitation of Wikipedia's operational freedoms. In 2013, internet advocacy groups prevented the imposition of an anti-piracy bill in Taiwan, which the US Council on Foreign Relations describes as being "similar to the U.S. Stop Online Piracy Act (SOPA)." The CFR calls it "an amendment to the Taiwan Intellectual Property Office's Copyright Act [that] would have forced Internet service providers to block a list of domains or IP addresses connected to websites and services that enable illegal file sharing." Wikipedia objected to the Taiwanese government trying to protect individuals and companies from copyright infringement. "The plan would have allowed Taiwan's bureaucracies to create a blacklist for websites and peer-to-peer sharing tools like BitTorrent, rather than blocking individual videos and files as the law currently allows." Again we see the shared interests of Wikipedia and the US government, which wants to keep Taiwan open to US investments and refuses to recognize Taiwan as Chinese territory. "Most of the pressure for this legislation came from the recording industry, but the U.S. government also expressed concern over piracy in the U.S. Trade Representative's most recent National Estimate Trade Report." The CFR notes that "[t]he plan was abandoned after several large Internet companies, including Wikimedia Taiwan and Mozilla Taiwan, threatened to stage a day-long blackout similar to the Internet blackouts that took place in the United States against SOPA last year."[154]

NEOCOLONIALISM

According to the capitalist model, nations are "brands" that compete for investments, exports, foreign talent and international prestige. These are measured by the Alhit-Gfk Roper Nation Brand Index and the Country Brand Index. The South Korean Samsung company helped to develop the Nation Brand Double Octagon to measure nation substance and image. Lee and Chun argue that Wikipedia can help poorer countries with their national branding. They propose that unlike Facebook, Twitter and YouTube, which are limited in third-party access (Facebook), premised on visual data and loaded with lies (YouTube), acronyms or emoticons (Twitter), Wikipedia is open-access and professes to have editorial standards. Ergo, it is in researchers' minds the best popular website with which to measure real-time national branding. The authors examined the number of Indonesians and Vietnamese who viewed the English-language entries for "South Korea," "China" and "Japan"; the logic being that the latter three are bigger economies by GDP than the former two and tend to invest in the smaller countries. Thirty-seven percent of visits to the entry for South Korea concern politics, 33 society, 29 culture and just 1 economics. For China, 57 percent of users are interested in politics, 36 society, 6 culture and again 1 economics. For Japan, the least viewed of the three countries, 62 percent are primarily interested in the society, 22 culture, 14 politics and 2 economics.[155]

In 2018, *Wired* reported: "Almost a decade ago, we began mapping all of the content on Wikipedia and found that the site was a highly unequal representation of the world. There were many more articles about Europe and North America than there were about poorer parts of the world." It goes on to note that, "[f]or every article about Africa, there were twenty about Europe. That was despite the fact that Africa is three times larger than Europe, it has over twice the population, and has roughly the same number of internet users." It concludes: "The Wikipedia community has become increasingly aware of systemic barriers to participation, and a growing number of initiatives are seeking to counteract them and foster a more pluralistic representation of the world."[156]

From the outset, Wikipedia was never simply about disseminating free information. Rather, part of the goal was to inspire oppressed foreign populations to see a world outside the mental prisons imposed by their states' Ministries of Truth. That would be a fine objective, were it not for the fact that the end result of being inspired to free oneself is re-imprisonment in the US-led "free market" system championed by the likes of Wales. Noting how freed-up information inspired the Arab Spring, Wales told journalists about how pro-US-EU activists involved in Ukraine's Orange Revolution (2004) read Wikipedia. "It's one thing to go out on the street and demand change … It's another to say, 'O.K., we won, the bad guy's gone, now what?'"[157] That's where US-led information systems can help to replace the "bad guys"; i.e., with the wonders of the "free market." The Wikipedia Zero campaign ran on a zero-rating platform, meaning that users could get free internet access under certain conditions, namely if they used Google and Wikipedia. This violated net neutrality and was phased out in 2018. Countries and telecoms companies involved were typically poor and included Afghanistan's Roshan, Bangladesh's Banglalink, Iraq's Asiacell, Kenya's Orange SA, Kosovo's IPKO, Kyrgyzstan's Beeline, Pakistan's Mobilink, Saudi Arabia's Telecom Company, Thailand's dtac and Ukraine's Kyivstar.[158]

The US Agency for international Development (USAID) supports the soft-power form of neocolonialism. Often, USAID grant-programs in poor countries help to develop justice and law programs, civil society development and equality programs. Doing so can enable the absorption of oppressed populations, such as single mothers and homosexuals, into a different form of oppression, namely the US-led economic market system. In 2014, for instance, USAID sponsored a study with UCLA's Williams Institute on Sexual Orientation and Gender Identity Law and Public Policy. One report says: "When LGBT people are denied full participation in society because of their identities, their human rights are violated, and those violations of human rights are likely to have a harmful effect on a country's level of economic development."[159] Ergo, anyone promoting the rights of marginalized people in poor countries without also working with those people to liberate themselves from US economic domination is doing USAID's work knowingly or not.

On the Board of Wikimedia's Trustees sits Esra'a Al Shafei, founder of Majal (formerly Mideast Youth). Al Shafei is described as "promot[ing] expression for youth and underrepresented voices, and improve[ing] the lives of LGBTQ people in the Middle East and North Africa."[160] The website says Majal "addresses issues that receive little or no attention: From rights of the invisible lower income migrant workers, to the stigmatized Middle East LGBTQ community, to those seeking to express dissent through music."[161] Starting out as Mideast Youth, the organization was sponsored by TED Fellowships and Harvard's Berkman Center for Internet & Society.[162] US human rights policy in the Middle East and North Africa is a mixed bag. When human rights can be used as a weapon to criticize enemy states, like Iran, they feature in Western media. When allies commit human rights violations they are seldom reported, except when the US supports economic modernization programs in those states. According to the World Economic Forum: "Al Shafei currently serves on the Global Future Council on the Future of Human Rights at the World Economic Forum and is a Directors fellow at the MIT Media Lab."[163]

Consider how knowledge in poor countries is automated. By 2014, 732 bots had made 9.6 percent of Wikipedia's English-language edits, as had: 322 bots in German (10.2 percent), 228 Dutch (32.9 percent) and 216 French (22.9 percent). There is a colonial element to Wikipedia's use of bots. In poor countries, the number of bots and percentage of edits to Wikipedia entries are as follows: Bengali 31 (64.1 percent), Indonesian 23 (41.7 percent), Slovak 24 (50 percent), Swahili 34 (66.2 percent) and Vietnamese 25 (62.2 percent). The use of foreign (English-language) interwiki bots necessitates the establishment of English-language translations of each country's tailored bot policy.[164]

Funded by the European Union's Seventh Framework Programme and published by the International Monetary Fund, Ojanperä and colleagues proposed the creation of a Digital Knowledge Economy Index. They write that, "[e]ager to tap into economic and social opportunities potentially afforded by the information revolution, many governments of low-income countries have designed policies to guide their transformation into so-called 'knowledge economies'." Wikipedia fits into this model. From the neocolonial perspective, how can poor people be absorbed into the US economic system without the basic knowledge to allow them to compete? Here's where Wikipedia comes in. The authors note that "[p]olicy makers in many Sub-Saharan African (SSA) countries, in particular, are eager to tap into the new opportunities afforded by the information revolution, and both ICT sector policies as well as voices in the donor and private sectors are optimistic about the potentials of such a transformation." They note that the Knowledge Economy Index (KEI) "measures how close a country comes to having a knowledge economy with a score between 10 (best) and 0 (worst)." They note that "Sweden tops the list in the KEI scoring 9.43. For comparison, the US ranks 12th with a score of 8.77 and the highest-ranking African country is Mauritius at 67th with a score of 5.52."[165]

Paul Kagame, the US-British-backed dictator of Rwanda and fighter in the genocidal war in the Democratic Republic of Congo (2003-present) is quoted in a related IMF study: "In Africa, we have missed both the agricultural and industrial revolutions and in Rwanda we are determined to take full advantage of the digital revolution." The authors of the report note: "Given the centrality of technology and human capital in the knowledge economy, its measurement should feature an estimation of knowledge-rich digital activity."[166]

***

Let us now consider the inner workings of Wikipedia.

Chapter 2
The Hidden Costs of Free Information

In 2016, Wikipedia's founders and editors celebrated their digital child's fifteenth birthday. Around that time, Wikipedia had 200,000 editors, 48 million entries in 300 languages, and was read 15 billion times per month.[167] Twenty-seven million users were registered by 2015, and 20,000 new entries appeared each month. According to Pew, Wikipedia had 97.2 billion English-language page views. The non-English language world viewed the site much less often, with Ukraine's Wikipedia pages reaching 7 million views at the low end and Japan's reaching 15 billion at the high end. By 2015, Wikipedia was the 7th most viewed site in the world.[168] Wikipedia has a reputation for being left of center and progressive. "In almost all cases" analyzed in an academic, comparative study of Wikipedia and the respected *Encyclopædia Britannica*, it was found that "Wikipedia was more left-leaning." Eleven-percent of corporate-related Wikipedia articles were biased toward Democrats, as were 9% of government-related articles, 4% of education-, 4% of immigration-, and 3% of civil rights-related entries.[169]

With the exception of Islamic State (a.k.a., Daesh), the top ten most viewed Wikipedia entries in 2015 reflect the innocuous interests of tech-savvy, predominantly young people raised in the "capitalist" West: 1) list of deaths by year, 2) Wikipedia itself, 3) Facebook, 4) Daesh, 5) list of Bollywood films, 6) *Star Wars: The Force Awakens*, 7) the USA, 8) the 87th Academy Awards, 9) Google, and 10) *Game of Thrones*.[170]

The picture that emerges is one of a harmless, left-leaning, free encyclopedia relevant to the internet age. The reality is very different. That the entries might hold a "left-wing" bias towards, say, the Democratic Party, yields no information about the form and structure of Wikipedia or the nature of the Democratic Party. After all, the Democrats are split between the multibillionaire corporate donors who want it to be the party of big business, and the grassroots members who want it to be the party of working people. On the "left vs. right" issue, the same argument is made by right-wingers about mainstream media, namely that they have a "liberal bias." The opposite argument is made by left-wingers; that, as giant corporations, mainstream media are right-wing. So, a "left-right" analysis does not answer the question of bias. Mainstream television media in the US (with the exception of Fox) do have a liberal bias on cultural and party-political issues. But, as corporations, they have "right-wing" biases on most other issues:[*] the

---

[*] It should be noted that language is confused; a factor that makes communication between left and right groups difficult, if not impossible. For instance, war is considered by the grassroots left to be a right-wing agenda. But the so-called left-leaning liberal corporate media support war, making right-wingers believe that war is a left-liberal agenda. These linguistic inversions generalize across other fields, including the economy.

economy, foreign policy, the environment, workers' rights, and so on. Their biases are not necessarily the reflection of the political beliefs of their journalists, presenters, editors, CEOs, or even shareholders. Rather, they are an inherent consequence of corporations (private media conglomerates) selling their audiences to other corporations (advertisers). Unless media were democratized from the bottom up, nothing too radical either way (right or left) could emerge from such a power nexus. We find the same with Wikipedia.

Lerner and Lomi note that Wikipedia is "an emergent hierarchical order sustained by self-organizing sequences of text editing events." In social structures, status and reputation typically enable coordination more than conflict. Low-status Wikipedians are more likely than higher-status ones to have their work undone by peers in the future. "With more than 5 million articles visited each month by more than 500 million unique readers, Wikipedia is perhaps the most comprehensive knowledge repository available and one of the most popular web sites in existence."[171] Kumar and Shah studied false online information in an effort to develop technology to combat it. They cite one experiment suggesting that people are unable to distinguish fake stories from real ones, particularly when the fake stories are lengthy and well referenced. They cite tests in which "trained and trusted Wikipedia volunteers, called 'patrollers,' make the similar mistakes by approving long and well-referenced hoax articles for publication." On Wikipedia, they find that one percent of well-written hoax entries last up to a year before being detected as fake and removed. The average for hoax articles is three views per day, compared to 3.5 for non-hoaxes. One percent of hoaxes are viewed more than 100 times per day.[172] One case from 2005 that blended hoaxing with libel was the entry for a John Seigenthaler; a journal editor whom the entry falsely claimed was responsible for the assassinations of John F. and Robert Kennedy.[173]

To keep the organization in check, a body called the Wikipedia Cultural Diversity Observatory was established to list languages, ISO codes and other matters related to Wikipedia's cultural diversity. The Wikimedia Foundation and Catalan Agency for Business Competitiveness funded a study into Wikipedia's content. Authors Miquel-Ribé and Laniado write: "there was disagreement about the article 'Bronvaux,' a French municipality in the region of Lorraine, close to the German border and historically disputed between the two countries." German Wikipedia categorized the region as Historical Territory (German). "[T]he culture gap highlights a common difficulty in achieving a representation of cultural diversity, indicating that editors are often not able to cover concepts from other cultures." Researchers Rogers and Sendijarevic "compared an article dedicated to 'The Srebrenica Massacre' [1995] throughout different Wikipedia language editions, including English and Balkan languages. The study shows how the same article in different language editions adopts a different point of view to illustrate facts. Such points of view are sometimes unified, other times in total disagreement when it comes to the terminology employed and its political connotations."[174]

HOW WIKIPEDIA WORKS

By 2017, Wikipedia's entries totalled 38.79 million across 291 languages. Each day, around 860 new articles are added. Edits number 817 million and average 21.12 per page. In one month (June 2015) alone, over 374 million people visited Wikipedia. If published as books, Wikipedia's entries would have totalled 15,930 volumes by 2013.[175]

Professor José van Dijck notes that the "wisdom of crowds" philosophy that supposedly underpins Wikipedia should constitute a form of anarchism, in which everyone regardless of qualification is free and able to participate. In reality it does not. But neither is Wikipedia the Wales-controlled dictatorship suggested in the previous chapter. Instead, van Dijck likens the entity to a highly bureaucratic nation-state. The Wikimedia Foundation operates under US law, is directed by a board of trustees and raises money for Wikipedia's servers and equipment. Between 2006 and 2009, the Foundation morphed from a volunteer-led organization to a global institution with a centralized HQ and paid staff. With early supporters dropping off in protest over the Foundation's centralization, the Wikimedia Foundation is compared by van Dijck to the US Corporation for Public Broadcasting and to the Public Broadcasting System/Service in terms of its corporate-like structure within the supposed remit of providing a public service. One of the anarchistic elements of Wikipedia is content and trademark ownership being with the Wikipedia community as opposed to one or two individuals. However, researcher Mayo Fuster Morell notes that the community is "serendipitous."[176]

Prior to Wikipedia, a small group of academics were asked to assist in a free, online, open-content encyclopedia, originally called Nupedia. Co-founders Jimmy Wales and Larry Sanger established a protocol of peer-review based on openness and objectivity. Sanger and Wales had a split in opinion, with the latter preferring what became the Wiki model.[177] In 2001, Wikipedia described itself as "the free encyclopedia that anyone can edit." Freedom and mutual access to creativity and service are two principles with which anarchists of all shades would agree. Yet, Wikipedia never claimed to follow anarchist principles and, eleven years later, rejected them as partisan: "Wikipedia is NOT a soapbox, an advertising platform, a vanity press, an experiment in anarchy or democracy...," and so on (emphasis in original).[178] By the time its upper-echelon editors had reiterated the non-anarchism of Wikipedia, its lower-level registered users and contributors had reached 15 million and the number of entries 3.7m. Van Dijck describes Wikipedia as having "taken the road of systematized professionalization." Wikipedia's advocates used terms like "distributed collaboration" and "collaborative knowledge" to talk up its democratic merits. "The platforms' founders repudiated the notion of crowds producing Wikipedia." Until 2006, "the notion of a massive collective of contributors simply did not apply," with two percent of editors making 73 percent of the edits.[179]

Beginning 2006, elite usage declined. From the Marxist point of view explored by van Dijck, the hegemony of the "pioneers" allowed for the expansion of a "bourgeoisie" of digital settlers. These new users became the lower-level managerial class; a development typical of collaborative knowledge systems. Van Dijck divides Wikipedians into different classes. The lowest are blocked users, unregistered users, new users and autoconfirmed users. The middle-classes are the administrators, bureaucrats, stewards and bots. It is interesting that bots are higher on van Dijck's scale than humans. The elite of Wikipedia are the developers and system administrators.[180]

By 2010, 16 percent of all edits were made by bots.[181] "The most active Wikipedians are in fact bots," writes van Dijck, who compares this power concentration to other user-generated content platforms.[182] By 2010, the system administrators consisted of just ten people. Ten out of 15 million users. They manage and maintain Wikipedia Foundation Servers.[183] Introduced in 2002 to save on administration work, Wikipedia's editors employ an army of bots (457 in 2008) to make automated edits: 3RRBot, Rambot, SieBot, TxiKiBot and so on. One of the anarchistic elements of Wikipedia is the open-engineering of algorithmic tools. There are generally two kinds of bots: admin bots and coauthoring bots. Admin bots block spam, fix vandalism, correct spelling, discriminate between new and anonymous users, ban targeted users, and search for copyright issues and plagiarism. Tools that alert human editors include Huggle, Lupin and Twinkle.[184]

The coauthoring bots began with Derek Ramsey's Rambot, which pulled content from public databases and fed it into Wikipedia. Between 2002 and 2010, Rambot created 30,000 articles by pulling data from, among other places, the CIA's *World Factbook*.[185] Compared to proprietary algorithms such as EdgeRank and PageRank, Wikipedia's are open.[186] New editors are welcomed only "tactically." Of interest to the thesis of this book, that Wikipedia manufactures consensus, is the enculturation of new users. Within this system is a techno-elite that designs and operates the system that manages the myriad of users. This prompted organizational controls, including the distribution of permission-levels and the expansion of exclusion and blocking protocols. The growth of hierarchy resulted in rising complaints about what became a cumbersome bureaucracy, with the writer Nicolas Carr denouncing the supposed egalitarian expression of collective intelligence as a "myth."[187]

Meatbot is a pejorative computer geek term for a human. On Wikipedia, the English-language version contains the WP:MEATBOTS shortcut, which redirects to a subsection of its Bot Policy; which, ironically, has been edited by at least 38 bots. The Policy demands human editors "pay attention to the edits they make" and not to sacrifice quality for quantity. The Policy holds the given human responsible for the errors of the bot. Coded by Wikipedian programmers known as Pythons, bots have their own anonymity in some respects. Pythons have developed a bot-building tool known as *pywikipediabot* (Python Wikipediabot Framework). Their edits as distinct users in MediaWiki software do not appear. The bots help to dump all language material into a data repository called Wikidata. As noted, bots are charged with a variety of tasks, including having power over human users. R. Stuart Geiger questions the morality of attempting to put a bot on Wikipedia's Arbitration Committee, which deals with disputes, such as entry content, vandals and the banning of repeated rule-breakers.[188]

STRUCTURAL MISOGYNY

By 2008, 13% of Wikipedia editors worldwide were women. By 2011, 9% of contributors were women (15% in the US-English language version). Wikipedia's response to the gender imbalance was typically patronizing. It pledged to meet a female participation "target" of 25% by 2015. Empirical research found that many female contributors "reported feeling less confident about their expertise, less comfortable with editing others' work (a process which often involves conflict), and reacting more negatively to critical feedback than men."[189] This suggests that Wikipedia is a patriarchy. Highlighting the collaboration between the corporate talking shop, the World Economic Forum (WEF), and Wikipedia, the WEF notes: "Volunteers are working to raise the profile of famous women - who make up only 17 percent of Wikipedia's 1.5 million biographies, according to the Wikimedia Foundation, which hosts the online encyclopaedia - by writing more female biographies."[190] The lazy response would be to say that because women have been oppressed throughout history, men are more notable. But deeper research suggests that women have often been the inspiration behind many male-dominated achievements and, of course, been given little or no credit.[191]

Women tend to have less leisure time than men, working to look after children, elderly parents, the home and in full- or part-time jobs. Christina Shane-Simpson and Kristen Gillespie-Lynch reckon that these differences make it harder for women to participate in Wikipedia. They note that men tend to be more technology-oriented than women and self-assured in their alleged editing skills.[192] For instance, women were 30 percent more likely than men to express fear of criticism over their editorial skills and decision. Women are bullied, harassed, victimized and intimidated online more than men. This is not to suggest that women are incapable of self-defense, but abuse is off-putting. Studies of chatroom behavior suggest that men tend to display dominance more than women during communication.[193]

When it comes to content, women tend to favor a more positive tone than men; difference in content-styles can therefore lead to further male-female conflicts within Wikipedia. This has led to more female-articles being labelled "controversial" (presumably by male colleagues, who, as noted outnumber women). This also leads to more women being banned from Wikipedia in proportion to their numbers. In decision-making, women tend to seek to build consensus rather than give orders, unlike their male counterparts. This is also a problem in a hierarchy like Wikipedia, especially as administrators tend to communicate more with users who employ similar communicative styles. By 2016, little over under 23 percent of US Wikipedians working on the English-language site were women: a five-percent increase in female editors over a six-year period. Highlighting the gender imbalance, Shane-Simpson and Gillespie-Lynch write: "women may be less sure of their expertise, more often targeted for harassment, and more negatively affected by critical feedback than men. Consequently, women may contribute more during online discussions rather than through visible, article-based Wikipedia editing."[194]

In 2014, a number of female editors belonging to the Gender Gap Task Force were banned from Wikipedia, as was an editor who claimed that a male Wikipedian had been impersonating her on a pornographic website. Bryce Peake writes that the internal politics of Wikipedia is "a space where the primary focus is on the mastery of policy as a tool for domination—and not on the production of, or debates about, verifiable facts and actually existing knowledge."[195] Researchers Maude Gauthier and Kim Sawchuk write: "Sue Gardner, former Executive Director of the Wikimedia Foundation, describes Wikipedia's culture as sexist and intentionally intimidating towards women editors." Gauthier and Sawchuk are experts in ageism and feminism. They conducted an experiment in which they tried to create an entry for the UK-based advocacy group, the Centre for Women, Ageing and Media. The authors' entry was voted down by senior editors. One claimed that the organization had "[n]o coverage in reliable, nonaffiliated sources" and was therefore not a noteworthy organization. This is problematic because a male-dominated, neoliberal political economy that sees feminism and age as being against its interests would be unlikely to incorporate the Centre for Women, Ageing and Media into its cultural or propaganda system, meaning that few references to the organization will exist outside of specialist circles.[196]

But if Wikipedia editors selectively reject entries based on the subject's supposed obscurity, Wikipedia mirrors the unjust neoliberal culture in which it operates. Justifying their rejection, another editor said: "Very nearly every source here is still either primary or blogspotty." This, too, is problematic. Primary sources are often vital in their being direct carriers of information, as opposed to secondary sources which filter and frame the primary information. That Wikipedia's policy is to frequently reject primary-source material means that knowingly or not it acts like mainstream media and academia, selecting and reframing information as its editors see fit. Not only did Gauthier and Sawchuk find articles on different subjects that had not lived up to the standards imposed on their rejected work, they also noted that "one of the deleters was a partisan of the Men's rights movement and had had problems with a misogynistic impersonation of his account (which was disclosed on his userpage)."[197]

OF POLITICS AND CONTROVERSIES

Yasseri and the team calculated the most controversial subjects on Wikipedia. They write: "Wikipedia is more than just an encyclopaedia; it is also a window into convergent and divergent social-spatial priorities, interests and preferences." They studied 12 different language editions of Wikipedia and developed a Wikipedia Dispute Index. They identify several markers of controversy, the main one being "reverts"; i.e., when an editor undoes another's work. In English versions of Wikipedia, the most controversial topics were: 10) Christianity, 9) Race and intelligence, 8) Jesus, 7) United States, 6) Circumcision, 5) Global warming, 4) LWWE (wrestling), 3) Muhammad, 2) Anarchism and 1) George W. Bush. The authors write: "there is a positive role of the conflicts: if they can be resolved in a consensus, the resulting product will better reflect the state of the art then without fighting them out. However, there are examples, where no hope for a consensus seems in sight – then the struggle strongly limits efficiency."[198]

Category A controversies include politics, politicians, political movements and ideologies. Category A constitutes 25 percent of all controversial subjects. Category B accounts for 17 percent of contentious entries and includes geographical locations, countries, towns and cities; though there is likely to be overlap, given that the Occupied Palestinian Territories, for instance, fall into both geographical and political categories. Category C controversies constitute 15 percent and include religions, cults and beliefs; though, again there is overlap. Also overlapping is Category D, which includes history and historical figures and comprises 9 percent of highly disputed entries. Other category subjects include science, sport, literature (including newspapers), films and entertainers. Among all three language sets ((1) English-French-German-Spanish, (2) Czech-Hungarian-Romanian, (3) Arabic-Hebrew-Persian), the most controversial subjects are "Israel, Adolf Hitler, The Holocaust and God." The most controversial subjects on the French Wikipedia are: 10) Nuclear power, 9) God in Christianity, 8) Islamophobia, 7) The Muhammad al-Durrah incident (the killing of the eponymous 12-year-old filmed by a France 2 reporter in the Israeli-Occupied Palestinian Territories), 6) 9/11, 5) Sigmund Freud, 4) Jesus, 3) Jehovah's Witnesses, 2) UFOs, and 1) France's Presidential candidate, Ségolène Royal. The most controversial topics in Hebrew were: 10) Israeli PM Ariel Sharon, 9) Beitar Jerusalem FC (soccer), 8) the "Gaza War" (Operation Cast Lead 2008-09), 7) Daphni Leef, 6) Jewish settlement in Hebron (Israeli-Occupied Palestine), 5) Former and later PM Benjamin Netanyahu, 4) B'Tselem (Israeli human rights organization opposed to the occupation of Palestine), 3) the "Lebanon War" (2006), 2) Chabad messianism, and 1) Chabad.[199]

Some of the most controversial English-language Wikipedia entries in no particular order in the English, French, German and Spanish versions include the words Anarchism, Arab, Augusto Pinochet (former US-British-backed dictator of Chile), Czech, France, Global Warming, Homeopathy, Iran, Israel, Jerusalem, Jesus, Joseph Stalin, Language, Mexico,

Osama bin Laden, Pseudoscience, Psychoanalysis and Socialism.[200] Above, we explored Wikipedia's use of editing bots. Tsvetkova and the team noted that "some of the articles most contested by bots are about Pervez Musharraf (former president of Pakistan), Uzbekistan, Estonia, Belarus, Arabic language, Niels Bohr, Arnold Schwarzenegger. This would suggest that a significant portion of bot-bot fighting occurs across languages rather than within."[201]

REPUTATIONAL PRISONS

Supportive of big pharma, the English-language version of Wikipedia tends to attack alternative health practitioners and critics of Western foreign policy. For instance, a computer-user traced to the US Congress changed the word "dissident" in NSA whistleblower Edward Snowden's biographical entry to "traitor."[202] Given its popularity, ease of use, gravitas and promotion by the kind of MSM its editors often cite as sources (in a mutual reciprocity cycle), it is easy for individuals including critics of Western governments and corporations to be locked into Wikipedia's reputational prisons. For example, Susan Burke is a lawyer who brought cases against the US government on behalf of Iraqi torture and sexual abuse victims. One of Burke's civil cases involved Erik Prince, founder of the Blackwater mercenary company. In 2013, Burke announced that she was going to sue Wikipedia for defamation. Burke was hoping to unmask the identity of the two editors, "Zujua" and "CapBasics359," whom she believed could be working with Wikipedia on behalf of Blackwater.[203] Burke lost the case after the Court of Appeals in the District of Columbia reversed the judge's ruling on "Zujua's" attorney fees.[204] This means that in the US, potentially any anonymous person can write libelous material against another and invoke their right to "freedom of speech."

In the US, Section 230 of the Federal Communications Decency Act (1996) largely saves Wikipedia from libel cases because, unlike publishers which are not covered, Wikipedia is a service provider.[205] In 2008, the thesis was tested when literary agent Barbara Bauer tried to sue Wikipedia for defamation after the site allegedly insulted her. In addition to personal distress, such actions by Wikipedia could damage her business by casting doubt on Bauer's professional abilities. Wikipedia defended itself by invoking the Federal Communications Decency Act.[206] A year earlier, three French men attempted to sue Wikipedia when an entry described them as homosexual. But citing France's *Loi pour la confiance dans l'économie numérique* (2004), Judge Emmanuel Binoche ruled that service providers could not be sued for libel.[207] *The Register* notes that due to Britain's strict (in fact excessive) libel laws, which place the burden of proof on the accused not the accuser, Wikipedia's co-founder Jimmy Wales decided not to base the site's servers in Britain. *The Register* adds: "There certainly are good, thoughtful contributors at Wikipedia, yet huge swathes of material – encompassing biographies of living people – are governed by anonymous fanatics with an axe to grind."[208]

One such axe-grinder is Guerilla Skepticism, an organization run by Susan Gerbic, who once presented a workshop on skepticism adorned in a t-shirt which read, "Big Pharma Shillin'." In 2010, Gerbic began editing for Wikipedia in an effort to counter largely harmless eccentrics: ufologists, flat Earthers, anti-vaxxers and other nonconformists who represent a miniscule fraction of the broader population. Like the religious dogmatists of old who persecuted heathens, the worshippers of today's power systems are terrified of tiny numbers of dissidents. Now working with 100 colleagues across multiple languages,[209] Gerbic and her so-called skeptics are skeptical of little people, not of big power, such as the US government, intelligence agencies, mainstream media or multimillion dollar drug companies that kill tens of thousands of people and distort market prices.

Another with an axe to grind is the mastermind behind a vulnerable adult called Andrew Philip Cross, who edits as "Philip Cross." Some have pointed to the correlation between the progressive individuals targeted for smear by Cross and their names being tweeted by the British *Times* writer and former hedge fund investor, Oliver Kamm. Kamm strenuously denies that he is behind Cross and has hinted at legal action against those who make the allegation.[210] Others point to the coincidence that each Cross target is a Kamm critic. Having made 130,000+ edits to the entries for anti-war pundits, journalists, academics and politicians, the allegedly obese, immobile and autistic Cross[211] appears to be used by a political Svengali, an individual or perhaps individuals (not Kamm, Kamm assures us), to the distress of Cross's parents. Cross refers to his targets as "goons"[212] and over a fifteen-year period has edited the entries for: the former politician, George Galloway (top target); the UK-based media analysis website, MediaLens (second most targeted, with Cross writing 80 percent of the Wikipedia entry's content on the group); the veteran, prize-winning journalist, John Pilger; veteran Middle East correspondent, the late Robert Fisk; the British Labour Party's former leader, Jeremy Corbyn; ex-UK Ambassador to Uzbekistan and human rights whistleblower, Craig Murray; and anti-Syria war research academic, Dr. Piers Robinson. American targets include the Pulitzer Prize-winning journalists Chris Hedges and Glenn Greenwald.

In addition to trying to create the general impression of progressive, anti-war critics of Western foreign policy as mentally unhinged, factually inaccurate and not representative of the majority of British people, Cross has directly aided British and American state propaganda by minimizing Anglo-American war crimes. For instance, the Iraq Body Count (IBC) is an organization notorious among anti-war campaigners for underestimating the number of dead as a result of the US-British invasion in 2003. Cromwell and Edwards of MediaLens have worked to expose this. Cross removed all references to their work from Wikipedia's entry on the IBC. When proposed on Twitter, that Cross might be a proxy for British intelligence, such as Government Communications Headquarters or the Ministry of Defence's secret social media warfare unit, the Joint Threat and Intelligence Research Group, Jimmy Wales responded: "Evidence matters. Conspiracy ranting is cheap crap."[213]

THE CORPORATE PUBLIC RELATIONS MANUAL

"Wikiwashing" is the art of cleansing a biographical entry of negative information. The Texas-based Wiki-PR hires editors and created 250 fake accounts to create or contribute to entries regarding its clients. A Trustee of the Wikimedia Foundation UK stepped down after it was revealed that he had been paid by the Gibraltar Tourist Board.[214] Corporate interference has broad impacts on group dynamics and participation. The number of active editors was down from 51,000 in 2007 to 31,000 in 2013. Wiki-PR says that its edit entries for 12,000 clients, allegedly included Priceline and Viacom; as we have seen, Viacom is a big Wikimedia donor. Other companies offering editing services include MyWikiPro, Wikiexperts, Freelancer and Elance. One editor, Morning277, spent years writing and editing 6,000 unchallenged articles for companies and individuals. Being paid editors "is not against the rules," said Wiki-PR's CEO Jordan French in 2013.

It was late as 2012 that Wikipedia updated its guidelines on prohibiting articles written by undisclosed public relations firms. The PR firm Sunshine Sachs was reportedly successful in erasing references to Mia Farrow's political activism in Ecuador. Mike Wood is a freelance Wikipedia editor who boasts of creating entries for giant US corporations, including major banks. Wood says that the presence of PR editors made established editors more suspicious of new members. In 2012, it became clear that the climate of hostility toward the new members was causing a drop in volunteerism: by about 10,000 between 208 and 2015. Jimmy Wales edited his own page to refer to himself as the founder of Wikipedia; erasing references to Larry Sanger's role. Wikipedia is more popular among readers of media articles than WebMD. By 2015, half of all US physicians had consulted it as a source. The Oxford University Press-published book chapter entitled "Marbug and Ebola" published in 2011 had been plagiarized from a Wikipedia entry from 2006.[215]

By 2013, 30,000 people per month edited Wikipedia but since 2003, only 1,000 administrative roles have been created. Leslie Cafferty, Vice President of Corporate Communications at Priceline, said: "We are using [Wiki-PR] to help us get all of our brands a presence because I don't have the resources internally to otherwise manage" the company's Wikipedia profile. Emad Rahim, Dean of Colorado Technical University's College of Business and Management, describes himself as "a brand": "a thought leader" who hired Wiki-PR to use Wikipedia as a tool for self-promotion only to find that his entry was targeted for deletion. Wikimedia Foundation Global Communications Office's Matthew Roth said: "The Wikimedia Foundation is monitoring the sockpuppet investigation." Sockpuppeteering "isn't in the spirit of Wikipedia."[216] By 2014, Wikipedia had changed its guidelines and even sent a cease and desist letter to Wiki-PR's CEO, Jordan French, in an effort to minimize corporate tinkering.[217]

Wikipedians Gemma Griffiths (Wikimedia UK, ex-Motorola PR specialist) and Paul Wilkinson (in PR since 1987), co-authored a document teaching PR consultants how to use Wikipedia: The Chartered Institute of Public Relations' *Wikipedia Best Practice Guide*. It is worth quoting at length as it not only shows how corporations blatantly utilize Wikipedia for their own ends, it shows the blurred distinctions between the corporate world and the supposedly neutral encyclopedia, with Griffiths and Wilkinson actively explaining how to use the organization to repair reputational damage. "Wikipedia has established a strong brand and has become a destination site on the web. It also ranks highly for search." The report notes that "[t]hese two features combined mean that Wikipedia has a significant reputational impact for any individual or organisation that is discussed in its articles." What are the poor corporations to do? "Errors in traditional media can be dealt with swiftly through well-established processes. Correcting content in a Wikipedia article requires engagement with the community and, crucially, adherence to its rules." Errors means exposing corporate wrongdoing. The report goes on to note that "[t]he reputation of an organisation can be attacked in a matter of hours through changes to its Wikipedia page." But this goes for defenseless individuals, too, not just potentially multimillion dollars companies that can muster a sophisticated counterattack.[218]

The report continues: "Monitoring Wikipedia pages for modifications has become a key part of managing the reputation of an organisation. In reality rogue attacks on Wikipedia pages are few and far between but when they occur an organisation has no option but to seek redress via the community's own workflow." As we have seen, companies and intelligence agencies have sought to untarnish their "brand" by editing Wikipedia. "The relationship between the public relations industry and Wikipedia is an uneasy one although there have been numerous efforts in recent time to bring the two constituencies closer together." The report goes on to note that "[a] group of public relations practitioners has created a group called the Corporate Representatives for Ethical Wikipedia Engagement (CREWE) to lobby [co-founder Jimmy] Wales and the wider Wikipedia community to review the community's processes and policies in favour of improved corporate engagement." The authors go on to explain how lobby groups have succeeded in using the encyclopedia to improve their public image. "This remains a work in progress although thanks to the efforts of CREWE and organisations such as the [Chartered Institute of Public Relations] in the UK and the [Public Relations Society of America] in the US the relationship and understanding between Wikipedia and the public relations industry is much improved."[219]

In terms of aiding social progress beyond the shallow sloganeering of culturally liberally causes like feminism and gay rights, one of the serious problems with Wikipedia is its insistence on a prospective entry's "notability." If no-one has ever heard of a grassroots political movement, dissident or work of literature that challenges power, probably because power has suppressed that information, it is unlikely to appear on Wikipedia; unless an influential editor or administrator permits it. The PR manual notes: "The subjects of articles should also meet Wikipedia's notability criteria – a test used by editors to decide whether a topic can have its own article. If no reliable third-party sources can be found on a topic, then it should not have a separate article. This helps avoid indiscriminate inclusion of topics." So, if one authors a radical book of high quality reviewed by niche academics but not MSM, it will disappear into the memory hole because Wikipedians will not permit an entry to be created. This reinforces the wider system of marginalizing dissenting voices and reinforcing the members of the established order, such as popular authors.[220]

Another problem is Wikipedia's libeling of defenseless individuals. Companies and wealthy people can pay PR hacks to counter Wikipedia's smears. Co-founder Jimmy Wales himself says: "If something has been written about your client, tell them your client has a response, or a response that has been published elsewhere and should be on the site." Consider the implications. The supposedly neutral Wales is giving advice to PR companies on how to limit the damage done to their clients' reputations. "Talk to the community with respect. State your job title, identity, interest and company. Escalate with kindness. This is effective almost always." One particularly shocking case of corporate-Wikipedia collaboration was that of Arturo Silva; a member of BP oil's corporate communications team in Houston, Texas. Silva created a transparent user account, named Arturo at BP. The PR manual notes that "he earned barnstars from other Wikipedians for his openness …

He then used his 'userspace' on this account to draft improvements to the relevant BP articles which he then linked from their talk pages." Consider the ethical implications of Wikipedia allowing planet-destroying corporations to gloss their profiles. Silva "wrote everything from a neutral point of view and importantly always provided credible third party references for everything he wrote."[221]

This adds another problem for the so-called neutrality principle. Oil companies pollute as part of their corporate practices. That is an objective fact. Ergo, when trying to "balance" objective reality with denials from polluting companies, the process of balancing lends support to an unjust system. "This is precisely what is recommended in the CIPR guidelines and the idea is that this information is then checked by independent 'Wikipedians' and eventually incorporated into the actual Wikipedia user page by those independent third party editors." The PR manual goes on to note that, "[d]espite his effort to ensure the articles retained a neutral point of view, there were still contributors who remained suspicious of 'big business' and would prefer for it not to be included as a 'significant view' at all. However, his approach is commendable for erring on the side of caution." The PR manual also says that Silva was not unique in adopting this approach. Verizon Communications' PR director, Bob Varettoni, joined as User:VZBob. Wikipedia introduced disclosure guidelines as late as 2014, but at the time of writing has not prohibited the editing of entries by paid hacks or PR consultants.[222]

Part II
Content Analyses

Preface

As noted in the general Introduction, the subjects in this section were selected for their universality and bipartisanism. Many of the Wikipedia entries on these subjects are now locked, meaning that if one compares my quotes from Wikipedia to the entries online today, they will be the same. Where they differ, however, please copy and paste the given Wikipedia entry's URL into Archive.org's Wayback machine and look for versions dated between December 2018 to March 2019, when this research was conducted.

Chapter 3
USA vs. Russia

Russia is America's enemy. The US State Department says: "In response to Russia's ongoing violations of Ukraine's sovereignty and territorial integrity, including Russia's occupation and attempted annexation of Crimea, the United States has suspended most bilateral engagement with the Russian government on economic issues."[223] The US Defense Department says: "Long-term strategic competitions with China and Russia are the principal priorities for the Department, and require both increased and sustained investment, because of the magnitude of the threats they pose to U.S. security and prosperity today, and the potential for those threats to increase in the future."[224] The US Congressional Research Service says: "Over the course of 2014, the U.S. government rolled out targeted economic sanctions on Russian individuals and entities in critical commercial sectors in response to that country's annexing of the Crimean region of neighboring Ukraine and its support of separatist militants in Ukraine's east."[225]

Wikipedia and its organizers are largely US-based. We would therefore expect that political entries would be biased in favor of the US and, where Russia is concerned, anti-Russian to a greater or lesser extent. Yet, such bias would violate Wikipedia's supposed neutrality. So, one simple test to determine the neutrality of Wikipedia is to compare entries for the foreign relations of the United States[226] and Russia.[227] If the encyclopedia is neutral, both entries will be approximately equal in the degree and scope of their praise and criticism. The US and Russia are two very different nation-states in terms of their histories, geographic and demographic sizes, global influence, and foreign policy objectives. For Wikipedia entries on very different types of nations to be objective, we would expect Wikipedia to require entries on the foreign relations of each nation-state to conform to a common set of criteria. Such criteria could include questions like: How much each nation spends on its military and its foreign aid budget; the number of other nations with which it has positive and negative relations; the number of UN resolutions adopted against the nation; and so on. But no such set of criteria appear to exist for Wikipedia entries on any country. The lack of criteria makes it easy for authors and editors to violate the supposed neutrality principle.

Predictably, we find that Wikipedia's use of language to describe Russia's foreign relations is more negative than the language used to describe the foreign relations of the US. The general picture that emerges is that the US is flawed but generally good and liked by other nations. Russia is generally bad and liked only by so-called rogues, like China.

SPECIAL RELATIONSHIPS

For the subsection "Foreign relations" of its entry "United States," Wikipedia says: "The United States has an established structure of foreign relations." The use of the words "established" and "structure" conveys authority and the supposed respectability of the US. The US "...is a permanent member of the United Nations Security Council and New York City is home to the United Nations Headquarters." Compare this language to the subsection "Foreign relations" in the entry for "Russia": "The Russian Federation is recognized in international law as a successor state of the former Soviet Union [USSR]. Russia continues to implement the international commitments of the USSR, and has assumed the USSR's permanent seat in the UN Security Council." Wikipedia's reference to the USSR and the tacit implication that contemporary Russia is continuing the policies of the Soviet Union gives the impression that the old Red Menace is alive and well.

The source for the claim that Russia "is recognized in international law as a successor state of the former Soviet Union" is the British Foreign Office; a hardly impartial source. This seems to be a strange source, given that the UK Foreign Office is not an arbiter of international law. Perhaps a legal reference from an authority, such as the UN or the International Court of Justice, is included in the source? It is not. In fact, the source does not even mention the USSR.[228] The webpage's See Full Profile link does, however, lead to the correct source.[229] Citing no sources itself, the British Foreign Office claims:

"The Russian Federation (Russia) is recognised in international law as continuing the legal personality of the Soviet Union (USSR) which was dissolved on 31 December 1991. The Russian Federation is currently divided into some 80 administrative units officially entitled subjects of the Federation. However, a programme of regional mergers is underway."[230]

Notice the difference in tone in the original source compared to how it is rendered in the Wikipedia entry. Either way, pointing out that Russia is a successor to the USSR is like pointing out that the United States is the successor to the original Union.

Using generalizing language, Wikipedia portrays the US as a popular, much-liked nation: It "has a 'Special Relationship' with the United Kingdom and strong ties with Canada, Australia, New Zealand, the Philippines, Japan, South Korea, Israel, and several European Union countries, including France, Italy, Germany, and Spain." Let's consider some of these examples.

With regards to Britain, the entry omits what the source actually says about the so-called Special Relationship, namely that it was initially based on the transfer of British imperial power to the US after WWII and now includes British possession of US-controlled nuclear weapons systems as a mutually-beneficial guarantor of US-British elite interests. The source (its content omitted by Wikipedia) quotes the US State Department, which said in 1948: "The United Kingdom, the Dominions, Colonies and Dependencies, form a worldwide network of strategically located territories of great military value, which have served as defensive outposts and as bridgeheads for [US] operations."[231] So, the Special Relationship is actually beneficial to elite US military interests.

To continue with the military theme: The UK, Australia, Canada, New Zealand, and the US constitute the so-called Five Eyes; a global surveillance system based on US infrastructure and technical capabilities.[232] The Five Eyes reference is omitted from the Wikipedia reference to these countries. When it comes to the Philippines, the source in the Wikipedia entry explains the real reason for "strong" US-Philippine relations, namely the predictable uses of the Philippines to serve US military purposes; again, omitted from the entry. When we click the link, we find that the source says:

> "The United States and the Republic of the Philippines maintain close ties stemming from the U.S. colonial period (1898-1946), the bilateral security alliance, extensive military cooperation, and common strategic and economic interests ... The bilateral security relationship has gained prominence as a key link in the evolving U.S. foreign policy "pivot" or "rebalancing" toward Asia, and the two sides are discussing bolstering U.S. access to Philippine military facilities."[233]

The Wikipedia entry also omits what its source says about the reasons for the "strong" relationship between the US and Japan. The source says:

> "Japan is a significant partner of the United States in a number of foreign policy areas, particularly in security concerns, which range from hedging against Chinese military modernization to countering threats from North Korea. The alliance facilitates the forward deployment of about 50,000 U.S. troops and other U.S. military assets based in Japan."[234]

It should be noted that the annual threat assessments given by the Pentagon to Congress regularly confirm that China is a *regional* power with *regional* ambitions, not a global power threatening US hegemony. It should also be noted that, for decades, the US has unilaterally rejected peace offers and negotiations by and with North Korea.[235] Wikipedia's emerging pattern of omitting the content of the given source is repeated for South Korea. Again, the following appears in the source, but not in the Wikipedia entry:

> "South Korea (officially the Republic of Korea, or ROK) is one of the United States' most important strategic and economic partners in Asia. Congressional interest in South Korea is driven by both security and trade interests.

Since the early 1950s, the U.S.-ROK Mutual Defense Treaty commits the United States to help South Korea defend itself. Approximately 28,500 U.S. troops are based in the ROK, which is included under the U.S. 'nuclear umbrella'."[236]

So, the impression we get from this part of the entry on US "Foreign relations" is that the US is generally benign and much liked by nations that have special relationships with it. This is a form of propaganda by omission: the simple omission of the military and strategic interests of US policymakers in those countries. (The reasons for close US-Israeli relations are more controversial and not easy to resolve or argue in the limited space here.)

OMITTING THE STRATEGIC INTERESTS

How does this presentation compare to the entry for Russia's "Foreign relations"? "As the successor to a former superpower, Russia's geopolitical status has often been debated, particularly in relation to unipolar and multipolar views on the global political system," the entry reads. "While Russia is commonly accepted to be a great power, in recent years it has been characterized by a number of world leaders, scholars, commentators and politicians as a currently reinstating or potential superpower." Notice that the US is formally committed to a military doctrine of world domination, called Full Spectrum Dominance by the

Pentagon,[237] yet this is not only absent from the Wikipedia entry on the US, but when it comes to the entry on Russia, the latter's alleged hegemonic tendencies are emphasized.

The "world leaders" claim is sourced to two leaders, Israeli PM Benjamin Netanyahu and the late Hugo Chávez of Venezuela, who at the time in 2009 recognized South Ossetia as Russian, following the Russo-Georgian war in the previous year. The article notes "Russian isolation" internationally over its actions in South Ossetia and paints Chávez in isolation over his claim that "Russia is a superpower." So, in this case, Wikipedia makes Russia seem more powerful that its own source actually says it is. The Wikipedia authors omit Chávez's observation that *the US* wants "to control the whole world."[238] So, according to the source, but not the Wikipedia entry's rendering of it, Russian *regional* expansion, such as it is, should be seen in the context of US *global* expansion. The other source actually quotes Netanyahu as saying that Israel would like to cooperate with Russia. Presumably this was omitted from the Wikipedia entry because it doesn't fit the anti-Russia narrative.[239]

The "scholars" who say that Russia is an emergent power is actually a single scholar, Ronald Steel; a Professor at the University of Southern California. In keeping with its seeming, undeclared policy of omission, again the Wikipedia editors omit what Steel actually says. Invoking John Quincy Adams, Steel says that the US should not be looking for "monsters to destroy." The context in which Steel made the remarks is also omitted. Steel said: "...the conflict in Georgia showed how rational Russia's concerns over American meddling in its traditional sphere of influence are, and that Washington had better start treating it like the great power it still is."[240] This is quite different from Wikipedia's claim that "scholars" consider Russia to be an emerging superpower.

According to Wikipedia, the US "works closely with fellow NATO members on military and security issues and with its neighbors through the Organization of American States and free trade agreements such as the trilateral North American Free Trade Agreement with Canada and Mexico." No sources are provided and no further information is given. The phrase "works closely with" suggests that the US is a mutual partner in NATO and other organizations. The reality is that the US dominates NATO and that NATO is a tool of US global hegemony, particularly though not exclusively where Russian geostrategic interests are concerned. The US continues to be the biggest NATO contributor (spending 3.57% of GDP in 2017), followed by Greece (which spends 2.36% of its tiny GDP on the military), the UK (2.12%), Estonia (2.08%), and so on.[241] A report on the history of NATO strategy by the RAND Corporation notes that:

> "...the Alliance off well in the early 1950s by creating an integrated military structure, securing a lasting U.S. military presence in Central Europe, accepting U.S. leadership on strategy, and agreeing on the rearmament of West Germany. Having hunched itself on the path of a sustained military buildup in Central Europe, however, it dramatically switched

gears in the mid-1950s. Influenced by fiscal considerations and by the belief that nuclear weapons could deter all forms of aggression, it wholeheartedly embraced the U.S.-designed nuclear strategy (MC 14/2) that called for massive retaliation against nearly any provocation and relegated conventional defenses to the sidelines."[242]

The Brookings Institution cites "bandwagon" theory and notes that other powers rely on the US in NATO for their sense (though not reality) of collective self-defense: "...States facing an external threat will ally with the strongest power – usually a nation that others perceive as more likely to win a conflict." The report says that NATO "...has roots in the bandwagoning rationale as some of its aspirants found the allure of joining with the United States following World War II attractive, especially given the economic and military devastation wrought during the war."[243]

Turning to the Organization of American States (OAS) mentioned in the Wikipedia entry, official and semi-official sources, this time ones not cited by Wikipedia, provide an insight into the reality of the US role. The Congressional Research Service explains: "The United States historically has sought to use the OAS to advance economic, political, and security objectives in the Western Hemisphere. Although OAS actions frequently reflected U.S. policy during the 20th century, this has changed to a certain extent over the past 15 years." So, again, we see that the real interest that US elites have in international forums is to exploit them to its advantage. This picture is obscured, and in fact eliminated, by Wikipedia. Why have US relations with OAS countries changed in the last 15 years? One reason is the so-called Pink Tide, which refers to the Latin American movement's non-commitment to full communism and socialism (which are symbolized by the color red, hence it was only a "pink" tide). The Pink Tide was a series of economic and social reforms across Central and South America, led by socially progressive, though sometimes politically dictatorial, governments. The Pink Tide reversed decades of brutal, US-led neoliberal policies and lifted millions out of poverty. It also closed markets to many US corporations, hence the designation of the Pink Tide's figurehead, Hugo Chávez, as a demon.[244]

Turning to NAFTA, the North American Free Trade Agreement: The Wikipedia entry again gives the false impression that the US is a neutral actor in the NAFTA alliance. Predictably, the official documentation demonstrates that NAFTA was designed to promote US corporate interests. In a document on the subject, the Congressional Research Service again states: "NAFTA established trade liberalization commitments that set new rules and disciplines for future FTAs [free trade agreements] on issues important to the United States, including intellectual property rights protection, services trade, dispute settlement procedures, investment, labor, and environment."[245] In its assessment of NAFTA 20 years on, the US Chamber of Commerce noted the success of NAFTA for US businesses: "With new market access and clearer rules afforded by NAFTA, U.S. services exports to Canada and Mexico have tripled, rising from $27 billion in 1993 to $82 billion in 2011."[246] So much for benevolence in US foreign policy. (It is also worth noting that both the Chamber and Wikipedia, at least in this entry, omit the tragic consequences of NAFTA for many US workers, whose jobs were outsourced to Mexico.)

Finally, the Wikipedia entry praises the US contribution to international aid: "...In 2008, the United States spent a net $25.4 billion on official development assistance, the most in the world." It qualifies: "As a share of America's large gross national income (GNI), however, the U.S. contribution of 0.18% ranked last among 22 donor states." However, it compensates for painting US aid contributions in a bad light by adding: "By contrast, private overseas giving by Americans is relatively generous." But the source cited in the entry is more complicated. It actually analyzes government aid in the context of both private donations and investments. It says:

> "Foreign aid or (development assistance) is often regarded as being too much, or wasted on corrupt recipient governments despite any good intentions from donor countries. In reality, both the quantity and quality of aid have been poor and donor nations have not been held to account ... Aid is often wasted on conditions that the recipient must use overpriced goods and services from donor countries. Most aid does not actually go to the poorest who would need it the most. Aid amounts are dwarfed by rich country

protectionism that denies market access for poor country products, while rich nations use aid as a lever to open poor country markets to their products. Large projects or massive grand strategies often fail to help the vulnerable as money can often be embezzled away." (Bullet points omitted)[247]

The report also quotes Arabella Fraser of Oxfam as saying: "...aid flows are largely dictated by geo-strategic concerns rather than by efforts to reduce poverty."[248] Omitting this, the Wikipedia entry's use of the words "private overseas giving" is ambiguous. Is it corporations (i.e., private donors) that give "generously" or is it ordinary people? The source, however, is unambiguous: American citizens—not the government or corporations—are big foreign charity donors:

"…the generosity of the American *people* is far more impressive than their government. Private aid/donation typically through the charity of individual people and organizations can be weighted to certain interests and areas. Nonetheless, it is interesting to note for example, per latest estimates, Americans privately give at least $34 billion overseas— more than twice the US official foreign aid of $15 billion at that time." (Emphasis in original)[249]

RETURN OF THE RED MENACE

Compare Wikipedia's pretty picture of the USA (which it paints by omitting what much of its own sources say) to that of Russia. According to Wikipedia, Russia "... maintains diplomatic relations with 191 countries and has 144 embassies. The foreign policy is determined by the President and implemented by the Ministry of Foreign Affairs of Russia." This gives the impression that, unlike the pluralistic US, Russia's foreign policy is determined by a single person. However, the cited source actually says that, since the collapse of the Soviet Union:

> "...the different departments of the Foreign Ministry have gotten used to the idea of conducting their 'own' foreign policy. In light of the fact that the Russian Federation entities and major economic agents have their own interests abroad, the picture becomes even more variegated. As a result, in addition to the single foreign policy line there arises some 'simple average' of sharply contrasting initiatives that exist in parallel with – and occasionally opposite to – the main policy vector set down by the President."[250]

So, rightly or wrongly, the source actually says that Russian foreign policy has become more not less pluralistic, albeit among Russian elites and conditional over time. Contrary to the picture painted by Wikipedia of an all-powerful President Putin, the source says: "...the executive is forced to deal with questions of strategy while the head of the state, who puts forward ideas and initiatives, lacks the time or the means to shape them into a single political line which would be consistently adhered to by all of the state bodies." The source even goes as far as blaming the West, in part, for Russia's alleged expansionist policies, noting the behavior of NATO: "...many of the emerging problems are largely the result of past mistakes. A typical example is the admission of new NATO members. Russia should have sought legal restraints against NATO expansion to the East, i.e. including new members from among the former Soviet republics." All of this is omitted from the Wikipedia entry.

Recognizing its peaceful international relations, Wikipedia says that Russia "...participates in the Quartet on the Middle East," with the UN, EU, and USA. It is also involved in "the Six-party talks with North Korea. Russia is a member of the Council of Europe, OSCE, and APEC. Russia usually takes a lead role in regional organisations such as the CIS, EurAsEC, CSTO, and the SCO." But the Wikipedia entry goes on to say that the once-friendly, post-Soviet relationship with the US and NATO "...has significantly deteriorated due to several issues and conflicts between Russia and the Western countries." It doesn't say what these "issues" and "conflicts" are. If we read the sources for the claim, they turn out to focus on Russian-NATO relations over the Ukraine issue. The source for this part of the entry is the not-exactly-impartial NATO itself.[251] The other source is the *Daily Beast* website, the entire article of which is based on a single tweet from President Trump, who says:

> "Our relationship with Russia is worse now than it has ever been, and that includes the Cold War. There is no reason for this. Russia needs us to help with their economy, something that would be very easy to do, and we need all nations to work together. Stop the arms race?"[252]

The entry is presented chronologically. It then reverts to US-Russian relations from 2002. It claims: "The NATO-Russia Council was established in 2002 to allow the United States, Russia and the 27 allies in NATO to work together as equal partners to pursue opportunities for joint collaboration." What is the source for this alleged equality? It is NATO, again.[253] Interestingly, the NATO source says that the so-called equality emerges from the context of discussions about shared counterterrorism strategies, not about NATO strategies generally. Wikipedia omits this and in doing so, creates the false impression that Western organizations are trying to accommodate the devious Russia.

After noting Russia's so-called special relationship with China, Wikipedia then goes on to say that Russia sells India military equipment. Noted above is the absence of the strategic interests that the US has in its "special relationships." This gives that the impression that Russia's foreign policy is driven by the interests of its elites and by *realpolitik* (which it is), unlike the US, whose motives are somehow pure and egalitarian (which they are not).

Unlike the entry for the US, the entry for Russia's foreign relations includes a paragraph on human rights. "An important aspect of Russia's relations with the West is the criticism of Russia's political system and human rights management (including LGBT rights, media freedom, and reports about killed journalists) by Western governments, the mass media and the leading democracy and human rights watchdogs." Firstly, notice the use of the word "important." The West, meaning Western elites (meaning US elites), supposedly considers human rights in Russia to be important, but "the West" is not defined; neither is the context in which the word important is used. Are Russia's abuses of domestic human rights "important" enough for Western governments to sanction the Russian government? Evidently they are not. Targeted sanctions were introduced against Russia in response to its annexation of Crimea, not due to Russia's domestic abuses. Secondly, consider the tacit implication, that "the West" (whatever that's supposed to mean) has a moral authority to pass judgement on the actions of non-Western states. The further implication is that the West has a clean record on domestic human rights. Thirdly, consider the omission of the opinions of non-Western nations regarding Russia's human rights abuses. The implication is that only the US and its allies can voice opinions worthy of consideration on human rights issues. The further implication is that China, for example, is a human rights abuser (which it is), unlike the US, so China (or any non-Western nation) has no moral authority to speak about Russia's abuses.

"In particular," Wikipedia continues: "such organisations as Amnesty International and Human Rights Watch consider Russia to have not enough democratic attributes and to allow few political rights and civil liberties to its citizens." When we check the source, we find that the Amnesty International report cited by Wikipedia does indeed mention all of the things attributed to Russia and more.[254] But consider Wikipedia's hypocrisy in arbitrarily including a paragraph on Russia's human rights abuses while omitting such a paragraph for its entry on US foreign relations. In 2009, the same year as the Amnesty report cited by Wikipedia, Amnesty said of the US:

> "Fifty-nine people died after being shocked with Tasers, bringing to 346 the number of such deaths since 2001. Although these deaths were commonly attributed to factors such as drug intoxication, medical examiners concluded that Taser shocks caused or contributed to at least 50 deaths. Many of those who died were subjected to multiple or prolonged shocks, were under the influence of drugs and/or had health or other problems which could have made them more susceptible to the adverse effects of such devices. Tasers

were also frequently used against people who did not pose a serious threat...

[T]he UN Committee on the Elimination of Racial Discrimination ... expressed deep concern that racial, ethnic and national minorities, especially Latino and African American people, were "disproportionately concentrated in poor residential areas characterized by sub-standard housing conditions, limited employment opportunities, inadequate access to health care facilities, under-resourced schools and high exposure to crime and violence" ...

Mexican national José Medellín was executed in Texas ... in violation of the USA's treaty obligations and an order by the International Court of Justice (ICJ). José Medellín was never advised by local officials of his right as a detained foreign national to seek consular assistance, as required under the Vienna Convention on Consular Relations. In 2004, the ICJ ruled that the USA had violated its obligations under the Convention in the cases of José Medellín and 50 other Mexican nationals on death row in the USA."[255]

And this excludes US foreign human rights abuses. If the entries for Russia and US shared a principle of neutrality, we would expect some recognition on the part of Wikipedia that many countries express concerns about human rights in the US, as they do about Russia. Unlike the Amnesty report, the HRW report cited by Wikipedia does not discuss Russia's domestic human rights abuses generally. Rather, it talks specifically about Russian atrocities in Chechnya. Further, it is not a report, but rather, a video. Contrary to what the entry claims, "the West" had not condemned Russia's abuses in the war with Chechnya, according to the video, but actively *supported* them by refusing to assist Chechen civilians at various European rights courts to bring the Russian perpetrators to justice.[256] Here, the Wikipedia entry inverts what its source actually says.

In addition to omitting what Amnesty says about the US in the entry for US foreign relations (i.e., that international organizations are critical of how the US treats its citizens), Wikipedia also leaves out what HRW says. To quote HRW's global report from 2008 (same year as the HRW article on Russia):

> "The United States now has both the largest incarcerated population and the highest per capita incarceration rate in the world, with a rate five times that of England and Wales, seven times that of Canada, and more than 10 times that of Japan....
>
> The burden of incarceration falls disproportionately on members of racial and ethnic minorities. Black men are incarcerated at 6.5 times the rate of white men, and 11.7 percent of *all* black males age 25 to 29 are in prison or jail. (Emphasis in original)
>
> ... Women's rights in the United States suffered major setbacks at the Supreme Court

in 2007. One court decision severely restricted challenges to unequal pay (women earn only 77 cents for every dollar earned by men), another upheld the exclusion of in-home care workers from certain federal wage and overtime protections (89 percent of such workers are women), and a third upheld a ban on a medically approved late-term abortion method, adding to existing regulatory and financial obstacles to safe abortion."[257]

CONCLUSION

Finally, Wikipedia's entry on Russian foreign relations discusses Freedom House, acknowledging that the organization is funded by the US. There are a few problems, however. In the first place, the text references 2006. Secondly, the source text says 2004 (retrieved 2010). Third and finally, the link takes us to a report from 2009. Wikipedia says that Freedom House decrees that "Russia [is] 'not free', citing 'carefully engineered elections' and 'absence' of debate." But the Freedom House source is from 2004. At that time, Freedom House listed Russia as Partly Free, giving it five out of 10.[258] When we click on the Wikipedia link, it takes us to Freedom House's Russia 2009 page, which, despite ranking Russia as Not Free, gives it 5.5 out of 10 (1 being best and 10 worst).[259]

Wikipedia's editors take one approach to content concerning Russia and another when it comes to the USA.

Chapter 4
Nuclear War

A nuclear war and/or accident involving the launch and detonation of hundreds or even thousands of hydrogen bombs by two or more nuclear powers (Britain, China, France, India, Israel, North Korea, Pakistan, Russia, and the US) would end life as we know it. Pockets of humanity would survive in a radioactive wasteland, enveloped in dust clouds and, very likely, face a famine-inducing nuclear winter.[260] Indeed, the severity of the threat of nuclear war/accident is the very reason that states, all of which seek to maintain and expand their power where possible, not only continue to possess such weapons but maintain methods of delivering them;[261] the most important being the intercontinental ballistic missiles (ICBMs), which can reach targets anywhere on Earth within an hour or so.

Wikipedia has numerous entries for nuclear weapons, including the weapons themselves,[262] nuclear strategy,[263] antinuclear campaigning,[264] and the physics behind nuclear explosions.[265] These entries are full of propaganda. For example, the entry "Nuclear disarmament" contains a section entitled, "Nuclear disarmament movement." Despite the ongoing pressure from organizations like the Campaign for Nuclear Disarmament and the International Campaign to Abolish Nuclear Weapons to disarm, the section focuses on historical movements, freezing them in the time-context of the Cold War. The implication is that anti-nuclear activism is a thing of the past. Scientific organizations including the Bulletin of the Atomic Scientists, Pugwash, and the Federation of American Scientists are given short shrift (or not mentioned at all), implying that scientists (i.e., intelligent people) support nuclear weapons, when in fact many don't. The section on the World Peace Council (WPC), which had support among European civilians, implies that the civilians supported the WPC for ideological reasons; not because they really cared about disarmament, but because the Soviet Union, which directed the WPC, was "communist" and the majority of Europeans supporting it were "socialists."[266]

Encountering narratives that explore nuclear disarmament strategies and activities, as well as legal international obligations (i.e., things that could save us from annihilation), depends very much on which terms the reader enters into a search engine. If they search for "nuclear weapons," they are likely to find references to the aforementioned. However, if they search for "nuclear war," they are likely to encounter the following. This chapter explores the propaganda of Wikipedia's "Nuclear warfare" entry.

EXTINCTION AND NUCLEAR WINTER

The entry begins: "Nuclear warfare (sometimes atomic warfare or thermonuclear warfare) is a military conflict or political strategy in which nuclear weaponry is used to inflict damage on the enemy."[267] This summary is already problematic because for one thing, there has never been a nuclear war (though nuclear weapons have been used as demonstration- and test-weapons during war) and, for another, the summary presupposes that nuclear weapons have a potential role in warfighting.

Firstly, the threat of nuclear war serves the dual function of mutually-assured destruction (a perverse form of self-defense) and as a guarantor of lower-level operational freedoms.[268] Secondly, it is US strategy to develop lower-yield nuclear weapons for warfighting.[269] Ergo, Wikipedia's implication, that in nuclear warfare "...nuclear weaponry is used to inflict damage in the enemy," echoes US military propaganda. Nuclear weapons have never been used in warfighting. The atomic bombings of Hiroshima and Nagasaki were demonstrations of US power. They served no strategic purpose, militarily speaking. The following bombings of Hiroshima and Nagasaki, which used two different types of bomb, were an experiment using live human subjects.[270] Subtly, readers therefore get the wrong impression, that nuclear weapons are not about preventing a nuclear war under the mutually-assured destruction strategy, but rather, that nuclear weapons exist in order to fight wars. This is a dangerous misperception, one that the military is advancing, because the use of low-yield nuclear weapons to fight wars encourages other, nuclear-armed nations modernize their arsenals. It encourages non-nuclear states, like Iran, to consider acquiring nuclear weapons in self-defense against a US nuclear warfighting strategy.[271]

The entry then acknowledges that nukes are WMDs, the use of which could lead to long-term radioactive fallout and a devastating nuclear winter. Being from 1985, one of the sources for this claim is outdated.[272] The other is a generic (i.e., non-specialist) entry in the online edition of the *Encyclopaedia Britannica*.[273] Giving readers the impression that nuclear winter is only a theory and therefore nothing to worry about, the Wikipedia entry then states: "…Some analysts dismiss the nuclear winter hypothesis, and calculate that even with nuclear weapon stockpiles at Cold War highs, although there would be billions of casualties, billions more rural people would nevertheless survive." That's alright, then. Consider the overreliance on conjunctions and adverbs ("even with," "although" and "nevertheless"), as if to justify the unjustifiable. Interestingly, there are two sources for the nuclear winter hypothesis, one outdated and the other generic, as noted. There are *four* sources for the claim that nuclear winter is a bogus hypothesis, all of them even older than the sources that support the hypothesis.

It is worth considering the sources that informed the discussion on nuclear casualties and environmental damage. The first source is a paper published in 1982 by the physicist Dr. Brian Martin. Dedicating three paragraphs to potential climatic effects of nuclear war, Martin erroneously[274] bases his theory solely on previous particulate ejections by volcanoes and writes, of nuclear winter, that a stratospheric dust cloud released from nuclear explosions "seems unlikely to cause such climatic change." Martin also acknowledges that "simply not enough is known to predict with confidence all the global effects of nuclear war."[275] Yet, the Wikipedia authors omit Martin's admission that little is understood about this subject.

The entry includes his opinions as authoritative. The second source, also authored by Martin, argues that potential death-tolls resulting from nuclear war are exaggerated as part of a psychological ploy to undermine effective survival planning and post-war operations. By making people believe that no-one will survive a nuclear war, the US and (at the time) Soviet Union undermined defensive planning ("[e]xaggeration to justify inaction," as Martin calls it).[276] Wikipedia omits this crucial core of Martin's theory, making him out to be a minimizer of the seriousness of nuclear war in order to support Wikipedia's case.

As an aside, it is also interesting to note the double-standards that Wikipedia editors employ when using sources. Wikipedia marginalizes alternative researches as "conspiracy theorists" and alternative health practitioners as dangerous snake oil sellers, but the editors are happy to quote people with eccentric views when it suits them. Their source, Martin, writes, for instance: "In practice, poor non-white populations arguably would be better off without the attentions of white, western 'civilisation' - although nuclear war is hardly the way to achieve this." This does not conform to the standards of academic writing.

The third source is Dr. Robert Johnston's 1988 scenario (updated in 2003), which, like Martin's, states: "There is much public misconception concerning the physical effects of nuclear war--some of it motivated by politics." Like Martin, Johnston acknowledges that "...predictions described here are uncertain," though the Wikipedia entry does not mention this. Johnston argues that "there is no scientific basis for expecting the extinction of the human species." But there is no scientific basis for not expecting it, either. Johnston reveals that "[s]ources supplying the basis for this description include the U.S. Defense Nuclear Agency manual on nuclear weapon effects." So, in a roundabout way, Wikipedia is using US military data to reassure us against the idea (or at least counter the perceived wisdom) that nuclear war would be catastrophic. Other sources for Johnston's paper include "...scientific papers describing computer simulations of long-term effects published by groups ranging from the U.S. government to left-leaning scientific organizations, and research by a similar variety of groups on weapons characteristics and strategy."[277] Exactly what "left-leaning" means is hard to say in this context.

The final Wikipedia source on claims about nuclear winter and extinction comes from a 1975 book published by the US National Research Council. The Letter preceding the book acknowledges, as do the other sources, that "the assumption[s]" on which the study is premised are "of uncertain validity." The Letter also acknowledges that the report did not consider long-term consequences,[278] which are essential to evaluating extinction scenarios. Despite this, Wikipedia presents the counter-narrative (that we might survive nuclear war and do so without nuclear winter) as if its sources are self-assured and authoritative. To conclude the summary of extinction, the Wikipedia entry notes that "others have argued that secondary effects of a nuclear holocaust, such as nuclear famine and societal collapse, would cause almost every human on Earth to starve to death."

Again, the sources are outdated, undermining the validity of the argument. Plenty of more recent studies into nuclear winter not included in the Wikipedia entry, provide authoritative evidence, suggesting that nuclear winter is a likely outcome of even "limited" nuclear exchanges.[279]

ACCIDENTS AND FATALITIES

In the introductory paragraphs of the Wikipedia entry, the editors acknowledge that the US dropped two nuclear bombs; one on Hiroshima, the other on Nagasaki. Unusually, though not surprisingly in this context, the contributors provide no sources for the claim that (and the editors let the authors get away with it): "These two bombings resulted in the deaths of approximately 120,000 people." However, the common, estimated death toll for Hiroshima alone is 200,000. The US Department of Energy writes: "The five-year death total may have reached or even exceeded 200,000, as cancer and other long-term effects took hold."[280] Ergo, Wikipedia underestimates by nearly half the mass slaughter of Japanese people in one city alone. The intro then goes on to list other countries in possession of nuclear weapons, including Israel which, the entry correctly acknowledges, continues to deny that it possesses nukes. The intro concludes that:

> "After the collapse of the Soviet Union in 1991 and the resultant end of the Cold War, the threat

of a major nuclear war between the two nuclear superpowers was generally thought to have declined. Since then, concern over nuclear weapons has shifted to the prevention of localized nuclear conflicts resulting from nuclear proliferation, and the threat of nuclear terrorism."

The latter claim is not supported by sources and is only partially true. Nuclear strategists and theorists are concerned about localized detonations and terrorist possession of nukes, but they are also concerned about nuclear warfare, particularly given the strategic hostilities between the US and Russia over flashpoints like Ukraine and Syria.

For instance, in its annual report 2017, the *Bulletin of the Atomic Scientists* noted: "The United States and Russia—which together possess more than 90 percent of the world's nuclear weapons—remained at odds in a variety of theaters, from Syria to Ukraine to the borders of NATO; both countries continued wide-ranging modernizations of their nuclear forces, and serious arms control negotiations were nowhere to be seen."[281] Contrary to the impression given by the Wikipedia analysis, these crises were prioritized over nuclear terrorism threats. To give another example, also in 2017, the International Campaign to Abolish Nuclear Weapons (ICAN) won the Nobel Peace Prize. Their website's "The Facts" page states: "A single nuclear bomb detonated over a large city could kill millions of people. The use of tens or hundreds of nuclear bombs would disrupt the global climate, causing widespread famine."[282] Notice that, like the *Bulletin* but unlike Wikipedia, it places the onus on states that have the biggest stockpiles and means of delivery, not only on the terrorists whose nuclear reach (if they even had one) would be limited by comparison.

TYPES OF NUCLEAR WAR

The Wikipedia entry divides nuclear war into two camps: limited and full-scale.

Oddly, a source is given for the term (not definition) "limited nuclear war," but not for the term "full-scale nuclear war." The source for the use of the term "limited nuclear war" is an anti-Russian article in the *Bulletin of the Atomic Scientists*, the very organization that also warns of the dangers of continued nuclear possession and possibly brinkmanship over proxy wars in Syria and Ukraine. This exemplifies Wikipedia's selectivity when it comes to using sources. The source is anti-Russian in the context of which it is being used. By citing a source relating only to Russia on the question of so-called limited nuclear war, Wikipedia implies that only Russia would launch a limited a nuclear strike. The source, "Why Russia calls a limited nuclear strike 'de-escalation'," was written by Nikolai N. Sokov, ex-Soviet and Russian Minister of Foreign Affairs. Let's analyze it:

The source actually notes that Russia developed its own so-called limited capacities in the wake of US-NATO aggression in the Former Yugoslavia of the 1990s and in the context of the US modernizing its nukes. To put it simply, Wikipedia's source is used for the purposes of implicit anti-Russian propaganda (that "limited" nuclear war is solely Russian strategy and an aggressive one at that), yet the source itself says the opposite: that the cause of Russia's strategic shift towards "limited" capacity is due to US actions. Wikipedia omits this. Sokov writes that in terms of the US-British-led NATO destruction of Serbia in 1999: "The conventional capabilities that the United States and its allies demonstrated seemed far beyond Russia's own capacities." Given that Russia was fighting a bloody counterinsurgency war in Chechnya, it considered US moves in Serbia akin to its own in Chechnya. Sokov notes: "Moscow became deeply worried that the United States would interfere within its borders." Russia's new strategy was, in the event of full-scale attack by US forces, to retaliate with limited strikes of high value to the US ("tailored damage").

In 2008, Russia fought US-backed Georgian troops in defense of its *de facto* protectorate, South Ossetia. Russia's limited-strike nuclear policy threat "probably limited the West's options for responding to the 2008 war in Georgia," says Sokov. The ex-Foreign Minister then goes on to note that as the importance of nuclear weapons declined, following the end of the Cold War, the importance of rethinking defensive nuclear strategies increased due to US military operations in the Gulf (1991) and Serbia (1999). US "conventional weapons systems, unlike their nuclear counterparts, were highly usable ... The Russian response, begun even before the conflict over Kosovo had ended, was to develop a new military doctrine."[283]

The lesson (omitted by Wikipedia) is that aggression (the US in this case) provokes other nations into taking defensive measures. Wikipedia's paragraph on so-called limited strikes states:

> "…predictions argue that a full-scale nuclear war could potentially bring about the extinction of the human race, or at least its near extinction, with only a relatively small number of survivors (mainly in remote areas) and a reduced quality of life and life expectancy for centuries afterward. However, such predictions, assuming total war with nuclear arsenals at Cold War highs, have not been without criticism."

The source of the "criticism" is again Dr. Martin. The authors of the Wikipedia entry demonstrate their repeated reliance on the same sources for different topics. The entry then goes on to cite a study by the American Geophysical Union from 2006, which states that "limited" nuclear war on a regional scale could devastate the global climate. This creates cognitive dissonance because the previous paragraphs reported mixed opinions about the effects of nuclear war on the climate. This is either sloppy editing or a deliberate policy to neutralize the reactions of readers.

Turning to the entry's brief discussion of the "full-scale" nuclear war definition, the entry states: "a full-scale nuclear war … could consist of large numbers of nuclear weapons used in an attack aimed at an entire country, including military, economic, and civilian targets." "Large numbers" is not defined. The specific countries are not identified. "Such an attack would almost certainly destroy the entire economic, social, and military infrastructure of the target nation, and would probably have a devastating effect on Earth's biosphere." The only sources provided for the claim discuss biospheric destruction. The Wikipedia entry then draws attention to the possibility of accidental nuclear war, both on a limited scale or full scale, as a result of computer malfunction, human error, and/or brinkmanship. The paragraph elucidates specific cases, which are very real, but unlike its source it does not provide a specific number of real-life instances of near-accidental launches. The cited source is Dr. Alan F. Philips, writing for the Project of the Nuclear Peace Foundation. The article emphasizes supposed safety features incorporated in nuclear systems by the US and Soviet Union/Russia, such as the so-called hotline between the leaders of the two powers.

Philips's article is based on Scott D. Sagan's book, *The Limits of Safety*. It outlines 20 serious and minor accidents which, in the opinions of Sagan and Philips, could have initiated accidental nuclear war. These accidents include the so-called Suez Crisis Coincidence (1956), where the Soviets warned Britain and France that non-nuclear attacks on those countries were being considered by Moscow in response to formers' actions in the Middle East. The trouble is that around the same time several, unrelated but seemingly related events occurred, including the downing of jets. This confused the war and escalated the potential of nuclear usage. The second accident was the BMEWS Communications Failure (1961), when the Strategic Air Command and the North American Aerospace

Defense Command went dead, leading both organizations to believe that a possible nuclear attack was underway. And so on. The final and most recent event described in the article (the Wikipedia source) is the Russian False Alarm (1995), in which a Norwegian civilian research rocket was mistaken by Russian nuclear weapons operators for a nuclear attack. Despite using Philips's article as a source, none of these events are referenced in the Wikipedia entry. This is another case of propaganda by omission, in this case the minimization of the severity of the threat of nuclear accident. But the article itself minimizes the number of nuclear accidents and near-fatalities.[284] A much more comprehensive study is the one by Jaya Tiwari and Cleve J. Gray for the Center for Defense Information. (The document is increasingly difficult to find on Google). The authors use FOIAs and open source material to document 233 nuclear incidents over an 18-year period alone.[285]

DID NUKING JAPAN END WWII?

The Wikipedia entry for nuclear warfare then indulges in a curious blend of patriotic nostalgia and implication; that the WWII-era incendiary bombing of Japan was as, if not more, destructive than the atomic bombs dropped on Hiroshima and Nagasaki. This is true, but pointing it out in the context of nuclear weapons analysis only serves to justify the existence, and at worse use, of nuclear weapons. For example, the entry claims that the US "...was faced with the prospect of invading the Japanese home islands" in June 1945, as if the US had no choice in the matter. After detailing the extent of non-nuclear bombing raids on Japan (and by implication minimizing the importance of nuclear weapons), the article then cites fears of US troop casualties as a way of tacitly justifying the deployment of nukes as somehow saving lives. The entry states: "The Japanese government ignored this ultimatum, sending a message that they were not going to surrender. In response to the rejection, President Truman authorized the dropping of the atomic bombs."

Not only is the point about nuking Japan in response to its surrender rejection incorrect (a point to which we shall return), but one of the two sources provided by Wikipedia for the claim say something different. One of the sources is a now-declassified technical note on the readiness of the first nuclear weapon. The second is an academic history of what the author calls the "Hiroshima cult." The author notes that, contrary to the Wikipedia claim, the US would never accept Japanese surrender. To quote a passage of the book, omitted by the authors of the Wikipedia entry: "Military advice was strongly against a strict interpretation of unconditional surrender." For instance, the Joint Intelligence Staff believed that a literal interpretation of unconditional surrender "is unknown to the Japanese." By May 1945, Truman had "subtly modified the doctrine" by distinguishing between the Japanese government, military, and civilians. Truman's understanding of surrender was exclusively military surrender.[286]

The Wikipedia entry is written in such a way as to imply that nuking Japan was necessary to prevent a greater loss of life and end the war. Earlier, we stated that this is not true. Consider evidence not quoted or cited by Wikipedia:

Before Pearl Harbor, the event that allegedly brought the US into WWII, "[t]he U.S. military actively engaged in planning with the British, the British Commonwealth countries, and the Dutch East Indies for future combined combat operations against Japan," says economic historian, Dr. Robert Higgs. "Most important," Higgs continues:

> "…the U.S. government engaged in a series of increasingly stringent economic warfare measures that pushed the Japanese into a predicament that U.S. authorities well understood would probably provoke them to attack U.S. territories and forces in the Pacific region in a quest to secure essential raw materials that the Americans, British, and Dutch (government in exile) had embargoed."

Higgs goes on to point out that Japan's Foreign Minister, Teijirō Toyoda, communicated to Ambassador Kichisaburō Nomura, that:

> "[c]ommercial and economic relations between Japan and third countries, led by England and the United States, are gradually becoming so horribly strained that we cannot endure it much longer. Consequently, our Empire, to save its

very life, must take measures to secure the raw materials of the South Seas."[287]

Historian Mark Weber asks if, militarily, the use of atomic bombs and the murder of at least 200,000 people were necessary. "By any rational yardstick, they were not." Weber concludes that Japan had already:

> "been defeated militarily by June 1945. Almost nothing was left of the once mighty Imperial Navy, and Japan's air force had been all but totally destroyed. Against only token opposition, American war planes ranged at will over the country, and US bombers rained down devastation on her cities, steadily reducing them to rubble."

Weber notes that on 20 January 1945, "President Roosevelt received a 40-page memorandum from General Douglas MacArthur outlining five separate surrender overtures from high-level Japanese officials … In April and May 1945, Japan made three attempts through neutral Sweden and Portugal to bring the war to a peaceful end."[288]

The Wikipedia entry omits the Potsdam Declaration (July 1945), which proves that the use of nuclear weapons—then nearing the test-phase—was not only premeditated but a deliberate strategy. The impression given by the Wikipedia entry is that the use of atomic weaponry was some event into which the US stumbled. But the Declaration (point 13) reads: "We call upon the Government of Japan to proclaim now the unconditional surrender of all the Japanese armed forces, and to provide proper and adequate assurance of their good faith in such action. The alternative for Japan is prompt and utter destruction."[289] It is also worth noting that Wikipedia again presents a false image of a benevolent United States, when in fact the use of atomic weapons was calculated. Maj. Gen. Curtis LeMay, Commander of the 20th Air Force, intentionally prevented Hiroshima and Nagasaki from being conventionally bombed so that the efficacy of the new atomic weapons could be easily ascertained. LeMay said: "The assessment of the atomic bomb damage would not be confused by having to eliminate previous incendiary or high explosive damage."[290]

After the War, President Eisenhower conceded that: "The Japanese were ready to surrender and it wasn't necessary to hit them with that awful thing," referring to the atomic bomb. Brig. Gen. Bonnie Fellers said: "Neither the atomic bombing nor the entry of the Soviet Union into the war forced Japan's unconditional surrender. She was defeated before either these events took place." This echoed Admiral Leahy, Chief of Staff to Presidents Roosevelt and Truman, who said: "the use of the barbarous weapon at Hiroshima and Nagasaki was of no material assistance in our war against Japan ... The Japanese were already defeated and ready to surrender because of the effective sea blockade and the successful bombing with conventional weapons."[291]

AFTER HIROSHIMA

Wikipedia states: "Immediately after the atomic bombings of Japan, the status of atomic weapons in international and military relations was unclear. Presumably, the United States hoped atomic weapons could offset the Soviet Union's larger conventional ground forces in Eastern Europe, and possibly be used to pressure Soviet leader Joseph Stalin into making concessions." This gives a false impression of US benevolence and anti-imperialism; that there were no plans or ideas to use atomic weapons as the ultimate guarantor of US global hegemony: that, somehow, post-War US planners sat around scratching their heads over how best to live with the new weapons at their disposal. No sources are provided for this claim. Uncharacteristically, the editors have not (at the time of writing) inserted square brackets into the text requesting sources for the undocumented assertions. In giving this false impression of US naïveté, the entry tacitly denies the link between the possession of nuclear weapons and offensive foreign policy. The reality is that the highest echelons of the US military and political office understood perfectly well the implications of atomic weapons "in international and military relations."

An April 1945 memo written to the newly inaugurated President Truman states: "...we shall in all probability have completed the most terrible weapon ever known ... [T]he US is at present in the position of controlling the resources with which to construct and use it and no other nation could reach this position for some years." The memo notes that "it is practically certain that we could not remain in this position indefinitely." It cautions that other states are less moral than the US and, unlike the US, would use nuclear weapons to destroy entire cities (which, in reality, is what the US did; twice). "[T]he future may see a time when such a weapon may be constructed in secret and used suddenly and effectively with devastating power by a wilful nation or group." The authors of the memo deemed it "unrealistic" to approach international peace organizations to prevent further usage. The authors conclude that possession of the weapon "has placed a certain moral responsibility upon us which we cannot shirk."[292]

In his memoirs, President Truman wrote: "We were now in possession of a weapon that would not only revolutionize war but could alter the course of history and civilization." According to Truman, Secretary of War (they had more honest titles in those days), Henry L. Stimson, told Truman that, "If expectations were to be realized ... the atomic bomb would be certain to have a decisive influence on our relations with other countries."[293] Contrary to the nonsense that the US "hoped atomic weapons could offset the Soviet Union's larger conventional ground forces in Eastern Europe" (as Wikipedia claims), the fact is that the Strategic Air Command (SAC) planned for non-nuclear strikes on the Soviet Union initiated with nuclear strikes. A military history states: "Studies of war plans that assumed a major conflict with the Soviet Union spearheaded by an atomic strike employing SAC bombers ... From Hiroshima onward, Air Force leaders stressed that the atomic age had eliminated the time-honored American tradition of unpreparedness for war."[294]

The Wikipedia editors did, however, request sources and clarification on what they describe as the more "dubious" claims, that: "Many proposals were suggested to put all American nuclear weapons under international control (by the newly formed United Nations, for example) as an effort to deter both their usage and an arms race. However, no terms could be arrived at that would be agreed upon by both the United States and the Soviet Union." Emphasis is placed on Britain's top-secret nuclear attack strategy. Wikipedia's effect here is to deny, by omission, the fact that the US had similar strategies. The Wikipedia entry then quotes the dictator of China, Chairman Mao, on nuclear war annihilating half the world's population and bringing capitalist imperialism to an end. Mao quoted in Wikipedia:

> "Let us imagine how many people would die if war breaks out. There are 2.7 billion people in the world, and a third could be lost. If it is a little higher it could be half ... I say that if the worst came to the worst and one-half dies, there will still be one-half left, but imperialism would be razed to the ground and the whole world would become socialist. After a few years there would be 2.7 billion people again."

This quote reinforces the general tone, that the US possesses nuclear weapons defensively, that the world is full of nuclear-armed maniacs ready to strike. The book in which the Mao quote appears was written by Frank Dikötter. The trouble is, the authors of the Wikipedia entry leave out what Dikötter says next: "…[Mao] was bluffing, on this occasion and on others like it, but the point of all of the sabre-rattling was to show that he, not [Soviet leader] Khrushchev, was a more determined revolutionary."[295]

A paper in the journal *Strategic Studies Quarterly* explodes the Wikipedia-backed myths about US nuclear possession for strategic deterrence and mutually-assured destruction purposes. Contrary to the Wikipedia propaganda, it also reveals the superiority of US nuclear systems and their offensive capabilities:

> "During the 1950s, the US nuclear force far outmatched the meager Soviet arsenal. Until 1956, the Soviet Union had no weapons with the range to reach the United States, and even in the latter parts of the decade Moscow's rudimentary long-range nuclear arsenal was highly vulnerable to a nuclear disarming strike. The United States recognized its huge advantage and planned to fight and win World War III—if it occurred—by launching a massive nuclear disarming strike on the Soviet Union. Ironically, the era that spawned the term 'mutual assured destruction (MAD)' was not characterized by the condition of MAD; nuclear stalemate only emerged later."[296]

Similarly, a study for the US Air Force by the RAND Corporation agrees that warfighting, not just deterrence, was part of the US strategy. "Most U.S. and Soviet national security space systems developed in the 1960s were dedicated to supporting nuclear warfighting and deterrence missions."[297] This developed into the Single Integrated Operational Plan, which Wikipedia claims, without evidence, was a purely technical system not designed to exercise a first-strike.

Remarkably, the entries for the 1960s-present lack sources. At the time of writing, entire discussions lack sources concerning the Cuban Missile Crisis (1962), the establishment of the hotline, mutually-assured destruction theory, the development of ICBMs, and even potentially catastrophic errors in computer systems, which is totally uncharacteristic of Wikipedia entries. In addition to the lack of sources, there is also a remarkable lack of editorial request for sources and clarifications. The entry then goes on to discuss the development of nuclear weapons by China, France, India, Israel, North Korea, and Pakistan.

CONCLUSION

The average reader of Wikipedia's entry on Nuclear Warfare would get the impression that the US found itself in possession of nuclear weapons, as if by political accident (the history of the Manhattan Project is glossed over) and it had to therefore strategize defensively. Despite the fact that the first and only use of nuclear weapons was by the US (which it had to do to save soldiers' lives, the entry implies), it is the rest of the world that is immoral, volatile, and a threat to US interests. By omitting references to the law (e.g., the World Court Advisory Opinion of 1996, the Nuclear Non-Proliferation Treaty, etc.), the entry suggests that international legal obligations and opinions on the topic don't exist. The entry also implies that, contrary to reality, there are no contemporary mass movements supportive of multilateral disarmament.

Chapter 5
Climate Change

Given the general agreement among scientists and politicians worldwide, as reflected in the corporate media, that human activities do have detrimental effects on the climate, we might expect Wikipedia's entry on "Climate change"[298] to reflect the consensus. The other consensus is that humans must reduce CO2 emissions in order to limit the carbon content of the atmosphere and, in doing so, reverse global warming; global warming being a key driver of climate change. Our expectation is compounded by Wikipedia's reputation for being a "progressive" encyclopedia, as exemplified by its pro-Hillary Clinton edits as compared to its anti-Donald Trump entries. Even if we put aside alleged political ideology and accept that Wikipedia supposedly operates a policy of content neutrality, the objective reality of anthropogenic climate change means that Wikipedia's entry should reflect objective reality. There should be little room for skepticism and denialism.

Most people searching for the human impact on the climate are unlikely to search for "global warming" or "anthropogenic climate change." These and similar entries do exist on Wikipedia and go deeper into the human effects on the climate. However, the term "climate change" remains popular, though "climate emergency" is becoming increasingly common.

So, the question for Wikipedia is how to support US power (as underpinned by the climate-changing fossil fuels industry) while maintaining the encyclopedia's reputation of neutrality, objectivity, and progressiveness. What we find is that in the entry for "Climate change," the human role in inadvertently modifying global temperatures is minimized. The activity of the Sun and its cyclical effects on the climate are emphasized (thereby de-emphasizing the human role), as are non-human factors. The role of the fossil fuel industry is almost entirely absent. The sources are outdated and many claims rely on the same source. The definition of "climate change" is long and rambling, giving readers the false impression that the issue is more complicated and controversial than it is. But the entry's borderline climate change denialism is far from blatant. This particular entry represents one of the more subtle examples of Wikipedia's propaganda.

Before examining specifics, let's consider the informative case of Dr. William Connolley.

WHEN EDITORS GO TOO FAR

In this chapter, the term "climate change denial" is used, along with "denialists" and "denialism." Climate change "denial" is actually a broad spectrum, ranging from skepticism that human CO_2 emissions have much or anything to do with warming all the way to outright rejection of the evidence. For shorthand, the term "denialists" is used here, though it should be kept in mind that in some cases "skeptic" might be more accurate.

In 2005, the renowned journal *Nature* claimed that "Wikipedia comes close to *Britannica* in terms of the accuracy of its science entries."[299] The case of William Connolley is instructive. Connolley is a climate scientist who accepts and has written evidence in support of the theory of anthropogenic climate change. Connolley was a Wikipedia editor who, by the mid-2000s, was ruthlessly suppressing climate change denial on Wikipedia's entry pages ("edit wars"). Given the scientific consensus, that human activity significantly contributes to climate change, Connolley's edits seemed fair. *Nature* quotes Jimmy Wales in praise of Connolley's removal of edits made by climate change deniers. "It takes a long time to deal with troublemakers ... Connolley has done such amazing work and has had to deal with a fair amount of nonsense."[300]

This alleged bias against climate change deniers ("alleged" because the scientific consensus strongly suggests that anthropogenic climate change is real) led to criticism of Connolley by those who challenge the consensus. Climate change denier, Lawrence Solomon, wrote on the CBS website: "...on Wikipedia some folks are more equal than others ... Connolley routinely uses his editorial clout to tear down scientists of great accomplishment such as Fred Singer [another denier], the first director of the U.S. National Weather Satellite Service and a scientist with dazzling achievements. Under Connolley's supervision," says Solomon, "Wikipedia relentlessly smears Singer." Solomon concludes that on issues not limited to climate change, "there is no doubt where Wikipedia stands: firmly on the Left."[301]

So far, so good. By the mid-2000s, Wikipedia was giving tens of millions of people around the world the impression, enforced by mainstream media, that it was a left-leaning, people's encyclopedia holding consensus views on climate change. Those complaining about its alleged bias against climate change denial relegated themselves, in the eyes of the public, to the level of reactionary, "libertarian" types (many of them working indirectly for the Koch Brothers, as we shall see,) who are quite happy to burn fossil fuels and let the planet heat up beyond repair. But then, the cracks in Wikipedia's façade of progressive liberalism began to show.

Putting aside left-right ideology, the case of William Connolley demonstrates that dedicated editors and administrators shape Wikipedia in their own interests. Wikipedia is not, and never was, an open encyclopedia. The notion that "anyone can edit it" was loose, to say the least. Edit it to what extent? And how long will the edits last before senior editors and administrators re-edit and even ban users? By 2010, Connolley had reportedly edited more than 5,400 entries, most them relating to climate change. But Connolley got too big for his administrative boots and began banning contributors without good reason. These actions brought a case of arbitration against him.[302] Having gone from being praised in *Nature* for bringing the standards of the encyclopedia close to those of world-renowned volumes, Connolley was soon complaining to mainstream media that one's expertise on a subject counts for nothing in the eyes of Wikipedia's administrative clique.

From this we also learn that Wikipedia is a complex hierarchy, not a free and open system of contribution. Over the years, the quality and clarity of the entry on "Climate change" has declined. Let us now turn to the analysis.

IT'S THE SUN! OR IS IT…?

Wikipedia's entry, "Climate change," begins with four paragraphs defining the climate. This breaks from the norm of providing links to other entries. Ordinarily, the entry would say "see Climate," or similar. However, a relatively long explication of the meaning of the word "climate" includes, what amounts in some cases to, minimization of the role that humans play in current warming.

The entry begins: "Climate change occurs when changes in Earth's climate system result in new weather patterns that last for at least a few decades, and maybe for millions of years." Already, this contradicts the common, scientific understanding of climate; that the climate is a primary *driver* of weather patterns and that temperatures play a more important, underlying role than weather in the climate; weather being one of the many effects of climate. Disturbingly, this echoes President Trump's denialism. Recall that future candidate Trump said: "Many people don't even think there is such a thing as 'climate change.' It's called weather."[303] Both Trump (in a simple way) and Wikipedia (in a more complicated way) emphasize the role of weather. As President, Trump said of storms: "we had years where we had none, and then over the last couple of years we had more. And hopefully, we'll go back to many years where we have none. But we have been hit by the weather, there's no question about it."[304] Trump conflates climate change and severe weather.

It is important to stress that unlike Trump, Wikipedia does *not* claim that weather and climate are similar, if not the same. However, the entry on "Climate Change" is suffused with enough confusion to mix weather and climate, and to raise doubts about the extent of the human contributions to warming and thus climate change. Another example is the statement from the Wikipedia entry: "The climate system receives nearly all of its energy from the sun, with a relatively tiny amount from earth's interior." Like the Trump quotes, this echoes the statements of climate change deniers, who point to solar activity as the main driver of climate change. In this context, such deniers imply that human CO_2 and other emissions are insignificant. Compare Wikipedia's statement to those of high-profile climate change deniers, like Dr. Tim Ball, who writes: "Recent stories claim the Sun is not the cause of global warming or climate change. It is a classic example of exploitation of public lack of knowledge."[305] Or consider MIT's Professor Richard Lindzen:

> "Sceptics also are much more open to the numerous known causes of climate change, including long-period ocean circulations, solar variability, and the various impacts of ice, and do not regard carbon dioxide as the climate's

ultimate 'control knob.' The main difference between these first two groups, however, is that the second group openly opposes catastrophism while the first group does not."[306]

By making a generic reference to solar activity and its effects on climate change, the Wikipedia entry subtly questions the relevance of anthropogenic warming. Later, under the heading "Causes of climate change," the entry states: "On the broadest scale, the rate at which energy is received from the Sun and the rate at which it is lost to space determine the equilibrium temperature and climate of Earth." The entry provides no sources for the claim about the Sun, instead providing two sources for the second claim, that solar energy and Earth energies are distributed via oceanic flows. One source for this claim is from the 1980s' and relies on US Navy data. It also relies on *estimates* of oceanic meridional surface temperatures.[307] The second source is now a decade old and relies on "numerical experimentation" and specifically examines the role of ocean gyres and the energy transport of atmospheric midlatitudes.[308]

A LONG, RAMBLING DEFINITION

The introductory paragraph then goes on to note that, "When the incoming energy is greater than the outgoing energy, earth's energy budget is positive and the climate system is warming." No sources are provided for this claim, which reinforces the notion that present warming is being driven by the Sun.

Again, without including a source, the entry defines climate as the "long term averages of weather." The examples given are the El Niño southern oscillation, Pacific decadal oscillation, and Atlantic multidecadal oscillation. One cannot help but wonder if these examples were chosen due to their historic variabilities and unpredictability. By selecting historically unpredictable weather events, the authors of the entry tacitly imply that climate is and always has been unstable. While this is true, by implying that major variability depends on solar and space activity, the entry by default minimizes human contributions to climate change.

Notice the equivocal language of the third paragraph, which is when we get to climate *change*, as opposed to definitions of climate. The entry states: "Human activities can also change earth's climate, and are presently driving climate change through global warming. There is no general agreement in scientific, media or policy documents as to the precise term to be used to refer to anthropogenic forced change; either 'global warming' or 'climate change' may be used." Raising the point of disagreement among climate scientists about specific elements of climate change, while using the word "can" instead of "is," further minimizes the human impact. Interestingly, the equivocal paragraph is the first to provide sources. This technique, perhaps deliberate, gives readers the impression (albeit unconsciously) that the previous statements are axiomatic and therefore require no sources. When needed, however, the authority of evidence (real or not) is invoked by the inclusion of sources.

The source on which the claim is based makes clear that: "... there is a strong, credible body of evidence, based on multiple lines of research, documenting that climate is changing and that these changes are in large part caused by human activities."[309] This acknowledgement begs the question as to why the statement was confined by the authors and editors of the Wikipedia entry to the endnotes.

As if to undermine the credibility of the next claim, that climate researchers use climate proxies (e.g., carbon levels buried in permafrost) to study the effects of CO_2 on modern climate change, the single presented source is an outdated one from 1999.[310] A more recent study, for example by Tesi et al. (not included in Wikipedia's entry), notes that "[r]ecent hypotheses, based on atmospheric records and models, suggest that permafrost carbon (PF-C) accumulated during the last glaciation may have been an important source for the atmospheric CO_2 rise during post-glacial warming."[311] This is important because proving such links would provide empirical evidence that CO_2 does in fact significantly drive modern warming. From this we could deduce that human CO_2 emissions make significant contributions to climate change. So, why is it ambiguously presented in the entry?

"However," Tesi et al. continue, "direct physical indications for such PF-C [permafrost-carbon] release have so far been absent." As a result, the team studied "the Laptev Sea (Arctic Ocean) as an archive to investigate PF-C destabilization during the last glacial–interglacial period. Our results show evidence for massive supply of PF-C from Siberian soils as a result of severe active layer deepening in response to the warming." A few years earlier, DeConto et al. noted that, "Between about 55.5 and 52 million years ago, Earth experienced a series of sudden and extreme global warming events (hyperthermals) superimposed on a long-term warming trend." If the authors can determine the cause of the ancient warming, they can aid our current understanding of climate change. The authors conclude:

> "...the Early Eocene hyperthermals occurred during orbits with a combination of high eccentricity [an Earth-science term relating to an axis and relative ellipsis] and high obliquity [the change in axial tilt]. Corresponding climate–ecosystem–soil simulations accounting for rising concentrations of background greenhouse gases and orbital forcing show that the magnitude and timing of the PETM [Palaeocene-Eocene Thermal Maximum] and subsequent hyperthermals can be explained by the orbitally triggered decomposition of soil organic carbon in circum-Arctic and Antarctic terrestrial permafrost."[312]

Why, given the existence of such detailed and contemporary articles demonstrating the historical and thus contemporary connections between warming, climate change, and CO2, do the Wikipedia authors and editors rely on outdated, single-sources?

USING OUTDATED SOURCES

Further expanding the definition of climate change, the Wikipedia entry says that climate change simply means "change in the statistical properties (principally its mean and spread) of the climate system." The source is the Intergovernmental Panel on Climate Change (IPCC). But the IPCC report says much more than that. The so-called statistical properties, says the IPCC report, persist "for an extended period, typically decades or longer ... Climate change may be due to internal processes and/or external forcings." The report, cited in but not actually quoted by the Wikipedia entry authors, notes that "[s]ome external influences, such as changes in solar radiation and volcanism, occur naturally and contribute to the total natural variability of the climate system." However, it also states that, "[o]ther external changes, such as the change in composition of the atmosphere that began with the industrial revolution, are the result of human activity."[313]

Like the entry for "Nuclear warfare," the Wikipedia entry on "Climate change" also contains blatantly contradictory statements which neutralize the opinions of readers. Having noted El Niño as an example of weather instability in the Earth's climate systems, the entry then states: "...fluctuations over periods shorter than a few decades ... do not represent climate change." This renders the previous statement useless.

Curiously, the entry says that anthropogenic climate change is also known as global warming. It then provides a link to that entry. But the entry for "Global warming" is different to the entry for "Climate change." If climate change and global warming are the same, why include two separate entries?

The source for the claims about anthropogenic climate change is Article 1 of the UN Framework Convention on Climate Change (1994), which does not say what the authors of the Wikipedia entry claim it does. Rather, Article 1 of the Framework places emphasis on human activity: "…'Climate change' means a change of climate which is attributed directly or indirectly to human activity that alters the composition of the global atmosphere and which is in addition to natural climate variability observed over comparable time periods." Why, then, does the Wikipedia entry focus on drivers of climate change beyond human activity, given that one of its own sources emphasizes the human role? There is only one reference to the specific word "anthropogenic" in the cited Article 1 of the Framework: "... 'Greenhouse gases' means those gaseous constituents of the atmosphere, both natural and anthropogenic, that absorb and re-emit infrared radiation."[314]

The Wikipedia entry then claims that the term climate change has been politicized to "become synonymous with anthropogenic global warming." But the entry provides no sources. Lack of sources is all-too-common for Wikipedia entries that challenge elite US interests, be they government or corporate. A source is, however, provided for the next claim, that: "Within scientific journals, global warming refers to surface temperature increases while climate change includes global warming and everything else that increasing greenhouse gas levels affect." The inclusion of a source for references to non-human related warming activities implies that the authors of the entry seek to divert attention from the human activities that cause warming (i.e., things we can change at the expense of fossil fuel corporations, and thus US global economic and military power,) and lead us to other causes of climate change about which we can do nothing, including solar and volcanic activity.

The single source provided is the US National Aeronautics and Space Administration (NASA). But, again, it is an old source from more than a decade ago. Astonishingly, the source says something completely different to Wikipedia's rendering of it. Recall that Wikipedia claims that the politicization of the term "climate change" means that it is now almost exclusively used in the context of human activity. But NASA defines global warming as "the increase in Earth's average surface temperature due to rising levels of greenhouse gases." It defines climate change as "a long-term change in the Earth's climate, or of a region on Earth." The NASA article concludes that "...temperature change itself isn't the most severe effect of changing climate." It notes that of equal, perhaps greater, importance for human survival are "[c]hanges to precipitation patterns and sea level." Consequently, "scientific research on climate change encompasses far more than surface temperature change. So," compared to global warming, "...'global climate change' is the more scientifically accurate term." Crucially, given the age of the article, NASA cautions: "This material is being kept online for historical purposes. Though accurate at the time of publication, it is no longer being updated."[315]

Given that NASA advises us to look for more updated sources, it is ironic that the Wikipedia authors and editors do not apply the same standards. If they did, they would look for more recent and potentially more accurate publications. As an aside, the authors of the Wikipedia entry on "Climate change" write a brief history of the now-defunct term "*climatic* change."

> "A related term, 'climatic change', was proposed by the World Meteorological Organization (WMO) in 1966 to encompass all forms of climatic variability on time-scales longer than 10 years, but regardless of cause. During the 1970s, the term climate change replaced climatic change to focus on anthropogenic causes, as it became clear that human activities had a potential to drastically alter the climate."

Without a source (and to the credit of the editors, who state that a citation is needed), the authors erroneously claim that, "Prior to the 18th century, scientists had not suspected that prehistoric climates were different from the modern period." However, one of the entry's previous sources says the opposite. Mike Hulme writes:

"The idea of climate change – whether of natural or human origin – has a genealogy that can be traced back to Greek civilization. Not only were changes in climate discerned by Greek scholars, but these early observers were also able to trace causation to human actions in the world. For example, in the third century BCE, Aristotle's student Theophrastus observed and documented local changes in climate induced by human agency: the clearing of forests around Philippi in Greece warmed the climate, while the draining of marshes cooled the climate around Thessaly."[316]

MINIMIZING THE HUMAN IMPACT

The Wikipedia entry directs readers to the entry on "Global warming" for an expanded discussion of "Human influences." But this seems obfuscatory, given that most people now use the term "climate change" instead of "global warming," and are therefore more likely to search for "climate change" and encounter the Wikipedia entry of the same name. The small subsection on human influences notes: "The scientific consensus on climate change is 'that climate is changing and that these changes are in large part caused by human activities'." The source is the nearly-decade old National Research Council report, which Wikipedia had quoted earlier. As noted in the previous chapter, we see an overreliance on single sources.

A second source for the quote, that anthropogenic climate change "is largely irreversible," is a paper from 2009. The Wikipedia entry quotes the paper as if it is futile to try to stop and reverse the human contribution to climate change. The sense of futility encourages the continued use of fossil fuels under the erroneous assumption that little can be done to reverse climate change. As noted, certain Wikipedia statements indirectly echo former President Trump's denialism. More recently, the National Highways and Traffic Safety Administration (NHTSA) published a 500-page draft environmental impact statement.[317] The *Washington Post* comments that the NHTSA authors conclude that as the planet's climate fate is sealed, so the NHTSA thinks it is justified in advocating for maximum profit at the expense of emissions caps.[318] But what the 2009 Wikipedia source actually says is that anthropogenic climate change is only irreversible under certain circumstances; that is to say, if we reduce emissions now, climate change is reversible. Wikipedia is giving the wrong impression. To quote the source (which the entry cites but doesn't quote):

> "Among illustrative irreversible impacts that should be expected *if* atmospheric carbon dioxide concentrations increase from current levels near 385 parts per million by volume (ppmv) to a peak of 450–600 ppmv over the coming century are irreversible dry-season rainfall reductions in several regions comparable to those of the 'dust bowl' era and inexorable sea level rise." (Emphasis added).[319]

Wikipedia leaves that bit out, giving the impression that all is hopeless, so like Trump and the NHTSA, let's not even try.

After quoting again the National Research Council and emphasizing the claim that "much remains to be learned," the subsection on human impacts then claims that science has studied fossil fuels, aerosols, cement manufacturing, animal husbandry, termites, and deforestation, and "the roles they play" in climate change. Notice the twofold propaganda of 1) diverting attention from the role of fossil fuels by including references to animals and termites, and 2) the lack of clarification that fossil fuels play the major role in human-caused climate change. A third, tacit propaganda factor could also be argued, that rural people (who raise animals and use massive amounts of land) are being tacitly blamed for climate change via Wikipedia's absence of detailed criticism of urban practices and fossil fuel usage. Interestingly, the source for the claim about cement production and its role in climate change states the following:

> "In comparison with other influences, the effects of solar variations on present global warming are small. Indirect estimates suggest that changes in the brightness of the Sun have contributed only a few percent of the global warming since 1750. Direct measurements show a decreasing solar intensity over recent decades, opposite to what would be required to

explain the observed warming. Solar activity has declined significantly over the last few years, and some estimates suggest that weak activity will continue for another few decades, in contrast with strong activity through the 20th century. Nevertheless, the possible effects on warming are modest compared with anthropogenic influences."[320]

This is important to note because, true or not, the Wikipedia entry on "Climate change" opens by emphasizing the alleged role of solar activity on the Earth's climate systems. But here one of the entry's sources is saying the opposite. Instead of raising matter, the authors of the entry just ignore it.

Compare Wikipedia's current, rambling subsection on the impact of humans on climate change to the earlier, 2003 subsection, the entirety of which reads:

"Anthropogenic factors are acts by humans (Homo sapiens) that change the environment and influence the climate. The major factor is CO_2 emission from fossil fuel combustion IPCC. Other factors include forest alterations, and agricultural or other changes that affect the Earth's albedo or the carbon cycle."[321]

Notice that, unlike the more recent entries, the older one emphasizes the human uses of fossil fuels. The more recent entry's claim that deforestation, termites, etc., "are also of concern in the roles they play—both separately and in conjunction with other factors—in affecting climate, microclimate, and measures of climate variables," is supported by a single source: an editorial in the *New York Times*. But the editorial says nothing about climate variability and the role of different factors in climate change. It is an article about US involvement in the Paris Climate Change Summit 2015. The article blames the lack of action on the part of Brazil and China for the failure of the US Congress to legislate the previous Kyoto Protocol.[322]

After "Human influences" (204 words), the entry then explores "Orbital variations" (182 words), "Solar output" (460 words), "Volcanism" (441), "Plate tectonics" (237 words), and "Other mechanisms" (163 words). So, out of six climate change causes, the entry ranks the one that we as a species can do the most about (i.e., our own CO_2 emissions) third, as measured by word count (assuming word count reflects importance).

OMISSION: CATASTROPHIC IMPACTS

The entry concludes: "According to the IPCC, human-caused global warming is driving climate changes impacting both human and natural systems on all continents and across the oceans." But, as we have seen, it's not just the IPCC that draws this conclusion. So, why is this one the only source cited? "Some of these impacts include the altering of ecosystems (with a few extinctions), threat to food production and water supplies due to extreme weather, and the dislocation of human communities due to sea level rise and other climate factors." These sweeping generalizations omit the specific human consequences of climate change. "Taken together these hazards also exacerbate other stressors such as poverty." But the stressors exacerbate more than poverty, as we shall see. The entry concludes: "Possible societal responses include efforts to prevent additional climate change, adapting to unavoidable climate change, and possible future climate engineering." Notice the generalizing language. Below, we shall look at some specific cases. The entry makes no reference to grassroots actions or to specific ways of preventing "additional climate change," like fossil fuel reductions and the expansion of renewables. Instead, the quick-fix solution of geoengineering, which would allow oil companies to continue polluting, is tacitly advocated.

Consider a tiny sample of the kind of specific effects omitted by Wikipedia:

Cook et al. anticipate that current trends in climate warming will dry the northern hemisphere by nearly double. Increased potential evapotranspiration (PET) intensifies drying in locations where rainfall has already reduced and "drives areas into drought that would otherwise experience little drying or even wetting from precipitation trends alone." Cook et al. note that "PET amplification effect is largest in the Northern Hemisphere mid-latitudes, and is especially pronounced in western North America, Europe, and southeast China." [323] Beardy and Chester note the impacts that drought in the US could have on domestic food supplies. "In addition to Phoenix and Tucson, cities including El Paso, Las Vegas, Los Angeles, and

San Diego rely on Arizona for several types of agricultural products such as animal feed and livestock, meaning that disruptions to Arizona's agriculture also disrupt food supply chains to at least six major cities."[324]

With regards to China, Yu et al. note: "Unsustainable water management, especially groundwater management, could potentially cause disastrous consequences in both food production and water supply in extreme events." They conclude: "Our simulations project a rise of 2.5~3.3% in average rice, maize, and wheat productivity before 2050 but decrease thereafter if climate warming continues. The frequency of extreme agricultural droughts in China is projected to increase."[325] The UN Framework Convention on Climate Change says: "Given that more than 80 per cent of global agricultural land is rain-fed, 21 the projected changes in water quality and quantity due to climate change are expected to have a significant impact on the agricultural sector, in terms of agricultural productivity and hence affecting food security."[326] The UN Food and Agricultural Organization predicts increased migration from central and east Asia, and from sub-Saharan Africa, as a result of climate change-related drought:

> "Heat amplifies the potential for migration across a range of water stresses. This has been shown to be the case in country-level studies in Pakistan, Indonesia, the Philippines, Mexico, West Africa and South Africa, as well as global comparative studies ... Indonesia and the

Philippines, anomalously high temperatures amplified the migration effect of both drought and extreme rainfall."[327]

Australia's Climate Council notes that worldwide, "Climate change is influencing all extreme rainfall events. The warmer atmosphere holds more moisture, about 7% more than previously. This increases the risk of heavier downpours." It further states that "[s]torm surges are becoming more devastating because of climate change and rising sea levels. Many coastal flooding events are associated with simultaneous high sea level events and heavy rainfall events in the catchments inland of coastal settlements."[328] Jevrejeva et al. state that globally, "Warming of 2°C will lead to an average global ocean rise of 20 cm, but more than 90% of coastal areas will experience greater rises. If warming continues above 2 °C," the authors explain, by the year 2100, "sea level will be rising faster than at any time during human civilization, and 80% of the global coastline is expected to exceed the 95th percentile upper limit of 1.8 m for mean global ocean sea level rise."[329] This means that coastal communities will be driven from their homes and flee inland. A report by the British think tank, the Overseas Development Institute, together with the UN Development Program, cites a case-study from Vietnam of how local populations deal with sudden flooding. These events "increase the likelihood that people will migrate internally (either temporarily or permanently), whereas people may seek to adapt to slow-onset events in situ". However, in low-lying areas like Indonesia and Bangladesh, "people are temporarily relocating in response to extreme weather events like flooding, but migrating on a longer-term basis when confronted with creeping environmental stress and repeated slow-onset events like prolonged heat and drought during key agricultural seasons."[330]

Climate change-related sea levels and flooding also mean that wealthier nations with the ability to pump water and build flood barriers will spend more time and money on defenses and adaptation strategies. The European Environment Agency states: "The sea surface temperatures off Europe's coastlines are rising faster than those in global oceans." It notes that "[w]ater temperatures are one of the strongest regulators of marine life and increases in temperature are already causing big changes under water, including significant shifts in the distribution of marine species."[331]

OMISSION: THE ROLE OF OIL COMPANIES

The Wikipedia entry on "Global warming" does briefly reference the role of oil companies in funding climate change denial. But, as noted, given that most people now use the term "climate change" as opposed to "global warming," people are more likely to encounter the entry examined in this chapter. For instance, Wikipedia has an entry entitled "ExxonMobil climate change controversy," but does not link to it in its main "Climate change" entry, which is odd given the role of fossil fuel companies and the size of Exxon as a corporation.

The major energy companies have known about their role in contributing to climate change since at least the early-1980s, when Exxon Research and Engineering Company circulated a memo entitled, "CO2 'Greenhouse Effect'." The memo, omitted from Wikipedia's entry on "Climate change," stated that although uncertainty remained over the precise contributions of CO2 to the greenhouse effect:

> "Atmospheric monitoring programs show the level of carbon dioxide in the atmosphere has increased about 8% over the last twenty-five years and now stands at about 340 ppm. This observed increase is believed to be the continuation of a trend which began in the middle of the last century [the 1800s] with the start of the Industrial Revolution. Fossil fuel combustion and the clearing of virgin forests (deforestation) are believed to be the primary anthropogenic contributors."

It goes on to note that CO2 creates a greenhouse effect by absorbing the Sun's infrared rays. The more CO2 there is, the warmer the climate. The memo goes on to note an unequal warming distribution, with the polar icecaps increasing their temperatures. The memo highlights concern for Exxon because "[m]itigation of the 'greenhouse effect' would require major reduction in fossil fuel combustion," meaning a loss of profit. "Making significant changes in energy consumption patterns now to deal with this potential problem ... would be premature."[332]

Exxon went on to fund climate change-denier propaganda (including think tanks linked to Professor Richard Lindzen, noted above. Lindzen said that Exxon was "the only principled oil and gas company I know in the US."[333]) Other oil and gas companies, as well as entrepreneurs, have long-financed climate change-deniers, a crucial fact omitted by Wikipedia. The Campaign Against Climate Change notes of billionaire energy investors, Charles and David Koch:

"The 'Kochtopus' has been involved in undermining every kind of environmental progress but in particular it has opposed climate change legislation, for instance in New Hampshire and in California where it backed the infamous Prop 23 which threatened (but failed) to push back climate change legislation In fact a Greenpeace report in 2010 (Koch Industries: Secretly Funding the Climate Denial Machine) found that they are now the leading funder of climate change disinformation, outdoing even ExxonMobil. A follow-up report in 2011 found that the Kochs are still spending vast amounts of money opposing bills to control pollution, most notably supporting Proposition 23 - a move to abolish laws controlling greenhouse gas emissions until unemployment fell below a certain level."[334]

CONCLUSION

Wikipedia's entry is too long, too equivocal, and underplays the role of humans in climate change. While not denying the human role, it represents one of the more subtle cases of borderline-denial propaganda. It is also an example of bad scientific practice, given the age of many of the sources. The frequent and expansive references to solar and volcanic activity reflect the crudest of today's denial propaganda; but, again, it's not so simple because the entry doesn't actually deny the human role. At the very least, it minimizes our impact. This minimization can only serve the interests of the big polluters.

Chapter 6
Al-Qaeda

Real or not, terrorism is regarded as a serious and ongoing threat to US and indeed international security.[335] Experts worry that groups including Al-Qaeda and Islamic State (a.k.a. Daesh) could come into possession of nuclear weapons. The damage caused by a terrorist group detonating a nuclear weapon, which experts assume they would buy from Pakistan or from one of the ex-Soviet Republics, would not be anywhere near as severe as a nuclear war between nation-states. However, it would cause enough damage to kill hundreds of thousands of people and annihilate an entire city. In addition to the perceived nuclear threat, there are ongoing concerns about civilian casualties in Western countries resulting from suicide bombings and other forms of terrorism. (Let's, for a moment, put aside this solipsistic view that excludes the far greater terror that is state-military aggression.)

The reality is that the US and Britain created what they later dubbed "Al-Qaeda" as a proxy against the Soviet Union. Let's examine the Wikipedia entry on "Al-Qaeda" and in particular, its "History"[336] section, as well as the section entitled, "Alleged CIA involvement."[337]

DEBATING ORIGINS & ETYMOLOGY

Unusually for a Wikipedia entry, the piece on "Al-Qaeda"[338] is not chronological. It begins with the organization's structure (which it claims has changed in recent years), moves on to its strategy, traces the origins of its name, continues with the organization's ideology and religious "compatibility" with broader Islam, before finally examining its history. The entry concludes with Al-Qaeda's alleged influence and activities. This splatter-effect makes it hard to form a coherent narrative. The lack of structure also makes it difficult to analyze the entry. The reality is that a coherent narrative, one of US-British creation and protection of the group, can be formed and analyzed. For that reason and, in the context of assessing the extent of pro-US bias in Wikipedia entries, this subchapter examines Wikipedia's claims about Al-Qaeda's origins (which can be found in the entry's section entitled, "History").

Wikipedia states: "The origins of al-Qaeda can be traced to the Soviet War in Afghanistan (December 1979 – February 1989)." Already, this is problematic because history does not fit into neat timeframes. In his book *Devil's Game*, for instance, journalist and historian Robert Dreyfuss documents long-standing US connections with Islamic extremist groups, dating from at least the 1950s. Dreyfuss notes British support given to the extremist Wahhabis who founded modern-day Saudi Arabia at the turn of the last century. Mujahideen translates as "freedom fighters." These were the US-British-allied guerrilla terrorists who fought a dirty war against the Soviets in Afghanistan throughout the '80s. Given Britain's historical role in Afghanistan, Dreyfuss also points out that when the US launched the proxy war against the Soviets, the British, who were also part of the operation, called upon their Mujahideen *jihadi* sleeper cells in Afghanistan and in Soviet states to aid the "holy war."

The evidence suggests that Osama bin Laden, later blamed by US media and politicians for 9/11 and other terror attacks, was a minor figure in the *jihad*, compared to forces directly trained by the US and Britain; as we shall see. The Mujahideen faction that joined bin Laden's group never actually called itself "Al-Qaeda." So, to say that the organization can be traced specifically to the Soviet invasion is stretching the truth. One of the sources for both claims—that the organization referred to itself as "Al-Qaeda" and that it formed during the Soviet invasion—is a US court case (*USA v. Usama bin Laden et al.*). Cited by Wikipedia, the transcript includes the testimony of one Jamal Ahmed al-Fadl who identifies the name of his group as "Al-Qaeda." In the transcript, he says that he joined in 1989 or 1990.[339] The chronology is important because although he may have *joined* bin Laden's group, for convenience he might have heard it called "Al-Qaeda" by foreign sources or he might have testified that the group used that name. It is also sleight-of-hand on the part of the Wikipedia entry authors to use this as a source and claim that "Al-Qaeda" existed in Afghanistan during the Soviet occupation, given that one of the people on which the claim is based went to Afghanistan for *jihad*, just as the war was ending. In reality, most of the *jihadis* who invaded Afghanistan did so prior to the Soviet invasion, as we shall see.

A previous reference cited by Wikipedia concerning the etymology of the group is one of Peter L. Bergen's books. Bergen does not actually say what Wikipedia claims he says. Wikipedia claims that Al-Qaeda began as a group in 1988, a decade into the Soviet occupation; which rather contradicts the previous claim that it traces its origins to the Soviet invasion in December, 1979. Rather, Bergen refers to a document supposedly concerning one Wadei al Haj (a.k.a., Wadih el Hage, a.k.a., Abdel Saboor), who lived in Arizona and who trained in Afghanistan for five years, including training with traps and explosives.

Bergen comments that the document "illustrates how from its earliest days al Qaeda had an interest in recruiting Americans." But this does not prove that the members specifically called themselves "Al-Qaeda." Omitted by Wikipedia, the next document purports to be a discussion between bin Laden and Abu al Rida "regarding the establishment of the new military group." The document merely states: "general camp, special camp, Qaeda (base)." It doesn't serve as a founding document or even proof that a specific group was founded at all. In fact, other experts consider "Al-Qaeda" to be a loose affiliation of *jihadis*.[340] Indeed, in Bergen's book, bin Laden is quoted as saying the opposite of what Wikipedia claims: "...We have not started an organization or an Islamic group ... We were able to give political power to the Mujahideen." (The Mujahideen were the US-British-backed *jihadis* that invaded Afghanistan, as mentioned above.) The strongest evidence is al Rida's statement: "Initial estimate, within 6 months of al Qaeda (the Base), 314 brothers will be trained and ready." The document from November 1988 doesn't prove that the *jihadis* called themselves "Al-Qaeda," but rather, that they were training at a base.[341]

Like the first source, the second source for the claim, that Al-Qaeda was created during the Soviet occupation of Afghanistan (the BBC), actually says the opposite: "Al-Qaeda, meaning 'the base', was created in 1989 as Soviet forces withdrew from Afghanistan and Osama Bin Laden and his colleagues began looking for new jihads" (but this isn't accurate, either). So, according to the BBC, the organization was not created during the Soviet occupation, but at the end of the occupation. The Wikipedia entry conveniently leaves out what the BBC says next: "During the anti-Soviet jihad Bin Laden and his fighters received American and Saudi funding. Some analysts believe Bin Laden himself had security training from the CIA." Contrary to the claim that "al-Qaeda" is or was a specific group, the BBC further states:

> "This loose connection between groups has raised a question of definition. When we talk about al-Qaeda do we refer to an actual organisation or are we now talking about something closer to an idea? ... Some analysts have suggested that the word al-Qaeda is now used to refer to a variety of groups connected by little more than shared aims, ideals and methods."[342]

MARXISM WAS TO BLAME!

Next, the Wikipedia entry claims that "[t]he United States viewed the conflict in Afghanistan in terms of the Cold War, with Marxists on one side and the native Afghan mujahideen on the other."

Given Wikipedia's alleged reputation for insisting on the use of mainstream and scholarly sources, it is a break in protocol for the single source for this claim to be the History Commons website;[343] a site run by the Center for Grassroots Oversight (CGO).[344] Contrary to the claim, the source cited by Wikipedia says nothing about Marxism or even the Cold War. In fact, the US State Department said at the time (in sources not cited or quoted by Wikipedia), quite the opposite; that the US did not view the war through the prism of Cold War Marxism. A telegram from April 1978 states: "While large numbers of Afghan military officers have been exposed to Soviet training in the USSR or have had contact with Soviet military advisors in Afghanistan, it is unknown how many may have become Marxist or pro-Soviet."[345] A CIA memo, again written prior to the invasion and again not cited or quoted by Wikipedia, states: "Moscow would favor the eventual creation of a Marxist state in Afghanistan along the lines of a Cuba or Vietnam. At this point, however, the Soviets are probably more concerned with the new government's stability in power and with minimizing the damage to Soviet interests."[346] A telegram written in September 1979, two months prior to the invasion states: "For 18 months now we have watched this Marxist party (PDPA) devour itself. An Afghan official last night quietly described the leadership to an Embassy officer

as a 'bunch of scorpions biting each other to death'."[347]
And so on.

Interestingly, the Wikipedia entry dedicated to the "Soviet-Afghan War" is more honest, at least in the opening definition:

> "The Soviet–Afghan War lasted over nine years, from December 1979 to February 1989. Insurgent groups known collectively as the mujahideen, as well as smaller Maoist groups, fought a guerrilla war against the Soviet Army and the Democratic Republic of Afghanistan government, mostly in the rural countryside. The mujahideen groups were backed primarily by the United States, Saudi Arabia, and Pakistan, making it a Cold War proxy war."[348]

(Though the "Soviet-Afghan War" entry then goes on to claim that the Soviets committed "genocide" in Afghanistan.)

Returning to the "Al-Qaeda" entry, Wikipedia's deception continues: "This view led to a CIA program called Operation Cyclone, which channeled funds through Pakistan's Inter-Services Intelligence agency to the Afghan Mujahideen." The "view" never existed, so it could not have involved the decision to launch Operation Cyclone. Furthermore, the cited source (History Commons) doesn't even say that. Notice that the US involvement is minimized by the reference to Pakistan's ISI; and the British involvement is suppressed entirely. In the real world, the view that informed the decision to create the Mujahideen was articulated twenty years later by US President Jimmy Carter's National Security Advisor, Zbigniew Brzezinski:

> "According to the official version of history, CIA aid to the Mujahadeen began during 1980, that is to say, after the Soviet army invaded Afghanistan, 24 Dec 1979. But the reality, secretly guarded until now, is completely otherwise: Indeed, it was July 3, 1979 that President Carter signed the first directive for secret aid to the opponents of the pro-Soviet regime in Kabul. And that very day, I wrote a note to the president in which I explained to him that in my opinion this aid was going to induce a Soviet military intervention."[349]

Actually, one of Wikipedia's sources (John K. Cooley)[350] writes that operations involving *jihadis* in opposition to the Soviets began in 1978, even earlier than Wikipedia and Brzezinksi claim.[351] Brzezinksi bragged that training, arming, funding, and organizing international terrorists "had the effect of drawing the Russians into the Afghan trap ... The day that the Soviets officially crossed the border, I wrote to President Carter: We now have the opportunity of giving to the USSR its Vietnam war."[352]

This vital admission, widely quoted (in, for example, Cooley's book), is missing from the Wikipedia entry.

Having minimized the US role and hitherto suppressed the British role, the entry then mentions the Saudi role in Operation Cyclone: "The US government provided substantial financial support to the Afghan Islamic militants. Aid to Gulbuddin Hekmatyar, an Afghan mujahideen leader and founder of the Hezb-e Islami, amounted to more than $600 million. In addition to American aid, Hekmatyar was the recipient of Saudi aid." The links with Hekmatyar went further than that. Hekmatyar met with and British PM Margaret Thatcher. (In fact, Wikipedia's entry "Gulbuddin Hekmatyar"[353] notes his connections to Britain's MI6 and PM Thatcher.)

More confusion abounds. Wikipedia states: "At the same time, a growing number of Arab mujahideen joined the jihad against the Afghan Marxist regime, which was facilitated by international Muslim organizations, particularly the Maktab al-Khidamat (MAK). In 1984," it continues, "MAK was established in Peshawar, Pakistan, by bin Laden and Abdullah Yusuf Azzam." How could the prior events have happened at the same time as an organization that was founded later, in 1984? Furthermore, the source (the respected website, GlobalSecurity.org)[354] states that bin Laden was a "key member," not a founder. Notice also the reference to the so-called Marxist regime that the *jihadis* opposed, even though the State Department records prove that the US planners knew at the time that the Soviet-backed regime in Afghanistan called itself "Marxist" and was not Marxist in any practical sense, but was, in fact, fraught with in-fighting.

INFLATING BIN LADEN'S ROLE

The entry then re-emphasizes Saudi funding before claiming that bin Laden funded operations out of his own pocket. The source for this latter claim is Bruce Riedel, a former CIA analyst who has every interest in downplaying the CIA's role.

Having omitted entirety the role of the US-British-organized Mujahideen in Afghanistan (who attacked civilians and used Blowpipe missiles), and having minimized the US role, the Wikipedia entry then deviates totally from the main point about the future "Al-Qaeda's" role in Afghanistan, and talks about the group, MAK (mentioned above) and its spreading to the USA. The entry goes on to note that infamous *jihadis* connected to MAK and operating in the US include the "Blind Sheikh," Omar Abdel-Rahman. The Wikipedia entry omits the fact that Rahman was whisked away from an Egyptian jail, after he tried to kill the President Hosni Mubarak, and was brought into the US and protected by the CIA. Interestingly, one of the sources for the claim that the *jihadis* came from 43 different countries, also says (contrary to the Wikipedia claim), that MAK was established in 1980 (not 1984) by bin Laden's ally, Abdullah Azzam, not by bin Laden himself. Instead of addressing these historical gaps in knowledge and encyclopedic inconsistencies, Wikipedia just ignores them.

The entry tries to, or at least has the effect of, shifting responsibility for the explosion of *jihadi* lunatics in the '80s away from the US and onto the shoulders of MAK. But one of the sources used—though not actually quoted—by Wikipedia, reveals the importance of the US role. It says that Pakistan's President, Zia al-Haq:

> "...accept[ed] – with the encouragement of the United States – millions of dollars in Saudi money tainted with the proselytizing message of Wahhabism, a fundamentalist sect of Sunni Islam. The most prominent player in that transfer of oil wealth to sustain a jihad against the infidel Russians was Osama bin Laden. He had arrived in Peshawar, Pakistan – with the blessings of Saudi royalty – to fight the jihad. In collaboration with his revered leader, Abdullah Azam, he set up in February 1980 the Maktab al-Khidmat (MAK) or Services Center, a support organization for Arab volunteers for the jihad in Afghanistan that would later evolve into al-Qaeda in 1989."[355]

This changes the picture entirely. Contrary to the evidence presented in the best books on the topic, the Wikipedia entry claims that bin Laden was responsible for training and organizing the majority of foreign fighters. This gives the impression that the US had some minimal role in funding early operations, but that the major initiatives and financing were taken by and came from the Pakistani and Saudi governments, and that the individuals responsible for creating "Al-Qaeda" were those linked to MAK.

This implied view of history is total nonsense. John K. Cooley's book *Unholy Wars* describes a sophisticated hierarchy of training, at the top of which sat the US Navy SEALs and Green Berets, as well as the UK's SAS. They flew thousands of *jihadis* from dozens of countries into Afghanistan and Pakistan. They also trained the top commanders at US bases. The SAS trained other *jihadis* in the mountains of Scotland in preparation for mountain warfare in Afghanistan. The CIA and MI6 provided on-the-ground rifles, communications systems, and even Stinger missiles. The British media could not report on it because the government slapped a Defence-Notice on the operations (censorship of British media). Wikipedia simply ignores this evidence.

Wikipedia's source for the absurd claim, that Operation Cyclone was mainly the work of bin Laden, is a *Forbes* article from September 2001. Incredibly, the article states that it relies on Russian intelligence for information on bin Laden, as well as declassified online information: "some of the information on the Net may be deliberate misinformation," the source admits. "This is field intelligence and is, therefore, unconfirmed. The following biography is based on such material as well as information published in the West."[356] Wikipedia leaves out that crucial bit.

Wikipedia states: "Experts debate the notion al-Qaeda attacks were an indirect result from the American CIA's Operation Cyclone program to help the Afghan mujahideen." "Experts" do not debate this at all: Cooley, Jason Burke,[357] Steve Coll,[358] and others are perfectly clear that late-70s', anti-Soviet operations created today's well-trained, global threat by the US and Britain equipping tens of thousands of extremists and their prodigies, some of whom formed a group later known as "Al-Qaeda." To its credit, the Wikipedia entry quotes Robin Cook, the UK's former Foreign Secretary, who resigned from Tony Blair's government over the decision to invade Iraq in 2003. Shortly before his death in 2005, Cook wrote that "Al-Qaeda" translates as "the computer file" of the fighters trained by the US; and UK, he might have added.[359]

The Wikipedia subsection on what it calls alleged CIA involvement (read: CIA involvement) also quotes Munir Akram, Pakistan's Permanent Representative to the UN, as saying that US operations led to the empowerment of radical Islam. The evidence and argument (including quotes) supporting the fact that US involvement helped create "Al-Qaeda" amounts to just 146 words. In contrast, the word count making the contrary claim totals 316. This is designed to make, or least has the effect of making, US involvement seem largely inconsequential. But the propaganda is even more subtle than that. Notice that (betraying its supposed neutrality) Wikipedia has gone from arguing against the importance of the US role in empowering radical Islam and the creation of "al-Qaeda" to the more specific and less relevant question of whether US (and British) involvement empowered bin Laden personally.

Given that the article already establishes (falsely) that bin Laden was the main organizer of the *jihad*, it then makes the US role in modern *jihad* seem even less significant by claiming that the US never directly supported bin Laden. The real question is, did the US and Britain create a global *jihadi* network whose commanders and followers are responsible for a significant amount of global terrorism today? The answer is unequivocal.

SOME MISSING PIECES

In addition to leaving out the British involvement and evidence that Operation Cyclone preparations began long before the Soviet invasion in December 1979, the Wikipedia entry omits primary documents that confirm connections between Osama bin Laden and the US military. Let's consider a few such documents. Recall the earlier analysis, that the Wikipedia entry diverts attention from the US role in creating "Al-Qaeda" and the Mujahideen, and shifts the blame to bin Laden; whom it ridiculously implies was responsible for much of the *jihad* in Afghanistan and thus the creation of Al-Qaeda. But that's not what the US Congressional Research Service (CRS) says. To quote the CRS, referring to the Soviet occupation:

> "During this period, most U.S. officials perceived the [*jihadi*] volunteers as positive contributors to the effort to expel Soviet forces from Afghanistan, and U.S. officials made no apparent effort to stop the recruitment of the non-Afghan volunteers for the war [such as bin Laden and his followers]. U.S. officials have repeatedly denied that the United States directly supported the non-Afghan volunteers. The United States did covertly finance (about $3 billion during 1981-1991) and arm (via

Pakistan) the Afghan mujahedin factions, particularly the Islamic fundamentalist Afghan factions, fighting Soviet forces."

Contrary to what Wikipedia says:

"By almost all accounts, it was the Afghan mujahedin factions, not the Arab volunteer fighters, that were decisive in persuading the Soviet Union to pull out of Afghanistan. During this period, Bin Laden, Azzam, and Abd al Rahman were not known to have openly advocated, undertaken, or planned any direct attacks against the United States, although they all were critical of U.S. support for Israel in the Middle East."[360]

A report for the Combat Studies Institute at Fort Leavenworth confirms the existence of significant links between bin Laden and the US (tacitly denied by Wikipedia. The extent of those links is not discussed. The extent of the links likely explains the heavy redactions in other reports concerning the origins of Al-Qaeda.) To quote study:

"Within the context of the Cold War, the United States overlooked the theological underpinnings of the mujahidin fighters and covertly assisted in their arming and training.

Beyond the fundamental ideological differences, the United States (specifically the Reagan administration) saw the mujahidin and their success in the Afghanistan war as an opportunity to stem communist expansion and weaken the Soviet Union. Only after the demise of the Cold War and the rise of transnational terrorism did links between the United States and Osama bin Laden surface in the context of the Afghan war in the 1980s. The Afghan war provided an excellent training ground for militant Muslims to become battle hardened and demonstrate their faith in the concept of a perpetual jihad."

It continues:

"The origins of Al Qaeda are of profound significance to the status and structure of the organization today. During the Soviet Union's war in Afghanistan, mujahidin fighters 'portrayed the event as a holy war,' which resonated throughout the Islamic world. Islamic freedom fighters committed to ejecting the foreign invaders from Afghanistan converged from around the globe to fight the Soviet Union. In addition to the indigenous support from various local Islamic sources, the mujahidin received substantial support from the US, European, and Saudi Arabian governments. The experiences gained by mujahidin fighters in Afghanistan served as a common force in the creation of Al Qaeda's network. The success in Afghanistan led militant Muslims to assume a 'heady sense of confidence' and belief that they assisted in the demise of the once-powerful Soviet Union. The development of an *esprit de corps* among the radical mujahidin led to an intensified belief in the concept of the jihad. The Afghan war provided bin Laden with a "rolodex" of willing participants in his vision for the future."[361]

A partly-declassified draft National Security Council (NSC) report contradicts the Wikipedia claim about the origins and etymology of "Al-Qaeda." It states: "Bin Ladin had drawn on his family's wealth and donations from sympathetic merchant families in the Persian Gulf region, to organize the Islamic Salvation Foundation, or al-Qa'ida ('The Base')." Recall that Wikipedia is quoted as saying that the US role in indirectly creating Al-Qaeda continues to be "debated." The NSC document states: "Many of the men who became key members of the al-Qa'ida leadership met and fought alongside him in Afghanistan against the Soviets."[362] Extraordinarily, the document states (before a heavily redacted section): "Bin Ladin came to the attention of the CIA as an emerging terrorist threat during his stay in Sudan from 1991 to 1996." The redaction is either designed to cover up significant CIA connections with bin Laden or to cover up the possibility that bin Laden was hardly active in Afghanistan and that his presence has been inflated by 9/11-era propaganda.

CONCLUSION

The Wikipedia entry on "Al-Qaeda" minimizes the US role in creating (what became) the organization as a proxy force in the late-1970s, omits entirely the significant British role (even though some of the entry's sources explore this issue), shifts the burden of responsibility onto Osama bin Laden (who, in reality, appears to have been a comparatively minor figure), and avoids discussing the effects of Mujahideen actions on Afghan civilians and the Soviet war crimes they provoked.

Other interesting omissions, which require further discussion, include: the CIA Bin Laden Unit's chief, Michael Scheuer, telling the BBC that between 1998 and 1999, the CIA had ten "easy opportunities" to kill or capture bin Laden, and that the White House (then under Bill Clinton) prevented them from moving on the target;[363] the curious fact that the FBI's post-9/11, bin Laden "Wanted" poster did not reference bin Laden's alleged connections to the 9/11 attacks;[364] and, even more astonishingly, the fact that an updated FBI "Wanted" poster formally records bin Laden as "Deceased" as of November 2001, when the poster was last updated.[365]

Chapter 7
Iraq Blockade

It is hypocritical of Wikipedia to denigrate and marginalize so-called conspiracy theorists and alternative health practitioners while promoting other, far more dangerous fringe beliefs; in this case, the fringe theory that the US-British blockade imposed upon Iraq (1990-2003) was not the underlying cause of the mass-deaths of infants in the country. It is appalling, though not surprising, that Wikipedia supports near-genocide denial. ("Near" because the blockade was not genocide in the sense that the perpetrators were intending to kill every Iraqi. But the scale of the killing was on a level comparable to 20th century genocides, notably the extermination of Armenians by Turks, which also killed approximately one million people.) The reason for Wikipedia's near-genocide denial is a basic one: the US has power, unlike fringe conspiracy theorists and alternative health practitioners, and Wikipedia generally supports US power.

"Sanctions" on Iraq (a major blockade in reality) were a war crime that killed at least half a million Iraqi children. The blockade lasted from 1990 until the US-British invasion in 2003. Wikipedia questions the humanitarian effect of the sanctions, making its entry a serious case of war crime denial. So, what are the Western elites' interests in Iraq and what really happened in the 1990s? At the time of writing, the Wikipedia entry for "Sanctions against Iraq"[366] omits several crucial facts: The background interests of the US and Britain in Iraq's oil; the fact that Iraq's dictator, Saddam Hussein, had been armed and fully supported by the US and Britain all the way up to the day of his invasion of Kuwait in 1990; and the breadth of the sanctions (blockade) and their collapsing of Iraqi society.

To deny the death-toll wrought by the sanctions, the entry not only omits the above information, it even cites marginal revisionist literature disputing the impact of the sanctions. The impression that the average reader gets from the entry is that: the sanctions were controversial, but not as bad as others claim; the sanctions were justified in relation to the dangers posed by Saddam Hussein; and that the United Nations, which simultaneously administered the sanctions under pressure from the US and revealed their human impacts, committed fraud. The message is that if the US does something in terms of its foreign policy, it is axiomatically justified. Let's fill in the blanks before analyzing the entry.

OIL INTERESTS, SADDAM HUSSEIN & KUWAIT

Wikipedia's entry omits the fact that Western forces have invaded and interfered with Iraq since at least the 1830s, when the British Empire brought what the colonialists called "civilisation" to the "sons of lawlessness."[367] Oil became, and remains, the West's main interest in Iraq, which is the second largest source of oil in the Middle East (second to Saudi Arabia). Oil was described in 1947 by the British Foreign Office as a "vital prize for any power interested in world influence or domination."[368] By the end of the Second World War, gaining control of a nation's oil had less to do with importing it and using it for domestic markets, and more to do with controlling global oil prices and denying enemies and their banks access to the potential revenues.

During the Cold War, the CIA worried that, "Since Western European oil requirements could not be adequately met from other sources" in the event of oil-producing states like Iran and Iraq taking control, "the USSR would thereby have considerable bargaining power in seeking to acquire strategic materials and dollar exchange."[369] The CIA later discussed the complexities of international oil markets and how to lean on other nations to produce more or cut back on production, depending on the circumstances: "Countries outside the Gulf having the most surplus capacity--Libya, Nigeria, and Venezuela ... would raise output only after prices start rising." The report notes that "Libya, with one-fourth of the surplus outside the Gulf, might withhold its spare capacity for political reasons," namely as a weapon against the US. This document exemplifies the kind of thinking in US policymaking circles.[370]

Iraq's Gen. Bakr and his close ally, Saddam Hussein, came to power in Iraq in a soft coup in July 1968 as Baath Party "socialists" (dictators in this case). In 1979, Saddam seized power. During the Iran-Iraq War (1980-88/89), the CIA was championing

Saddam's role in regional "stability," which means that Saddam fostered a predictable enough political landscape to suit US interests. "Unless a powerful figure emerges, Iraq without Saddam risks a return to the political instability that existed before Bakr and Saddam gained control." The CIA goes on to note that "weaker Iraqi leaders are likely to ... be reluctant to press for closer ties to the United States. Moreover, Iraq would become more hostile toward Israel."[371]

The commitment to "stability" didn't seem to apply to the Iran-Iraq War, other than the perverse "stability" that arises for the US when two regional powers fight. Via Israeli conduits, the US under President Reagan supplied Iran with weapons. But the US, under CIA auspices, was also sending arms to Iraq under CIA Director, Robert Gates. The aim was to prop up the regime against a possible invasion of secular Iraq by the Islamic Republic of Iran.[372] But Reagan's regime went further. The CIA and Defense Intelligence Agency provided Saddam with intelligence on Iranian troop movements so that Saddam could use chemical weapons (sarin gas) against his enemies.[373] In the UK, Prime Minister Thatcher's regime also helped to build up Saddam Hussein's arsenal. This led to the Parliamentary *Scott Report* (1996), much of which remains secret.[374]

Iraq's War with Iran ended in 1989. Both sides were devastated and both sides claimed victory. Saddam Hussein also hated his neighbor, Kuwait. The modern territorial boundaries of the nation-state of Kuwait were an invention of the Anglo-Ottoman Convention of 1913, which divided Kuwait into two zones (one of which also borders Saudi Arabia). The boundaries were further settled by British colonial official, Sir Percy Cox, via his memorandum of 1923. Iraq's sovereign claims to Kuwait were raised by the revolutionary leader, Abdul Kassem in 1961. Kassem refused to recognize the 1913 agreement or the Cox memo.[375] Known as the Kuwait Crisis among the small number of scholars who pay attention to the period, the British mobilized 7,000 troops to protect Kuwait (read: UK oil interests) from an invasion by Iraq. By then, Kuwait was the largest oil producer in the region and believed to be the fourth largest regional source of oil;[376] after Saudi Arabia, Iraq, and Iran. The British response highlights the strategic importance of Kuwait to US-British corporate interests.

By the time he came to power, Saddam was accusing Kuwait, rightly or wrongly, of illegally drilling for oil inside Iraq's internationally-recognized boundary. Up until the day of Saddam Hussein's invasion of Kuwait in August 1990, top-ranking US officials were openly praising the dictator and ally. In July 1990, President Bush wrote to Saddam Hussein expressing his hopes that the two nations could forge closer relationships in the context of mounting Iraq-Kuwaiti tensions:

> "The United States and Iraq both have a strong interest in preserving the peace and stability of the Middle East. For this reason, we believe that differences are best resolved by peaceful means and not by threats involving military force or conflict. I also welcome your statement that Iraq desires friendship rather

than confrontation with the United States. Let me reassure you, as my ambassador [April Glaspie], Senator [Bob] Dole, and others have done, that my administration continues to desire better relations with Iraq. We will also continue to support our friends in the region with whom we have had long-standing ties. We see no necessary inconsistency between these two objectives. As you know, we still have certain fundamental concerns about certain Iraqi policies and activities, and we will continue to raise these concerns with you in a spirit of friendship and candor."[377]

Bush's conciliatory tone did not go down well with the bloodthirsty Pentagon and neocons in the background, who found themselves closer to the centers of power when Bush's son, George W., became President in 2001. The Pentagon reportedly tried to block the letter as it conveyed US "weakness."[378]

Saddam Hussein invaded Kuwait in August 1990. The US and Britain moved in swiftly to use the invasion as a pretext to maintain a lengthy military occupation of Iraq (to ensure control over the country's oil) in the form of: the military-backed embargo (1990-2003); the daily, illegal no-fly zone bombings by US and British jets (1991-2003); the invasion and occupation (2003-2011); and the re-occupation and bombing under the pretense of countering Daesh (2014-present).

SANCTIONS AS A PRETEXT

The professed reasons for the sanctions (blockade) against Iraq kept changing. The economic sanctions, according to a US Navy report, had multiple professed objectives, which changed according to circumstances. These included: the withdrawal of Iraq forces from Kuwait; the prevention of Saddam Hussein's potential threats to other neighbours; the imposition of a UN weapons inspection regime to end Saddam Hussein's US-British-enabled weapons of mass destruction program; and compel Iraq to set up a compensation fund for Kuwait. The UN Secretary-General, Boutros Boutros-Ghali, said: "the objectives for which specific sanctions regimes were imposed have not always been clearly defined. Indeed they sometimes seem to change over time."[379]

After the adoption of UN Security Council Resolution 665, the US imposed what the study Navy called "the first internationally sanctioned 'full blown maritime intercession regime' ever used in an attempt to diffuse an international crisis and return to the status quo." The Navy also reported that blockades are considered an act of war, hence the reluctance on the part of US officials to refer to it as a "blockade" and the use of the substitute word "sanctions."[380] It is a violation of international law (the UN Charter 1945) to use financial or military means to change the government of a foreign, sovereign nation. But as the world's superpower, the US (and its loyal follower Britain) does as its elites choose.

In 1991, President George H. Bush's Deputy National Security Advisor, Robert Gates (later

Obama's Defense Secretary), said: "...all possible sanctions will be maintained until he [Saddam] is gone."[381] A year later, Bush said: "...I remain determined to keep the pressure on Saddam until a new leadership comes to power in Iraq."[382] Madeleine Albright was the Secretary of State for Bush's successor, Clinton. She said: "...there is nothing, short of the removal of Saddam Hussein from power, that would persuade the Clinton administration to set time limits on sanctions [sic]."[383] This important context—the illegality and immortality of the blockade and its ulterior motive to simultaneously weaken Iraq while *de facto* keeping Saddam in power—is all omitted from the Wikipedia entry on the sanctions.

The cruellest hypocrisy was that the US authorized Saddam to crush a Shia-Kurdish 1991 rebellion that many believe would have overthrown him, had it succeeded.

The most comprehensive set of sanctions in history, the blockade prevented virtually all imports: from building and medical materials (including painkillers and women's sanitary pads) to food and children's pencils (under the pretense that the graphite found in pencils could be used in Iraq's alleged weapons of mass destruction program).[384] The embargo wiped out at least half a million Iraq children in the first five years of its implementation and went on to collapse what was left of Iraqi society after the Gulf War 1991. Karl Mueller, a political scientist at Maxwell Air Force Base, and John Mueller, a Professor at Rochester University, wrote in the establishment journal, *Foreign Affairs*, that economic sanctions on Iraq "...may have contributed to more deaths during the post-Cold War era than all weapons of mass destruction throughout history."[385]

Along with the British blockade of Germany (1914-19), the embargo on Iraq was one of the worst economic crimes of the 20th century. It was also a blatant violation of the IV Geneva Convention (article 33) which prohibits collective punishments. The embargo is widely recognized to be a US-British initiative. Technically, it was administered by the United Nations, thereby rendering the UN, which is supposed to enforce international law, complicit in grave human rights violations on a scale described by its own administrators (Denis Halliday) as "genocidal." Three high-level UN officials (including Halliday) resigned in succession in protest over the blockade.

SANCTIONS: PURPOSE AND BACKGROUND

Shehabaldin and Laughlin wrote in the year 1998:

> "The Iraqi economic sanctions are the most effective of all economic sanctions in this century. The reasons are that Iraq is a small country, dependent on the export of one commodity (oil) and surrounded by unfriendly neighbours. These elements, and others, make sanctions very effective but at terrible cost of human misery and death."[386]

Given the wide acceptance, even in the Wikipedia entry, that the sanctions (blockade) were the most comprehensive in history, the logical conclusion is that mortality in the country would rise as a result of the complicated socioeconomic consequences. But we'd be mistaken to follow this logic, says Wikipedia.

The reality is that Iraq was a fragile economy. By 1990, 70% of its food was imported, meaning that any blockade would result in Iraq's circa 22 million people loosing almost all of their food sources. By 1990, Iraq's gross domestic product (GDP) was just 0.8 that of the USA's.[387] The sanctions cost Iraq two-thirds of its GDP.[388] Prior to the sanctions, Iraq was almost entirely dependent on oil exports. By blocking oil exports (until the oil-for-food program), the so-called international community sent Iraq's domestic fiscal and monetary policy into free fall.[389]

Abbas Alnasrawi[390] writes that other, historical factors contributed to the devastating effect of sanctions: the Iran-Iraq War (1980-88), which US and Britain armed and which led to a million deaths on all sides;[391] the militarization of Iraq's economy (again, with US-British support and enablement);[392] and the Gulf War 1991, in which US-British forces decimated some 50 percent of Iraq's military infrastructure.[393] Alnasrawi notes that throughout the 1970s, Iraq's economy became increasingly militarized, with three percent of Armed Forces personnel jumping to 21 percent by the end of the Iran-Iraq War. By 1980, an already high 20 percent of GDP on military spending was raised to 39 percent. The Iran-Iraq War crippled the economy to the point where the OECD and Soviet Union stepped in with credit and loans, turning Iraq into a debtor nation. Agriculture stagnated as many sector workers were drafted into the Armed Forces. The UN mission to Iraq that followed the Gulf War 1991 states that the US and Britain: "...wrought near-apocalyptic results upon what had been, until January 1991, a rather highly urbanized and mechanized society. Now, most means of modern life support have been destroyed or rendered tenuous."[394] As a result of a deliberate air war strategy to weaken the civilian infrastructure, Iraq's electrical energy output for homes, hospitals, schools, and so on, never exceed 25 percent of pre-war levels. Abbas Alnasrawi writes:

> "The sanctions included a ban on all trade, an oil embargo, a freezing of Iraqi government financial assets abroad, an arms embargo, suspension of international flights, and banned financial transactions ... In short, the embargo was intended to prevent anything from getting through to Iraq."[395]

According to Shehabaldin and Laughlin, the blockade pushed inflation above 8,000 percent per annum, rendering most food unaffordable. In August 1990, 1kg of wheat-flour cost (in Iraq dinars (IDs)) 0.005. By January 1998, the same amount of wheat-flour cost ID325, an increase of 650,000%. This generalizes. The price of: powdered milk rose from ID0.75 to ID1,500 (200,000%); baby milk (450g tin) from ID0.45 to ID450 (100,000%); rice 0.23 to 400 (173,913%); and beef ID6.83 to 2,2250 (32,943%). The average monthly income of a physician was ID4,000, meaning that buying a box of 30 eggs would leave the average physician with just ID1,000 at the end of the month. Prior to the sanctions, the average intake of powdered baby milk was 3.3 kilograms per month. After the sanctions were imposed, consumption halved. Consequently, by 1998 23 percent of all babies were born under 2.5kg, compared to 4.5 percent who were underweight prior to the blockade.[396]

On 1 September 1990, the regime of Saddam Hussein imposed a food rationing strategy to restore flour, rice, vegetable oil, sugar, tea, and baby milk to pre-blockade prices. The UN's Food and Agricultural Organization estimated that Saddam's strategy provided a per capita average of just 37% of the caloric intake of the pre-sanctions years.[397] Easily preventable and treatable diseases spread due to the blockade on medical equipment, including chemicals and basic pharmaceuticals.[398] Even UNSCR 706 (adopted in August 1991) recognized that world officials were: "Concerned by the serious nutritional and health situation of the Iraqi civilian population ... and by the risk of a further deterioration of this situation." As late as April 1995, the UNSC revisited the issue of sanctions, allowing Iraq (via UNSCR 986) to sell $2bn-worth of oil every six month (30 percent of which would be diverted to the Compensation Fund) to finance humanitarian needs. But Saddam Hussein rejected the deal, possibly over concerns about hyperinflation (i.e., not wanting to pump more worthless cash into the economy). UN Secretary-General Boutros Boutros-Ghali acknowledged that UNSCR 986 "...was never intended to meet all the humanitarian needs of the Iraqi people." By the end of 1996, however, Iraq was allowed to sell some oil again.

By 1996, cholera cases had increased by 831%. Prior to the blockade, there were 1,800 typhoid cases. After, there were 15,000. In 1989, there were 20,000 cases of dysentery. By 1997, there were over half a million.[399] In 1996, UN Under-Secretary-General, Martti Ahtisaari, stated: "It is unmistakable that the Iraqi people may soon face a further imminent catastrophe, which could include epidemic and famine, if massive life-supporting needs are not rapidly met."[400] By Middle East standards, Iraq was a secular society with comparably high work rates for women. But under the weight of the embargo, childcare and transportation costs meant that women had to drop out of the workforce.[401] By the year 2000, under the oil-for-food scheme, just $8.4bn-worth of goods made it into Iraq. This resulted in importation equivalents of $109 per person, per annum compared to pre-sanctions years, which averaged $508.[402]

Shehabaldin and Laughlin write:

> "The statistics provided by the United Nations speak for themselves about the size of the tragedy befallen on the Iraqis. It shows that as many as one million Iraqis, half of which are children may have died by the end of 1995 because of the sanctions. By the fall of 1996, at least 4,500 Iraqi children died each month, an average of 150 children a day."[403]

In addition to the crippling inflation, there was a brain drain and skills shortage, as professional Iraqis fled to other countries, including the US and Britain in search of work and survival. Alnswari notes that death estimates range between 500,000 and 1.5m. UNICEF notes that Iraqi infant mortality was 40 deaths per 1,000 live births in 1990. By 1998, it was 103.[404] Among the academics, international bodies, journalists, and governmental and non-governmental organizations that even know about it, the estimation that the US-British blockade on Iraq in the 1990s killed half a million children is not controversial. On-the-ground epidemiologists, UN officials from various bodies, and Western journalists all agree that the country collapsed under the weight of the blockade, which wiped out hundreds of thousands of lives.

But a small number of sanctions denialists dispute the facts. They do so by omitting and even inventing evidence to the contrary. The Wikipedia entry for the Iraq sanctions makes a big issue of the sanctions denialists, and fails to note that they are a fringe and expose their denialist propaganda. Instead, it lends credibility to the tacit assumption that when Britain and the US demolish a country, no one dies as a result. This shocking example of the denial of genocidal levels of death epitomizes the information warfare tactic of the editors of Wikipedia: When the US does something fundamentally illegal and immoral, any scrap of fake evidence can and will be used to justify or deny that wrongdoing. However, whenever anyone makes a claim against US foreign or domestic policy, it is legitimate to smear and marginalize them as a unreliable source presenting fake evidence. This exemplifies double-standards. Let's look at Wikipedia's claims before examining the facts.

WHAT WIKIPEDIA SAYS

The Wikipedia entry "Sanctions against Iraq" is part of a series on Baathism; the Baath party being Iraq's ruling government from 1968 to 2003, when the US and Britain invaded and overthrew the Saddam Hussein regime. It begins by stating, accurately, that:

> "The sanctions against Iraq were a near-total financial and trade embargo imposed by the United Nations Security Council on Ba'athist Iraq. They began August 6, 1990, four days after Iraq's invasion of Kuwait, stayed largely in force until May 22, 2003 (after Saddam Hussein's being forced from power), and persisted in part, including reparations to Kuwait, through the present."

It is good that the authors make clear that "sanctions" were in fact a blanket blockade. Deception soon follows, however. Providing no sources, it claims: "The original stated purposes of the sanctions were to compel Iraq to withdraw from Kuwait, to pay reparations, and to disclose and eliminate any weapons of mass destruction." As we have seen, several high-ranking US politicians made it clear that the blockade would continue until Saddam Hussein was gone. So, the stated aim was to pressure Iraqis into removing their government. (As noted, the reality is that the US and Britain used the blockade as a tool to destroy what was left of Iraq after the Gulf War. If the US authorities wanted Saddam Hussein removed, they wouldn't have authorized him to crush the 1991 Shia-Kurdish uprising aimed at overthrowing him.)

"Whereas it was widely believed that the sanctions caused a major rise in child mortality," the entry continues, beginning its descent into genocidal-levels of denial, "research following the 2003 invasion of Iraq has shown that commonly cited data were doctored by the Saddam Hussein regime and that 'there was no major rise in child mortality in Iraq after 1990 and during the period of the sanctions'." This is blatantly untrue and relies on the work of a small number of denialists. It is exposed below in the subchapter, "Denial."

Moving on to the section "Estimates of deaths due to sanctions," the entry then makes the ridiculous claim that "...effects of the sanctions on the civilian population of Iraq have been disputed." The effects of the blockade have only been "disputed" by a small number of denialists (Cetorelli, Dyson, and Spagat being the most notable). One of the sources provided for the fact that the blockade did have a devastating effect is the UN (the organization responsible for administering the embargo), which obviously acknowledges the impact of the blockade. The second source is a denialist (Spagat), cited in an effort to "balance" the reality of mass-deaths with alleged disputations. But the entry is deceptive in that the third source is quoted in the endnote as not denying the impact of the blockade, rather blaming the Iraqi government (true or not) for not spending the international assistance money on humanitarian needs.[405] The second source is the denialist, Michael Spagat.[406] The same arguments and sources given by Spagat (i.e., Zaidi and Fawzi; the International Study Team; the Working Group; and the Living Conditions Survey) also appear in Dyson and Cetorelli. So, to avoid repetition, this chapter analyses only the Dyson-Cetorelli paper, which Wikipedia cites.

The Wikipedia section on death-toll estimates then states the following. It is reproduced here at length to demonstrate that Wikipedia gives a platform to those who deny mass-murder:

> "Estimates of excess deaths during the sanctions vary widely, use different methodologies and cover different time-frames. The figure of 500,000 child deaths was for a long period widely cited, but recent research has shown that that figure was the result of survey data manipulated by the Saddam Hussein regime. A 1995 Lancet estimate put the number of child deaths at 567,000, but when one of the authors of the study followed up on it a year later, 'many of the deaths were not confirmed in the reinterviews. Moreover, it emerged that some miscarriages and stillbirths had been wrongly classified as child deaths in 1995.' A 1999 UNICEF report found that 500,000 children died as a result of sanctions, but comprehensive

surveys after 2003 failed to find such child mortality rates. A 2017 study in the British Medical Journal described 'the rigging of the 1999 Unicef survey' as 'an especially masterful fraud'. The three comprehensive surveys conducted since 2003 all found that the child mortality rate in the period 1995-2000 was approximately 40 per 1000, which means that there was no major rise in child mortality in Iraq after sanctions were implemented."

DENIAL

Let's consider what Wikipedia omits. Let's also expose the Dyson-Cetorelli distortions on which the above quote is based.

At the time of writing, the Wikipedia entry conveniently omits more recent evidence that reinforces or re-confirms the original claim: that the sanctions contributed to the rise in infant mortality. Writing in *The Lancet* in 2018, Farrokh Habibzadeh (an editorial consultant for the journal) claims that 1.5 million Iraqis died as a result of the blockade.[407] But two sanctions denialists, Dr Tim Dyson (a demographics specialist) and Dr. Valeria Cetorelli (another demographer who has written about the plight of Iraqi Yazidis under Daesh), begin their denialist paper with the statement:

"Since 2003, however, several more surveys dealing with child mortality have been undertaken. Their results show no sign of a huge and enduring rise in the under-5 death rate starting in 1991. It is therefore clear that Saddam Hussein's government successfully manipulated the 1999 survey in order to convey a very false impression—something that is surely deserving of greater recognition."

Already, this is methodologically flawed, if not preposterous. Since when has it been scientific practice to revise mortality rates in wartime, a war waged by Western powers? The language of the article is not scientific but indicates an agenda, namely the authors justify their motive for writing the paper in the context of so-called post-facts, "a world in which the truth is always trying to keep up with disinformation." The authors start with the false assumption and assertion (they provide no sources) that Saddam initiated a "deception ... to shake international opinion so that the UN economic sanctions would lifted." Untypical of academic papers, the authors use many adjectives: "evidence has exposed the fiction"; "more mundane truth has emerged"; "the original spectacular lie." Unusual language in a scientific paper or not, the question remains: are they writing truth? The authors denigrate what they smear as a "rapid assessment" of children's health in Iraq in 1991.[408]

That "rapid assessment" turns out to be one conducted by the Harvard Team, which published its findings in *The New England Journal of Medicine*. The Harvard Team visited various sites across Iraq "chosen independently of the Iraqi government," meaning that

Saddam's goons were *not* breathing down their necks and influencing the study, except in two southern cities (Basra and Az Zubayr). The latter cases were "apparently for security reasons." Due to smashed infrastructure, the Team had to rely "mainly on anecdotal reports." The denialists (Dyson and Cetorelli) seize on this methodological flaw to denounce the entire study. The denialists also claim that a second report on which the UN made its mortality claims was based on Iraqi propaganda. They claim that the second report made the erroneous assertion that 43 Iraqi infants in every 1,000 live births died prior to the sanctions. But this is not Saddam propaganda. The Harvard Team cite UNICEF's (not Saddam's or Saddam-influenced) data from 1990, suggesting that 42 Iraqi infants and 53 children per 1,000 died prior to the sanctions. The infant mortality report of UNICEF/Harvard Team was therefore almost identical to the UN reports, which denialists Dyson and Cetorello alleged is based on fake Saddam data.[409] (Below we shall see how these already-high mortality rates more than doubled by the mid-90s, despite what the denialists say.)

The next study with which the denialists Dyson and Cetorelli have a problem is by Ascherio et al. The latter article was corrected for a trivial error (corrected Dec. 1992), which reads in full: "Effect of the Gulf War on Infant and Child Mortality in Iraq (Special Article, N Engl J Med 1992:327;931-936). Dr. Tim Coté's institutional affiliation was given as the National Institutes of Health, implying support of the study by the U.S. government. Actually, Dr. Coté participated in the study as a private citizen, during an annual leave." The original article is clear that, at the time of the authors' writing (Sep. 1992), "...the effect of the war and the economic embargo on child mortality remains uncertain." The article states that 271 clusters of 25- to 30 households were surveyed to represent the broad Iraqi population. The authors also make clear: "The households were selected and the interviews conducted by an international team of public health professionals independent of Iraqi authorities." The authors blame the Gulf War and sanctions for what they describe as a threefold increase in mortality among children under five (or 46,900 children by 1992).[410]

The denialists Dyson and Cetorelli refer to Ascherio et al. as their collective title, the International Studies Team (IST). They smear a UN Food and Agricultural Organization (FAO)-sponsored study (conducted by Zaidi and Fawzi) because the researchers a) used IST data and b) conducted a field study with officials from the Iraqi Health Ministry, whom the denialists slander as "Saddam Hussein's government." The Zaidi-Fawzi-FAO study reckoned that 567,000 deaths had occurred by 1995. The denialists' level of propaganda by omission and denigration of the source material is shocking. They claim that Zaidi and Fawzi "hazarded an estimate," when in fact that 567,000 figure (right or wrong) is based on a careful analysis of pre- and post-sanctions infant and child mortality, as well as anthropometric data on stunting and comparative analyses with infant and child mortality in under- (or more accurately de-) developed nations, like Ghana and Congo.[411] The denialists omit this methodology. They fail to acknowledge that Britain's other leading medical journal (the *BMJ*) also carried the story, effectively endorsing the study's findings (Court 1995).[412]

The denialists further err in their claim that "[t]he FAO survey interviewed households that had been included in the IST survey in 1991." In fact, the survey merely cites the IST study as a baseline, along with references to other mortality studies in Iraq (which the denialists ignore). The denialists also claim that a subsequent letter by one of the authors (Zaidi) undermines the study because the letter acknowledges that stillbirths might not have been included. However, the denialists conveniently omit the fact that the authors of the letter (Zaidi and Fawzi) had already addressed that point: The stillbirths and higher-than-expected infant and child mortality figures (which led to apparent inconsistencies in their initial FAO report) are explained in the context of having been counted in the aftermath of the Gulf War (i.e., during a spike in civilian deaths), which the authors were careful to mention in the initial study as a dual cause (along with the sanctions) of the high mortality rates:

"Possible inclusion of stillbirths will have less of an impact on under-5 child mortality, which is supported by the fact that our presanctions under-5 child mortality rate' is comparable with what has been previously reported before the Gulf War. With the greater external consistency of our under-5 child mortality rate during the reference period our estimate of the excess number of child deaths is appropriate.

> Additionally, the excess number of child deaths probably underestimates the tragedy, since we extrapolated the mortality rates in Baghdad to the rest of Iraq, where living conditions are much worse."[413]

The denialists omit this. They also omit a letter in the same issue of the journal, written by Omar A. Obeid and Adbul-Hussein Al-Hadi (doctors of the Royal London Hospital and Sheikh-Omar Health Centre, Baghdad, respectively), who say:

> "The fall in weight in children more than 6 months of age manifested from the time of sanctions but before the bombing of Iraq's infrastructure. This decline can only be explained by the increase in food prices; children of weaning age and older are dependent on the family diet, which is usually poor."[414]

The denialists, Dyson and Cetorelli, claim that Zaidi's 1997 letter acknowledges flaws. However, of the higher and lower mortality estimates, Zaidi concludes, based on later on-the-ground surveying conducted by herself, that: "…accurate estimate of child mortality in Iraq probably lies between the two surveys."[415] Finally, the denialists attack a UNICEF study from 1999, which surveyed 23,105 Iraqi women. The denialists are careful to omit the conclusion of UNICEF's executive director, Carol Bellamy:

> "Even if not all suffering in Iraq can be imputed to external factors, especially sanctions, the Iraqi people would not be undergoing such deprivations in the absence of the prolonged measures imposed by the Security Council and the effects of war ... The large sample sizes -- nearly 24,000 households randomly selected from all governorates in the south and center of Iraq and 16,000 from the north -- helped to ensure that the margin of error for child mortality in both surveys was low."[416]

The denialists also omit Bellamy's plea to the government of Iraq to replace breastmilk substitutes with additional food. The failure to do so might have also contributed to malnutrition.

An analysis of the study concludes that in the south and center of Iraq, infant mortality rose from 47 per 1,000 live births pre-sanctions to 108. Under-5 mortality rose from 56 to 131. In the Kurdish north, however, infant and child mortality fell. The authors attribute this decline in the north to the positive effects of the oil-for-food programme.[417] The denialists make the unfounded allegation that the UNICEF study results for the south and center "were a deception." The structure of their claim is rather odd: they claim that a deception had been undertaken by UNICEF (for reasons not explained by the denialists), after which they make a number of claims about how the "deceptive" high mortality figures had influenced US and British policy towards Iraq. Only then do they present "evidence" for their claims. The denialists allegedly engage in deception (which they deny). First, they claim with zero evidence that mortality in Kurdistan had declined because of the end of Saddam's genocide against the Kurds. Maybe. Maybe not. But that has nothing to do with the impact of sanctions across the country as a whole. This issue is thrown in by the denialists and confuses things.

Next, they point to the UN's change in method for analyzing mortality. That's true, but for one thing the UN reports cited by the authors make reference to changing methodologies in the context of growing world populations. Neither report has anything whatsoever to do with Iraq or the context of reassessing mortality in wartime conditions.[418] Citing these reports as proof of deception is not only false, it is a non-sequitur. As further proof that the denialists are engaging in wilful deception, they fail to provide URLs for the UN sources (as if one can't Google them), unlike their other sources which they less blatantly mis-cite. The denialists go on to engage in more deception. Their source is the *New York Times*. The denialists claim that a census taken in the center and south of Iraq had been conducted by the government in 1997. From this, they make the logical leap (quoting US Census Bureau estimates) that: "...it looks like child mortality may not have been quite as high during the mid-to-late 1990s as has been thought." Is this science, quoting the government of the occupying power, which says "looks like" and "may not"? If we consult the *New York Times* article, we find that the article is actually talking about missing men; presumably they were murdered and "disappeared" by Saddam Hussein. There is reference to a 1997 census (which excluded Kurdistan). The *New York Times* actually states: "The new data on child mortality, of great interest to those who argued that United Nations sanctions were leaving Iraqi children underfed and without access to basic pharmaceuticals, are still being analyzed."[419]

The denialists were careful to omit this or note that no follow-up data were reported, indicating that the mortality rates were high after all. (If Iraqi government data proved that the sanctions had no effect, Western media would surely report that and have a field day?) The US Census Bureau Director is quoted as saying: "…on a preliminary basis it looks like the child mortality may not have been quite as high during the mid- to late 1990's as has been thought on the limited information we've had from other sources." The denialists use this paper-thin claim as evidence. Notice how the denialists are careful to omit the statement "…on a preliminary basis." Yet, the denialists are quick to dismiss the alleged preliminary data of others who support the notion that sanctions increased mortality.[420]

The Wikipedia-supported denialists (Dyson and Cetorelli) then engage in another non-sequitur by writing a paragraph about a study by the Working Group of an Independent Inquiry Committee. The study raises the possibility and then rejects the notion that the UN 1999 data had been tampered with. Contrary to what the denialists imply, the Working

Group absolutely does *not* accuse the UN of deliberately manipulating data. Contrary to the denialists' nonsense about lack of census data, the Working Group discusses several census studies in the context of infant mortality. On UN data from 1999 specifically, the Group states "...the lack of consistency between the adjusted 1987 [census] and 1997 [census] estimates for [mortality in the] 1980s suggests some under-reporting of deaf children (and consequently underestimation of child mortality) in 1997." [421] *Underestimation.* So, the denialists and the Wikipedia entry that quotes them as authoritative are the ones allegedly deceiving (which they deny).

The denialists engage in yet more non-sequiturs. They cite an Iraqi government Ministry of Planning and Development Cooperation from 2004, which they claim reports under-5 mortality rates from retro surveys from 1999 to 2003. They claim that the data are "surprisingly low," suggesting that it is further proof that the sanctions did not increase mortality. The reality is somewhat different. Presumably in an effort to make their source-material hard to find, the authors do not say which of the three volumes of the Iraqi Ministry report they are citing. After some work, it turned out to be volume II. The denialists do not provide a URL or page number. The report does say that infant and child mortality is lower than previous estimates, but then explains why. The denialists omit the explanation. Even worse, the report they cite actually confirms that infant and child mortality rose considerably, especially relative to neighboring countries. This suggests that indeed the blockade had an adverse impact. The authors of the report note:

"Once it turned out that there were indeed some omissions of births and deaths, it was decided to re-interview all households again with the small questionnaire."

The authors conclude:

"During the last 15 years [2004], infant and child mortality rates appear to have been steadily increasing. What is surprising is that one does not see an immediate rise, as depicted in other studies, after the 1991 Gulf war... Instead of a sudden jump to an extreme level, the [Iraq Living Conditions Survey] data indicates a progressive worsening of the situation for children. One should note that this should be seen in a context of declining infant and child mortality rates in neighbouring countries."[422]

All of this is omitted by the denialists.

Finally, the most ludicrous methodological approach is taken, namely the consultation of two additional reports on mortality, which the denialists claim only estimate prior infant and child mortality. So, estimates are bad when the results suggest that sanctions are responsible for increasing infant mortality, but they are good when presenting tables and graphs that supposedly show that sanctions had no effect. The denialists write: "The estimates for Iraq are based mainly on the 2004, 2006 and 2011 surveys." They reiterate their unfounded allegation against

UNICEF, that it tampered with data, and claim that they draw this conclusion based on different results to the UNICEF study drawn from their retro-active mortality reports: "In conclusion, the rigging of the 1999 Unicef survey was an especially masterful fraud. That it was a deception is beyond doubt, although it is still not generally known."[423] The denialists then make the logical leap to conclude that "the UN" (as if it's a centralized organization with a single party line) was engaged in a conspiracy to hide its "fraud" by adjusting Iraq's life expectancy from 57 to 70 in 2005.

Perhaps the greater evidence that the denialists engaged in bad scholarship is their blatant omission of all of the information about the social effects of the sanctions.

CONCLUSION

The Wikipedia entry for "Sanctions against Iraq" gives a platform to denialists who claim that the infant mortality caused by the US-British blockade of Iraq did not happen. This is one of the more shameful examples of Wikipedia's subservience to US state power.

Chapter 8
Israel-Palestine

The so-called Israel-Palestine "conflict" is widely regarded as an underlying cause of conflict and tension in the Middle East generally.[424] Palestinian statehood is a just cause for the majority of Arabs who inhabit the wider region. Because of its support from the US, Israel is seen by the majority of Arabs as the proxy nation of a foreign superpower that seeks to exploit Middle Eastern resources. This is understood in US military and intelligence documents, which note that *jihadis* exploit these grievances to help recruit volunteers.[425] Other causes in the Middle East are connected to the push for Palestinian statehood. For example, the corrupt and brutal Egyptian regime, which also receives US financial and military support,[426] and is also allied to Israel, oppresses the Egyptian population in the interests of US corporations (access to the Suez Canal in this case, following the British imperial legacy). Oppressed Egyptians, many of them Muslim, find common ground with majority-Muslim Palestinians, who are oppressed by Israel.[427] Likewise, Saudi dissidents (who are few in number, given the extreme brutality of the Saudi regime,) see their government as corrupt, and allied to the US and, increasingly, Israel. They, too, support the Palestinian cause.[428] And that's not to mention the four million

Palestinian refugees living in Lebanon, changing the demographics and politics of that country.

The so-called Israel-Palestine "conflict" is not a conflict at all. It is the occupation and annexation of one land and one people, the Palestinians, by another; the Israelis.[429] On this issue, Israel does not represent international Jewry. Most American Jews, for instance, want Israel to end its occupation, remove its colonies ("settlements"), withdraw its forces, and stay behind its own borders.[430] A plurality of Israelis and Palestinians support a two-state solution, in which Israel would withdraw its military forces from the Palestinian West Bank.[431] The entire world, minus Israel and its main enabler the USA, considers Palestine to be unlawfully occupied territory.[432] On the sole basis of objections to international legal opinion by two states (Israel, the occupier, and the US, the enabler), the issue is regarded as "controversial" or "disputed" in US media, including so-called liberal media. The only complicated factor is that Palestine existed before the modern invention of geographically defined "nation-states" with fixed borders, which were imposed on nations by the West. This means that when the modern, nation-state of Israel was founded in 1948 it, unlike Palestine, had roughly agreed-on borders (the 1949 Green Line).[433] The world, excluding Israel and the US, recognizes the right of Palestinian statehood (self-determination), but Israel's ongoing occupation and annexation of Palestine prevents this.

This chapter is about Wikipedia's twisting of the basic facts on this crucial, decades-long subject.

IN THE BEGINNING...

This chapter examines the introductory paragraphs of the Wikipedia entry, entitled "Israeli-Palestinian conflict."[434] The entry begins on "[the] ongoing struggle between Israelis and Palestinians that began in the mid-20th century." Oddly, given the volumes of scholarly work on subject, the source for this claim is a BBC timeline. Contrary to what Wikipedia claims, the BBC ridiculously traces the conflict back to "Biblical times," starting with 1250 BCE, when "Israelites began to conquer and settle the land of Canaan."[435] Recall that Wikipedia's entry begins by dating the "conflict" to the mid-1940s, not 1250 BCE. On the timeline, the BBC refers to the mid-1940s as a continuation of British imperial policy that handed control of the issue of the promise of a Jewish homeland in Arab-majority Palestine to the nascent United Nations in 1947. It says nothing about the "conflict" beginning at that point.[436]

Wikipedia continues: "The origins to the conflict can be traced back to Jewish immigration and sectarian conflict in Mandatory Palestine between Jews and Arabs." The reference is a single source: one article written for a History Research Honors Project. Wikipedia omits the fact that the source is relevant only to the 1882-1914 period. The author of the source says that perceived wisdom posits the origins of the "conflict" to the coalescence of British imperialism and the growth of Jewish nationalism among a small number of Zionist ideologues. But the author disagrees. Her disagreement is based on belief: "I believe that the conflict's origins can be traced further back in time" to Jewish migration to Palestine in the late-1800s. Belief or reality, the fact is that the source doesn't say what Wikipedia says it does.[437]

Making the "conflict" (which, in reality, is an occupation and annexation of Palestine) seem more complicated than it is (therefore advancing the US and Israeli position), the entry then states: "It has been referred to as the world's 'most intractable conflict', with the ongoing Israeli occupation of the West Bank and the Gaza Strip reaching 52 years." There are three sources provided for this claim. The first is a book, but the quote is not even from the book, as the source and endnote claims. It is from an *endorsement* for the book. The book is a theological analysis, not a real-world political analysis. In the volumes of scholarly work published on the topic, the source is not regarded as authoritative. It is deceptive on the part of the entry authors to include an endorsement as if it is part of the book. The endorsement, which makes its way into the Wikipedia entry quote, is from Dr. Chris Rice, Director of the Center for Reconciliation at Duke University's Divinity School. Notice that politicians, lawmakers, and geopolitical experts are not quoted. Notice also the attempt on the part of the Wikipedia entry authors to contextualize the "conflict" (occupation/annexation) as some obscure theological battle. Rice concludes his endorsement of the cited book by saying that the "holy land" is "the land where Jesus walked."[438]

The second source is a book by Dr. Virginia Page Fortna, who does indeed claim that the "conflict" is "intractable." But the Wikipedia authors leave out her reasons. Fortna writes (in relation to Israel's occupation of Syria and Palestine generally): After the

Six Day War (1967), which began the current occupation/annexation, "[t]he UN pushed for withdrawal [by Israel] back to the lines before the October resumption of hostilities, but Israel refused to withdraw from the captured territory. UN Security Council Resolution 242 (1967) calls for withdrawal from territories occupied [by Israel] in the Six-Day War [including the Palestinian Gaza Strip and the Palestinian West Bank]." As we shall see, Fortna errs in adding "... in exchange for a political peace settlement." The resolution (quoted below) does not say the Israeli withdrawal from territories it occupied in the War is contingent on exchange for peace. Nevertheless, Fortna adds, and Wikipedia omits: "...but this [i.e., the Israeli occupation/annexation] remains the heart of the political stalemate."[439]

The third and final source for the "intractable" claim is, once again, not an international relations expert, respected political figure (e.g., Desmond Tutu) or legal specialist, but rather, a psychoanalyst. The invocation of theology and psychoanalysis has the effect of obscuring the real, very simple, underlying cause of the violence, namely the Israeli occupation/annexation. The book is blatantly biased toward Israel, repeating US corporate media propaganda, that Palestine's then-leader, Yasser Arafat, rejected a "peace" offer by Israeli PM, Ehud Barak, at the Camp David Summit 2000. Arafat's decision is described by the author, Avner Falk, as "[t]ragic[...]" and Barak's offer as "generous." According to Falk, Arafat was wrong to demand that Israel abide by international law, namely UN Security Council Resolution (UNSCR) 242, which Falk references, but doesn't seem to realize that Palestinians are under no legal or moral obligation to accept offers from their occupiers/colonizers.[440] Rather, Israel is legally obliged to obey international law, UNSCR 242 being one of the main ones.

A MATTER OF LAW

The Wikipedia entry goes on to say that, "[d]espite a long-term peace process and the general reconciliation of Israel with Egypt and Jordan, Israelis and Palestinians have failed to reach a final peace agreement." No sources are provided and the context is omitted. The reality is that until 1982, Israel occupied Egypt's Sinai, having established a colony (Yamit), which it then dismantled. The sentence also omits the fact that both Israel and Egypt receive unprecedented US investments in their militaries ("aid," as it's erroneously called) and are therefore complicit in their shared interests against Palestine. The West Bank, which is now Palestinian territory, occupied and *de facto* annexed by Israel, was once controlled by Jordan,[441] whose regime is also now a close US ally, and historically a British one.[442] Wikipedia's presentation and omission of context gives the false impression that the Palestinians are the intractable ones. After all, if Israel can make peace with Palestine's neighbors, why not with Palestine? This false image works in the US-Israeli interest.

The entry claims that the "key issues" obstructing peace "are: mutual recognition, borders, security, water rights, control of Jerusalem, Israeli settlements,

Palestinian freedom of movement, and Palestinian right of return." These are issues, but not "key." The key issue is Israel abiding by international law (UNSCR 242 being one of the main documents) and withdrawing from Palestine. Relative peace will follow, as many Israeli military-intelligence experts agree (a point to which we shall return). Two sources are provided for the Wikipedia claims about key issues. The first is a statement by the Canadian government. Why the Wikipedia authors chose to reference the opinions of the Canadian government, as opposed to the governments of Djibouti or Holland, for instance, is not explained. Regardless of the motive for choosing a government (over, say, the libraries-full of UN documentation on the issue), the source actually *undermines* the Israeli position and confirms that the peace settlement is contingent on Israeli obligations under international. With the usual provisos about Palestinian terrorism, the Canadian government's statement also gives rhetorical support to Israel for political reasons (Canada being an investor in Israel and an ally of Israel's enabler, the USA), but the onus and obligations are on Israel.

The source states:

> "Canada does not recognize Israel's unilateral annexation of East Jerusalem ...
>
> Canada believes that a just solution to the Palestinian refugee issue is central to a settlement of the Israeli-Palestinian conflict, as called for in United Nations General Assembly

resolution 194 (1948) and United Nations Security Council resolution 242 ...

Canada does not recognize permanent Israeli control over territories occupied in 1967 (the Golan Heights, the West Bank, East Jerusalem and the Gaza Strip). The Fourth Geneva Convention applies in the occupied territories and establishes Israel's obligations as an occupying power, in particular with respect to the humane treatment of the inhabitants of the occupied territories. As referred to in UN Security Council Resolutions 446 and 465, Israeli settlements in the occupied territories are a violation of the Fourth Geneva Convention. The settlements also constitute a serious obstacle to achieving a comprehensive, just and lasting peace ...

Canada opposes Israel's construction of the barrier inside the West Bank and East Jerusalem which are occupied territories. This construction is contrary to international law under the Fourth Geneva Convention. Canada not only opposes Israel's construction of a barrier extending into the occupied territories, but also expropriations and the demolition of houses and economic infrastructure carried out for this purpose."[443]

To reiterate, Wikipedia leaves all of this out of its entry. The source doesn't say that Israeli military and colonial withdrawal from the occupied Palestinian territories, its dismantling of the annexation wall (or barrier or fence) and erection of security wall within its own internationally-recognized borders, are contingent on Palestinian behaviour; e.g., stopping terrorism and/or recognizing Israel: which Palestinian leaders do on conditional terms, as we shall see.

The second source for the Wikipedia claim, that Israeli "settlements" and Palestinian freedom of movement are key issues (as opposed to unilateral Israeli withdrawal), is based on an old (2007) World Bank report. The word "key" is not used in the text. The text discusses movement and access restrictions in the West Bank alone, not Gaza. It does not mention the Palestinian refugees living in Lebanon and elsewhere. The report gives a devastating analysis of Palestinian life in the West Bank under Israeli military occupation:

> "The practical effect of this shattered economic space is that on any given day the ability to reach work, school, shopping, healthcare facilities and agricultural land is highly uncertain and subject to arbitrary restriction and delay. In economic terms, the restrictions have created a level of uncertainty and inefficiency which has made the normal conduct of business extremely difficult and therefore has stymied the growth and investment which is necessary to fuel economic revival."

It goes on to note the "permit" system imposed by the Israeli occupiers/annexers and their collaborationist Palestinian elite allies. It raises the issue of Israeli military checkpoints that prevent freedom of movement in the Palestinians' own territory. It also discusses the construction of Israeli colonies "on private Palestinian land."[444] Again, Wikipedia omits all of this.

Bizarrely and inhumanely, the Wikipedia entry then raises the issue of tourism:

> "The violence of the conflict, in a region rich in sites of historic, cultural and religious interest worldwide, has been the object of numerous international conferences dealing with historic rights, security issues and human rights, and has been a factor hampering tourism in and general access to areas that are hotly contested."

The source is an old (year 2000) article published in the *LA Times*. Again, Wikipedia leaves out what the sources actually says. The source makes clear that Palestine is under an Israeli occupation. It discusses then-recent fighting: "Heavy fighting broke out between Israeli troops and Palestinians across the occupied territories earlier this month, and several Palestinians were killed."[445] As far as the Wikipedia entry is concerned, the areas in which tourism is affected "are hotly contested." The areas are not "hotly contested" by anyone except the governments of Israel and the USA.

THE BOGUS PEACE PROCESS

The Wikipedia entry's intro then moves onto the issue of the so-called peace process. "Many attempts have been made to broker a two-state solution, involving the creation of an independent Palestinian state alongside the State of Israel (after Israel's establishment in 1948)." This is technically true in the sense that many negotiations have been held (Oslo 1993, Oslo 1995, Camp David 2000, Taba 2001, and Annapolis 2007). No source is provided for the claim. It is, however, a falsehood, given that the technical interpretation of the truth is conditioned on the basic premise, which Wikipedia overlooks; that the Palestinians have no legal obligations on which an end to Israel's occupation/annexation is conditioned. One criminal cannot tell a court that they will stop committing crimes only if their co-accused stops. (Israel's claim that it must occupy Palestine for its "security" is challenged below, though again not by Wikipedia.)

Next, the Wikipedia entry states: "In 2007, the majority of both Israelis and Palestinians, according to a number of polls, preferred the two-state solution over any other solution as a means of resolving the conflict." The implication is that if both peoples want it and the Israeli government is capable of making peace with Jordan and Egypt, then the problem must lie with the Palestinian governments (Fatah in the West Bank and Hamas in Gaza). This is a convenient way of subtly shifting the blame from the sustained Israeli policy of annexation and colonization, and onto the shoulders of the victims; albeit corrupt victims, in the case of Fatah: and extremists, in the case of Hamas. (Hamas are no more extreme than Israel's major political parties. Successive Likud Platforms, for instance, refuse to recognize even the possibility of a Palestinian state.[446] Hamas, on the other hand, which has accepted peace with Israel conditioned on Israel's adherence to UNSCR 242, as we shall see, has a charter which calls for Israel's destruction,[447] but is uniquely demonized in Western media. Likud's refusal to even consider Palestinian statehood is barely if ever mentioned.)

The Wikipedia entry goes on to say: "The majority of Palestinians and Israelis in the West Bank and Gaza Strip have expressed a preference for a two-state solution." The source is an old one (2007) in *Haaretz*, one of Israel's major newspapers. But, again, the content of the source is omitted. The source reveals that, at least in 2007, ordinary Israelis are at odds with the elites that run their country in that most want to see Palestinians enjoying their own state:

> "Notwithstanding all the events in recent years, a majority of the Jewish public also views the Palestinians' demand for an independent state as justified - 62 percent (compared to 34.5 percent who see it as unjustified). As in the past, there is also a majority - 58 percent - that is sure or thinks Israel can permit the establishment of an independent Palestinian

state (32 percent think or are sure it cannot, and the rest do not know)."

But, unlike the Wikipedia interpretation, the reasons for alleged support for two-states among the populations of both nations are not clear:

> "All this apparently explains the belief of the majority of the Jewish Israeli public - 53 percent versus 26 percent - that, even if an Israeli-Palestinian peace agreement is signed based on the 'two states for two peoples' formula, the border between the two states should remain closed (5 percent prefer it be closed to Palestinians and open to Jews; 1 percent, open to Palestinians and closed to Jews; and 15 percent do not know)."[448]

The entry then states that "[t]he majority of Palestinians and Israelis in the West Bank and Gaza Strip have expressed a preference for a two-state solution." One of the sources for the claim is a book by Lev Luis Grinberg. Contrary to the claim in the Wikipedia entry, the book states: "Apparently the majority of Israeli and Palestinians stick to the two-state solution," which the author then derides, based on the opinion (not evidence) that the two-state solution is an "illusion." Wikipedia omits the crucial acknowledgment made by the author, that: "18 percent of Israeli citizens are Palestinian, and they cannot accept their inferior and discriminated status" as Arabs in a Jewish state. The author then expresses total ignorance (wilful or not) by assuming that a two-state solution would take place "within the borders of the Jewish state."[449] It would not. In a two-state solution, Israel would withdraw its military and colonies from the West Bank and its military control over Gaza, and allow contiguous travel between the two regions.

The second source is Alan M. Dershowitz's book, *The Case for Peace*, which, to the credit of the editors, is flagged as a potentially (read: definitely) "unreliable source."

Wikipedia then states: "Mutual distrust and significant disagreements are deep over basic issues, as is the reciprocal scepticism about the other side's commitment to upholding obligations in an eventual agreement." The source for this claim is the *Haaretz* article quoted earlier. It is a broad and sweeping statement, particularly given the reliance on a single source. The entry goes on to claim that, "Within Israeli and Palestinian society, the conflict generates a wide variety of views and opinions." No source is provided. Notice how the Israeli occupation/annexation of Palestine is referred to as a "conflict." Notice also the implication that the "conflict" (occupation/annexation) is somehow almost justified because not everyone affected is wholly against it (i.e., "...a wide variety of views" are expressed.) Exactly who these people are and what their alleged views are is not expanded upon. "This highlights the deep divisions which exist not only between Israelis and Palestinians, but also within each society," the entry continues. Given that Israel is occupying/annexing Palestine this sentence lets Israel off the hook. For one thing, it implies that somehow Palestinians have mixed feelings about the occupation. But in this context, the use of the word "about" is vague enough to be meaningless. What do the Palestinians think about the situation? What do they think about the occupiers and about their own corrupt governments? The truth is not hard to discern.

The fact of Palestinian government corruption and collaboration with Israelis gives the Wikipedia authors an excuse to shift the onus of responsibility from Israel to the Palestinian rulers. Likewise, it implies that perhaps Israelis bear no responsibility for the occupation because they have mixed feelings about the occupation, that perhaps many don't support it. This is all nonsense, of course. As noted above, Israelis want their successive governments to end the occupation/annexation of Palestine. But, during times of war, Israeli civilian approval for the mass slaughter of Palestinians exceeds 90% of the population.[450] ("Civilian" is a loose term in this context because Israel has a policy of national service.)

Next, the entry's authors abandon any ambiguity and lie outright. "A hallmark of the conflict has been the level of violence witnessed for virtually its entire duration. Fighting has been conducted by regular armies, paramilitary groups, terror cells, and individuals. Casualties have not been restricted to the military, with a large number of fatalities in civilian population on both sides." Civilian casualties not restricted to the military? Israel's deliberate policy is to *target* Palestinian civilians, both on a daily basis as part of its strategy to maintain the occupation of the West Bank, not to mention during its periodic massacres in Gaza.[451] In fact, Israeli commentators themselves refer to the strategy as "mowing the lawn."[452] At the start of the Second Intifada in 2000 (the Palestinian civilian uprising against the occupation), the casualty ratio was 1:2.5 (that's one to two-point-five) in Israel's favor, with the majority of Israeli deaths being military. In 2007, it was 1:25 (that's one to twenty-five) in Israel's favor. In 2009, after the Gaza massacre (Operation Cast Lead), the ratio changed to 1:154 in Israel's favor, again with the overwhelming majority being Palestinian civilians.[453] Death, injury, torture, kidnap, rape, and general humiliation of civilians is a logical consequence of military occupation/annexation, which is why the UN Charter regards national aggression as the ultimate war crime.

The entry then goes on to state: "There are prominent international actors involved in the conflict ... The two parties engaged in direct negotiation are the Israeli government, currently led by Benjamin Netanyahu, and the Palestine Liberation Organization (PLO), currently headed by Mahmoud Abbas." Notice how the onus is placed on "negotiation," not only Israel's legal obligation to end the occupation/annexation. Notice also the absence of commentary on the fact that Palestinians widely regard Abbas as a sellout collaborating with Israel to further the occupation and annexation of their homeland.[454]

The Wikipedia entry reads: "The official negotiations are mediated by an international contingent known as the Quartet on the Middle East (the Quartet) represented by a special envoy, that consists of the United States, Russia, the European

Union, and the United Nations." In reality, the Quartet is an ideological enabler of Israeli colonial expansion. In an insult to Arabs everywhere, its "peace envoy" was none other than arch war criminal, Tony Blair. It was formed in 2002 but only produced its first report in 2016,[455] in which Israel's legal obligations are cited indirectly as UN resolutions, but not called upon as being contingent for peace.

Since 1989, the main member of the Quartet—the USA—has unilaterally voted "No" on issues of Palestinian rights and statehood, almost every year at the United Nations General Assembly (the non-enforceable chamber of the UN).[456] It has also vetoed anti-Israeli UNSCRs. The EU (specifically the Parliament) supports Palestinian rights on paper,[457] but in reality trades with and invests in Israel and the occupied Palestinian territories,[458] making the EU complicit in war crimes. The Arab League has supported Palestinian statehood, in theory, in various statements.[459] But the reality is that the League is dominated by US and British allies who have no interest in taking action against Israel over its treatment of Palestinians. Recall the silence of the Arab League during Protective Edge (2014), for instance. By omitting the self-interest of these organizations, the Wikipedia authors reinforce the bogus suggestion that the "conflict" is so intractable that even the best minds of the most well-intentioned "international actors" cannot solve it.

All references to US-Israeli rejectionism are omitted. No sources are provided for the paragraph on the international interest in the "conflict."

THE SPLIT

The Wikipedia introduction to its entry, "Israeli-Palestinian conflict," concludes: "Since 2006, the Palestinian side has been fractured by conflict between the two major factions: Fatah, the traditionally dominant party, and its later electoral challenger, Hamas." But this is irrelevant to the fact that both Fatah and Hamas (as we shall see) have agreed to accept peace with Israel on the condition of UNSCR 242. By raising the issue of the Palestinian *de facto* civil war (beginning 2007) and not balancing it with remarks about fractures in Israel's political parties, the article once again shifts the responsibility for the occupation/annexation from Israel to the Palestine. In this case, the implication is that the peace talks have failed since 2007 because of the civil war. The entry goes on to note that "[a]fter Hamas's electoral victory in 2006, the Quartet conditioned future foreign assistance to the Palestinian National Authority (PA) on the future government's commitment to non-violence, recognition of the State of Israel, and acceptance of previous agreements." This implies that the Quartet has legitimacy and relevance.

The claim is totally false. "Hamas rejected these demands," it adds. The source is the US Congressional Research Service. As is all-too-common, the Wikipedia entry omits the crucial points of its source. Firstly, the source does not say that Quartet aid was conditioned on Hamas commitments to nonviolence. Secondly, it says that *US* aid, not Quartet aid, was contingent on Hamas commitments. US demands on Palestine have no objective relevance to Palestinians' legal obligations. Hamas correctly considers the US to be an enabler of the Israeli occupation of their would-be nation-state. In addition, the US had already deemed Hamas a Foreign Terrorist Organization. With regards to the Quartet, the source actually says that Quartet aid was conditioned on Fatah's renunciation of violence, not Hamas's. These were part of the negotiations, not "demands."[460] The entry says that these actions "resulted in the Quartet's suspension of its foreign assistance program, and the imposition of economic sanctions by the Israelis." The source for the latter claim is a book by Eve Spangler, but the claim is not addressed in the book. In fact, the Quartet is not even mentioned in the book or referenced in its Index.[461]

The Wikipedia entry then goes on to claim that Hamas "seized power" in Gaza following the US-Israeli-Fatah refusal to accept the legitimacy of the elections. It omits the reality: that Hamas was elected in a "process" that the international monitor, former US President Jimmy Carter, described as "honest, fair, and safe."[462] But Fatah refused to recognize the new government. To quote the false statements of Wikipedia: "...following Hamas's seizure of power in the Gaza Strip in June 2007, the territory officially recognized as the PA [Palestinian Authority, a.k.a. Fatah] was split between Fatah in the West Bank, and Hamas in the Gaza Strip." The entry provides no source for this distortion and concludes: "The division of governance between the parties had effectively resulted in the collapse of bipartisan governance of the PA. However, in 2014, a Palestinian Unity Government, composed of both Fatah and Hamas, was formed. The latest round of peace negotiations began in July 2013 and was suspended in 2014." Leaving aside the strange chronology, the article leaves out the fact that just one month after the formation of the Unity Government, Israel once again "mowed the lawn" in Gaza, slaughtering over 2,202 Palestinians (1,391 of whom were civilian),[463] as part of Operation Protective Edge, hardening Hamas's attitudes and weakening the Hamas-Fatah alliance.

A LEGAL & LOGICAL NOTE

Earlier, it was claimed by the author of this book that Israel's international legal obligations, specifically its end to the occupation and annexation of Palestinian territories, are independent of Palestine's obligations. Here is the complete text of the relatively short UN Security Council Resolution 242, which has been referenced frequently in this chapter:

> *The Security Council,*
> *Expressing* its continuing concern with the grave situation in the Middle East,
> *Emphasizing* the inadmissibility of the acquisition of territory by war and the need to work for a just and lasting peace in which every State in the area can live in security,
> *Emphasizing* further that all Member States in their acceptance of the Charter of the United Nations have undertaken a commitment to act in accordance with Article 2 of the Charter,

1. *Affirms* that the fulfilment of Charter principles requires the establishment of a just and lasting peace in the Middle East which should include the application of both the following principles:

(i) Withdrawal of Israel armed forces from territories occupied in the recent conflict;

(ii) Termination of all claims or states of belligerency and respect for and acknowledgment of the sovereignty, territorial integrity and political independence of every State in the area and their right to live in peace within secure and recognized boundaries free from threats or acts of force;

2. *Affirms further* the necessity

(a) For guaranteeing freedom of navigation through international waterways in the area;

(b) For achieving a just settlement of the refugee problem;

(c) For guaranteeing the territorial inviolability and political independence of every State in the area, through measures including the establishment of demilitarized zones;

3. *Requests* the Secretary-General to designate a Special Representative to proceed to the Middle East to establish and maintain contacts with the States concerned in order to promote agreement and assist efforts to achieve a peaceful and accepted settlement in accordance with the provisions and principles in this resolution;

4. *Requests* the Secretary-General to report to the Security Council on the progress of the efforts of the Special Representative as soon as possible.[464]

It was also stated earlier that both Fatah and the infamous Hamas have accepted peace with Israel (along with other Palestinian political groups), based on mutual acceptance of UNSCR 242. Fatah (a.k.a., the Palestinian Liberation Organization) formally accepted UNSCR 242, namely peace in exchange for Israel's abandoning of the territories it seized in 1988. In 2017, Hamas revised its much-criticized Charter. The new version explicitly accepts the territorial integrity of Israel, roughly the provisions of UNSCR 242:

> "...without compromising its rejection of the Zionist entity and without relinquishing any Palestinian rights, Hamas considers the establishment of a fully sovereign and independent Palestinian state, with Jerusalem as its capital along the lines of the 4th of June 1967, with the return of the refugees and the displaced to their homes from which they were expelled, to be a formula of national consensus."[465]

Finally, it was stated at the beginning of the chapter that numerous Israeli military and intelligence experts understand that prolonged occupation and cruel treatment of Palestinians jeopardizes Israel's security.

In 1995, Israel's Prime Minister, Yitzhak Rabin, was assassinated by a Zionist fanatic (Yigal Amir). Shortly before he died, Rabin told the Knesset that: "For 27 years we have been dominating another people against its will ... We cannot deny that our continuing control over a foreign people who do not want us exacts a painful price ... [T]he current situation creates endless possibilities for Hamas and the other organizations."[466] Rabin and his successors went on to further torture Palestine, despite growing internal dissent. In 2003, four former heads of Israel's internal Shin Bet security service (Yaakov Perry, Ami Ayalon, Avraham Shalom, and Carmi Gilon), warned that Israel is: "heading downhill towards near-catastrophe ... If we go on living by the sword, we will continue to wallow in the mud and destroy ourselves ... We must once and for all admit there is another side, that it has feelings, that it is suffering and that we are behaving disgracefully ... this entire behaviour is the result of the occupation."[467]

Breaking the Silence is "an organization of veteran combatants who have served in the Israeli military since the start of the Second Intifada [2000]." Breaking the Silence has collected 950 testimonies of Israeli soldiers. The organization states:

> "Cases of abuse towards Palestinians, looting, and destruction of property have been the norm for years, but are still explained as extreme and unique cases. Our testimonies portray a

different, and much grimmer picture in which deterioration of moral standards finds expression in the character of orders and the rules of engagement, and are justified in the name of Israel's security. While this reality is known to Israeli soldiers and commanders, Israeli society continues to turn a blind eye, and to deny that what is done in its name."[468]

In 2014, Israel's newspaper *Yediot Ahronot* published a letter signed by 43 soldiers from an elite Israeli cyber battalion:

"We, veterans of Unit 8200, reserve soldiers both past and present, declare that we refuse to take part in actions against Palestinians and refuse to continue serving as tools in deepening the military control over the Occupied Territories … Information that is collected and stored harms innocent people. It is used for political persecution and to create divisions within Palestinian society by recruiting collaborators and driving parts of Palestinian society against itself. In many cases, intelligence prevents defendants from receiving a fair trial in military courts, as the evidence against them is not revealed …

Millions of Palestinians have been living under Israeli military rule for over 47 years. This regime denies the basic rights and expropriates extensive tracts of land for Jewish settlements subject to separate and different legal systems, jurisdiction and law enforcement. This reality is not an inevitable result of the state's efforts to protect itself but rather the result of choice. Settlement expansion has nothing to do with national security. The same goes for restrictions on construction and development, economic exploitation of the West Bank, collective punishment of inhabitants of the Gaza Strip, and the actual route of the separation barrier."[469]

All of these facts are missing from the introduction of the Wikipedia entry on the so-called conflict, and indeed from the entire entry.

CONCLUSION

Wikipedia's entry on the so-called conflict is based on secondary, interpretive sources (such as books and articles) as opposed to primary sources (such as documents). Some of the sources are absurd (like the psychoanalytic and theological books) and few actually say what the entry attributes to them. The entry gives the impression that two equal parties are fighting an intractable war over land and rights. The brutal reality is almost totally obscured and, even worse, the responsibility is very often shifted to the victims, namely the Palestinians.

Conclusion

This book has argued that Wikipedia supports Western political and corporate interests by downplaying the seriousness of the threat of nuclear war/accident, engaging in borderline climate change- and genocide-denial, taking sides on issues concerning state power, and concealing the extent of US and British involvement in creating major terrorist organizations.

Wikipedia is structured in ways that allow its content to be shaped in such ways.

Chapters 1 and 2 presented a structural analysis of Wikipedia: who founded it and what interests they have; who funds the Wikimedia Foundation and their interests; who edits and re-edits Wikipedia; the relationship dynamics of the contributors vs. senior editors/bots; and the relationship between Wikipedia, US governmental departments, and US-based transnational corporations. It found that Wikipedia's structures are undemocratic and lean towards those with the time, energy, funding and/or motivation to spend much of their lives writing, editing, re-editing and censoring articles. The second part of the book presented a content analysis.

Chapter 3 compared Wikipedia's entries for the foreign relations of the US and Russia. It found that sources are highly selective and focus on Russia's oppression of homosexuals, for instance, without balancing the critique with a discussion of homophobia in the US. The entry for US foreign relations is striking in its lack of mention concerning US global objectives, such as Full Spectrum Dominance.

Chapter 4 discussed Wikipedia's handling of the topic of nuclear warfare. The Wikipedia entry downplays the significance of nuclear warfare and/accident by omitting the long history of accidental near-launches of nuclear-armed missiles. It also implies that the bombings of Hiroshima and Nagasaki were necessary in order to end the Second World War. The entry also paints the US as a victim of foreign aggression in an attempt to justify US possession of nuclear weapons by making inaccurate statements about US enemies. International law and nuclear limitation efforts are also omitted.

Chapter 5 argued that climate change is, together with nuclear war/accident, a major obstacle to decent, long-term survival. The Wikipedia entry borders on climate change denial. While it does not outright deny the human contribution to CO_2 emissions and their influence on global warming and thus climate change, the article over-emphasizes the role of the Sun and volcanoes in climate variation and uses equivocal language, all the while omitting references to fossil fuel companies and the anticipated social consequences of climate change.

Chapter 6 considered the history of the most notorious global terrorist group, Al-Qaeda. The Wikipedia entry makes it seem as if the US-British war against the Soviets (1979-89), which was fought in Afghanistan and made use of *jihadis*, had little to do with creating Al-Qaeda. Rather, the blame is shifted onto Osama bin Laden's then-comparatively inconsequential group, which others later dubbed "Al-Qaeda."

Chapter 7 analyzed the embargo imposed by the US and Britain on Iraq (1990-2003), which amounted to one of the worst economic crimes of the latter-half of the 20th century. It resulted in the deaths of over half a million infants. The entry gives a platform to revisionists who invent "evidence" and suppress real evidence. Here, Wikipedia is complicit in giving ideological support to near-genocidal levels of denial in an effort to make the US and its allies look good.

Chapter 8 concerned the so-called Israel-Palestine conflict, which in reality is the Israeli occupation/annexation of Palestine and the Palestinian struggle for self-determination. Wikipedia's introduction to the occupation/annexation ignore entirely the core issue: that every Palestinian act of terrorism and Israeli military "response" is taking place in the context of illegal Israeli occupation/annexation, meaning that Palestinian terror is a response to Israeli occupation/annexation. The US role in enabling Israel is omitted, Israel's legal obligations are not discussed and many of the sources either do not actually say what is attributed to them or they also say other, more important things that are ignored.

Wikipedia is not an open encyclopedia balanced by the wisdom of crowds. It is a tool of US state-military-corporate propaganda, albeit with competing and conflicting interests, which seeks to minimize US malevolence and maximize the horrors of US enemies. People need to start calling out Wikipedia for what it really is, to scratch beneath the surface and see who funds it, and, perhaps most important of all: to find ways of genuinely democratizing the organization.

Endnotes

[1] William Jordan, "British people trust Wikipedia more than the news," YouGov, 9 August 2014, https://yougov.co.uk/topics/politics/articles-reports/2014/08/09/more-british-people-trust-wikipedia-trust-news.

[2] Wikipedia, "Wikipedia: Wikipedia is not a reliable source," no date, https://en.wikipedia.org/wiki/Wikipedia:Wikipedia_is_not_a_reliable_source.

[3] Wikipedia, "A message to our readers about COVID-19," no date, https://en.wikipedia.org/wiki/Main_Page.

[4] Laura Donnelly, "Sage advisers used Wikipedia entries to model first Covid lockdown," *Telegraph*, 19 November 2020, https://www.telegraph.co.uk/news/2020/11/19/sage-advisers-used-wikipedia-entries-model-first-covid-lockdown/.

[5] Quoted in José van Dijck (2013) *The Culture of Connectivity: A Critical History of Social Media*, Oxford: Oxford University Press, p. 142.

[6] Quoted in Andrew Orlowski, "Wales and Sanger on Wikipedia: Hey, Jimmy. Didn't you just edit me out of history?," 18 April 2006, *The Register*, https://www.theregister.co.uk/2006/04/18/wales_sanger_interviews/.

[7] Marcin Sydow, Katarzyna Baraniak and Paweł Teisseyre (2017) "Diversity of editors and teams versus quality of cooperative work: experiments on Wikipedia," *Journal of Intelligent Information Systems*, 48: 601–632.

[8] Maude Gauthier and Kim Sawchuk (2017) "Not notable enough: feminism and expertise in Wikipedia," *Communication and Critical/Cultural Studies*, 14(4): 387.

[9] Christina Shane-Simpson and Kristen Gillespie-Lynch (2017) "Examining potential mechanisms underlying the Wikipedia gender gap through a collaborative editing task," *Computers in Human Behavior*, 66: 312-28, 313.

[10] Quoted in Bill Kovarik (2011) *Revolutions in Communication: Media History from Gutenberg to the Digital Age*, New York: Continuum, p. 325.

[11] Wikipedia (no date), "Hillary Clinton," https://en.wikipedia.org/wiki/Hillary_Clinton.

[12] Betty Boyd Caroli, "Hillary Clinton," Biographies, *Encyclopædia Britannica*, (online), https://www.britannica.com/biography/Hillary-Clinton.

[13] Michael Blanding, "Is Wikipedia More Biased Than Encyclopædia Britannica?," *Harvard Business School*, 19 January 2015, https://hbswk.hbs.edu/item/is-wikipedia-more-biased-than-encyclopdia-britannica.

[14] Kim Ghattas (2013) *The Secretary: A Journey with Hillary Clinton from Beirut to the Heart of American Power*, New York: Henry Holt, p. 270.

[15] Massimo Calabresi, "Hillary Clinton and the Rise of Smart Power," *TIME*, 7 November 2011, https://web.archive.org/web/20130924182428/http://content.time.com/time/magazine/article/0,9171,2097973,00.html.

[16] Quoted in Gayle Tzemach Lemmon, "The Hillary Doctrine," *Newsweek*, 6 March 2011, https://web.archive.org/web/20190928040034/https://www.newsweek.com/hillary-doctrine-66105.

[17] Valerie M. Hudson and Patricia Leidl (2015) *The Hillary Doctrine: Sex and American Foreign Policy*, New York: Columbia University Press, p. 60.

[18] Wikimedia Foundation (2018) *Independent Auditor's Report FY 2017-2018*, https://upload.wikimedia.org/wikipedia/foundation/6/60/FY17-18_-_Independent_Auditors%27_Report.pdf.

[19] Wikimedia Foundation (2015) *Communications Quarterly Review: Wikimedia Foundation - Q2 of FY14-15*, https://upload.wikimedia.org/wikipedia/commons/1/12/Communications_WMF_Quarterly_Review,_Q2_2014-15.pdf.

[20] Clinton Foundation (no date), "Leadership team: Craig Minassian," https://www.clintonfoundation.org/about/leadership-team#CraigMinassian.

[21] Chris Alcantara, "The most challenging job of the 2016 race: Editing the candidates' Wikipedia pages," *Washington Post*, 27 October 2016, https://web.archive.org/web/20161027154856/https://www.washingtonpost.com/graphics/politics/2016-election/presidential-wikipedias/.

[22] Exact rankings change all the time. Alexa, "The top 500 sites on the web," https://www.alexa.com/topsites and SimilarWeb, "Top Websites Ranking," https://www.similarweb.com/top-websites.

[23] In 2016, entrepreneur Mark Cuban told the Senate Judiciary Antitrust Subcommittee that Facebook is a dominant content-delivery business. The *New York Times* carrying the story also noted that 85 cents in every dollar of marketing goes to either Facebook or Google. Alphabet (which owns Google) owned 83 percent of the mobile search market shares in the US and nearly 63 percent of the US mobile operating systems. Despite providing just 11 percent of revenue to content creators, Google's YouTube provides 55 percent of audio and video streaming content (Jonathan Taplin, "Forget AT&T. The Real Monopolies Are Google and Facebook," *NYT*, 13 December 2016, https://www.nytimes.com/2016/12/13/opinion/forget-att-the-real-monopolies-are-google-and-facebook.html. Even the business journal *Bloomberg* opines that the big tech giants have "lost the monopoly argument." Lionel Laurent, "Apple, Facebook and Google Have Lost the Monopoly Argument," *Bloomberg*, 5 June 2019, https://www.bloomberg.com/opinion/articles/2019-06-05/apple-facebook-and-google-have-lost-the-monopoly-argument.)

[24] Google has over 90 percent of the search engine market share globally. There are 3.8 million Google searches per minute: or 2 trillion per annum. Bluelist.co (no date), "63 Fascinating Google Search Statistics," https://bluelist.co/blog/google-stats-and-facts/.

[25] In 2016, Alphabet teamed up with Britain's GlaxoSmithKline drug company to create a new life sciences company, Verily. Reuters, "Google parent Alphabet and U.K. pharmaceutical firm to create company focused on fighting diseases," 1 August 2016, https://business.financialpost.com/executive/smart-shift/google-

parent-alphabet-and-u-k-pharmaceutical-firm-to-create-
company-focused-on-fighting-diseases.

[26] "Established news outlets strongly dominate the results,
regardless of what a user is searching for. Of all the Google
News recommendations we collected, a full 49 percent ... were
to just five national news organizations: The New York Times,
CNN, Politico, The Washington Post and HuffPost. And those
five, much like other mainstream news organizations, tend to be
seen as center-left." Seth Lewis and Efrat Nechushtai, "Google
News Searches Aren't Politically Biased, but They Do Like
Mainstream Media," *LiveScience*, 31 August 2018,
www.livescience.com/63484-google-news-search-trump.html.

[27] In 2017, under the guise of countering "fake news," Google
implemented Project Owl. However, Vice President of Google's
search engineering, Ben Gomes, acknowledged another aim was
to "demote low-quality content" (quoted in Evan Popp,
"Independent Media Sites Seeing Decline in Traffic After
Change in Google's Algorithm," *Medium*, 9 December 2019,
https://medium.com/@evanpopp/google-changes-its-algorithm-
to-fight-fake-news-hurts-independent-news-sites-
a01b2d2ed32d). AlterNet's editor Don Hazen quit after staff
went public over his bullying, some of it sexually abusive in
nature. Prior to the revelations about his character, Truthdig
republished an article by AlterNet: "We were getting slammed
by Google's new algorithm intended to fight "fake news." We
were losing millions of monthly visitors, and so was much of the
progressive news media. Lost readership goes directly to the
bottom line" (Hazen, "Google's Threat to Democracy Continues
to Hit Alternative Media," *Truthdig*, 27 October 2017,
https://www.truthdig.com/articles/googles-threat-to-democracy-
continues-to-hit-alternative-media/). Kollibri Terre
Sonnenblume writes: "many leftist and progressive websites saw
double-digit percentage declines in the traffic referred to them
from Google searches. Among these were Alternet (-63%),
Democracy Now! (-36%), Common Dreams (-37%), Truth-Out
(-25%), The Intercept (-19%) and Counterpunch (-21%) [sic].
The steepest decline was experienced by the World Socialist
Web Site (wsws.org), whose search traffic fell by two-thirds"
("Cowardly New World: Alternative Media Under Attack by

Algorithms," *CounterPunch*, 26 October 2017, https://www.counterpunch.org/2017/10/26/cowardly-new-world-alternative-media-under-attack-by-algorithms/). For details of the techniques used, see Andre Damon and Niles Niemuth, "New Google algorithm restricts access to left-wing, progressive web sites," World Socialist Web Site, 27 July 2017, https://www.wsws.org/en/articles/2017/07/27/goog-j27.html. The algorithms continue to hit alternative health sites in favor of big pharma. See Maryam Henein, "Google Censors, Shadowbans, and Blacklists Alternative Health News," *Epoch Times*, 27 September 2019, https://www.theepochtimes.com/google-censors-shadowbans-and-blacklists-alternative-health-news_3098108.html.

[28] Seungwon "Shawn" Lee, Dessislava Boshnakova and Joe Goldblatt (2017) *The 21st Century Meeting and Event Technologies: Powerful Tools for Better Planning, Marketing, and Evaluation*, Ranton: CRC Press, p. 184.

[29] Google SearchLiaison on Twitter (1 June 2018): "Yesterday, we fixed an error in our Knowledge Panel about the California Republican Party that listed "Nazism" as one of the party's ideologies. We regret the error, apologize for it & want to explain how it happened" (https://twitter.com/searchliaison/status/1002654737135570944?lang=en).

[30] Amy Chozick, "Jimmy Wales Is Not an Internet Billionaire," *NYT Magazine*, 27 June 2013, https://www.nytimes.com/2013/06/30/magazine/jimmy-wales-is-not-an-internet-billionaire.html.

[31] Sultanate of Oman Ministry of Technology and Information, "Sultan Qaboos Award for Excellence in eGovernment 2014 winners announced," 4 December 2014, https://www.ita.gov.om/ITAPortal/MediaCenter/NewsDetail.aspx?NID=622.

[32] James Ball, "Wikipedia's founder calls for Richard O'Dwyer extradition to be stopped," *Guardian*, 24 June 2012, https://www.theguardian.com/uk/2012/jun/24/wikipedia-founder-richard-odwyer-extradition-stopped.

[33] *The Telegraph*, "Jimmy Wales: Wikipedia will use encryption to beat snooper's charter," 6 September 2012, https://www.telegraph.co.uk/technology/news/9524474/Jimmy-Wales-Wikipedia-will-use-encryption-to-beat-snoopers-charter.html.

[34] Wikipedia (no date), "The Holocaust," https://en.wikipedia.org/wiki/The_Holocaust.

[35] For an overview of the horror including the extermination of Jehovah's Witnesses, Afro-Germans, French prisoners, etc., see Doris Bergen (2016) *The Holocaust: A New History*, London: The History Press. For empirical proof in the form of International Business Machines' Hollerith punch-card system, which designated numbers for particular kinds of victim and extermination method, see Edwin Black (2001) *IBM and the Holocaust: The Strategic Alliance between Nazi Germany and America's Most Powerful Corporation*, Boston: Little, Brown and Co.

Details of the murder of 500,000 or so Gypsy-Roma can be found in: The first account seeking to give a voice to Gypsy-Roma, Donald Kenrick and Grattan Puxon (2009 [1995]) *Gypsies Under the Swastika*, Hatfield: University of Hertfordshire Press; Gunter Lewry (2000) *The Nazi Persecution of Gypsies*, Oxford: Oxford University Press (Gypsies in Germany, Hungary, Lithuania, Rumania, Slovakia and Yugoslavia); and János Bársony and Ágnes Daróczi (eds.) (2008) *Pharrajimos: The Fate of the Roma During the Holocaust*, New York: International Debate Education Association (Hungarian Roma).

For details about the murder of 300,000 or so disabled people as part of the Nazis' T4 and other programs: Suzanne E. Evans (2007) *Hitler's Forgotten Victims: The Holocaust and the Disabled*, London: The History Press and Evans (2004) *Forgotten Crimes: The Holocaust and People with Disabilities*, Chicago: Ivan R. Dee. On the thousands of homosexuals murdered, see Gunter Grau (ed.) (1995) *Hidden Holocaust? Gay and Lesbian Persecution in Germany 1933-45*, Patrick Camiller (trans.), London: Fitzroy Dearborn and Richard Plant (1986)

The Pink Triangle: The Nazi War Against Homosexuals, New York: Holt.

[36] Holocaust deniers used the internet as a medium to publish their writings within what Allington calls "a pseudoacademic framework to promote Holocaust denial as an alternative yet viable view." They established publications such as *The Journal for Historical Review*, which have a wider reach than print-journals. (William Allington (2017) "Holocaust Denial Online: The Rise of Pseudo-Academic Antisemitism on the Early Internet," *Journal of Contemporary Antisemitism*, 73: DOI: https://doi.org/10.26613/jca/1.1.4.) An early, pioneering article by Landesman argued that deniers labelled themselves "revisionists" to provide a veneer of legitimacy and that instead of outright denial, targeted their denialism toward specific aspects, such as questioning the six million figure (a clue that their denialism is primarily anti-Semitism as opposed to anti-homosexuality, etc.) or questioning whether or not the gas chambers were really just atrocity propaganda. (Betty Landesman (1998) "Holocaust Denial and the Internet," *The Reference Librarian*, 29(61-62): 287-99.) For a discussion on the legal difficulties that arise with cross-border media, notably the internet and policing a medium in which many if not most users are anonymous, see David Fraser (2009) "'On the Internet, Nobody Knows You're a Nazi': Some Comparative Legal Aspects of Holocaust Denial on the WWW" in Ivan Hare and James Weinstein (eds.) *Extreme Speech and Democracy*, Oxford: Oxford University Press, pp. 511-37.

[37] On 23 October 2015, the Editorial Board of the *New York Times* denounced the Prime Minister of Israel, Benjamin Netanyahu, for his repetition and expansion on previous allegations to the World Zionist Congress, that the Mufti of Jerusalem, Haj Amin al-Husseini (1895-1974), was responsible for the Final Solution by suggesting it to Hitler: "The Holocaust is not a history to tamper with, and now that he has heard the anguished outcry from people who understand that, Mr. Netanyahu should have the decency to acknowledge that he was wrong and out of line." The article is erroneously titled "Mr. Netanyahu's Holocaust Blunder" and can be found here: https://www.nytimes.com/2015/10/23/opinion/benjamin-

netanyahus-holocaust-blunder.html. The Pulitzer Prize-winning Professor Saul Friedländer's parents were murdered in Auschwitz. Hiding in a Catholic boarding school, he survived the Nazi Holocaust and emigrated to Israel in 1948. He is described by Israel's leading newspaper *Haaretz* as "The foremost Israeli and Jewish veteran historian of the Holocaust." In Israel, "Zionism has been taken, kidnapped even, by the far right," he says. "The right excels at using the Holocaust ... Since the 1970s when Menachem Begin described Yasser Arafat as a 'second Hitler,' we have seen how the political right in Israel has been using the Holocaust and its memory to justify more and more radical positions. It caused the left to refrain from even mentioning the Shoah." Quoted in Anshel Pfeffer, "'Zionism Has Been Kidnapped by the Far Right,' Says Holocaust Historian Friedlander," *Haaretz,* 18 May 2014, https://www.haaretz.com/jewish/.premium-israelis-you-re-being-hijacked-1.5248606. The original classic book on the subject, endorsed by the founder of Holocaust studies, Raul Hilberg, is Norman Finkelstein's (2000) *The Holocaust Industry: Reflections on the Exploitation of Jewish Suffering*, London: Verso.

[38] Christoph Hube, Robert Jäschke and Besnik Fetahu (2018) "Towards Bias Detection in Online Text Corpora" in Jo Bates, Paul D. Clough, Robert Jäschke and Jahna Otterbacher (eds.), *BIAS: Proceedings of the Workshop on Bias in Information, Algorithms, and Systems*, Sheffield, United Kingdom, March 25, 2018.

[39] Dariusz Jemielniak (2014) *Common Knowledge?: An Ethnography of Wikipedia*, Stanford: Stanford University Press, pp. vii-xiii.

[40] Gregory Kohs, "Secret Wikimedia Foundation donor list revealed," *The Examiner*, 24 April 2011, https://web.archive.org/web/20140817051132/http://www.examiner.com/article/secret-wikimedia-foundation-donor-list-revealed. The list can be found here: http://mywikibiz.com/Directory:Wikimedia_Foundation_secret_donor_list.

[41] Quoted Ben Stein, "In Class Warfare, Guess Which Class Is Winning," *New York Times*, 26 November 2006,

https://www.nytimes.com/2006/11/26/business/yourmoney/26every.html. That was before the financial crisis. A couple of years after, Buffett reiterated it: "there's been class warfare going on for the last 20 years, and my class has won. We're the ones that have gotten our tax rates reduced dramatically." Quoted in Greg Sargent, "There's been class warfare for the last 20 years, and my class has won," *Washington Post*, 30 September 2011, https://web.archive.org/web/20111005164900/https://www.washingtonpost.com/blogs/plum-line/post/theres-been-class-warfare-for-the-last-20-years-and-my-class-has-won/2011/03/03/gIQApaFbAL_blog.html.

[42] Consider the list of "libertarian" figures it endorses. Valerie Durham, "Newsmax Reveals the Top 100 Most Influential Libertarians List," FreedomFest, 1 June 2017, https://2019.freedomfest.com/newsmax-reveals-the-top-100-most-influential-libertarians-list/.

[43] Wikimedia Foundation (no date), "Benefactors," https://wikimediafoundation.org/support/benefactors/.

[44] The reviewer was Karin Lissakers. The quote and alternative perspectives can be found in Joseph P. Joyce (2013) *The IMF and Global Financial Crises: Phoenix Rising?*, Cambridge: Cambridge University Press, p. 70.

[45] Wikipdia (no date), "David Koch," https://en.wikipedia.org/wiki/David_Koch.

[46] The word "Kochtopus" does not appear in the entry, despite the "Kochtopus" (a portmanteau of Koch and octopus) being a serious piece of journalism that connects the tentacles of the brothers' business links and their impact on media and education. International Forum on Globalization (no date) "Kochtopus," http://ifg.org/kochtopus/. The Koch brothers had a two-decade strategy for blocking the development of electric vehicles in the US, including via propaganda and lobbying. (Ben Jervy, "How the Koch brothers got us here," *Bulletin of the Atomic Scientists*, 26 September 2019, https://thebulletin.org/2019/09/how-the-koch-brothers-got-us-here/). PR Watch reports: "New documents uncovered by the Center for Media and Democracy show that the billionaire Koch brothers have developed detailed personality profiles on 89

percent of the U.S. population, and are using those profiles to launch an unprecedented private propaganda offensive to advance Republican candidates in the 2018 midterms." Calvin Sloan, "Koch Brothers Are Watching You: And New Documents Reveal Just How Much They Know," PR Watch, 5 November 2018, https://www.prwatch.org/news/2018/11/13413/koch-brothers-are-watching-you-and-new-documents-reveal-just-how-much-they-know.

[47] Wikimedia Foundation (no date), "Benefactors," https://wikimediafoundation.org/support/benefactors/.

[48] Joe Pinsker, "The Covert World of People Trying to Edit Wikipedia for Pay," *The Atlantic*, 11 August 2015, https://www.theatlantic.com/business/archive/2015/08/wikipedia-editors-for-pay/393926/.

[49] Frances Di Lauro and Rebecca Johinke (2017) "Employing Wikipedia for good not evil: innovative approaches to collaborative writing assessment," *Assessment & Evaluation in Higher Education*, 42(3): 478-491.

[50] Matthew A. Vettera, Zachary J. McDowell and Mahala Stewart (2019) "From Opportunities to Outcomes: The Wikipedia-Based Writing Assignment," *Computers and Composition*, 52: 53-64.

[51] Meredith Drosback, "Telling the Untold Stories of African Americans in STEM," Obama White House, Archives, 23 February 2015, https://obamawhitehouse.archives.gov/blog/2015/02/23/telling-untold-stories-african-americans-stem.

[52] Knatokie Ford, "Honoring NASA's Katherine Johnson, STEM Pioneer," 30 November 2015, Obama White House, Archives, https://obamawhitehouse.archives.gov/blog/2015/11/25/honoring-nasas-katherine-johnson-stem-pioneer.

[53] Matt Bridgewater (2017) "History Writing and Wikipedia," *Computers and Composition*, 45(1): 36-50.

[54] Cristian Consonni, David Laniado and Alberto Montresor (2019) "WikiLinkGraphs: A Complete, Longitudinal and Multi-Language Dataset of the Wikipedia Link Networks," *arXiv:1902.04298*, https://arxiv.org/pdf/1902.04298. The authors say 5.9 million, but Wikipedia now celebrates 6 million.

[55] Unlike other conflicts in the region, "the Ethiopian occupation of Western Somalia (so-called 'Ogaden') remains a bitter bone of contention" (Louise FitzGibbon (1982) *The Betrayal of the Somalis*, Methuen: Rex Collings, p. 5). For an international perspective, see Ali Khalif Galaydh (1986) *Intragovernmental Negotiation: Soviet-Somali Relations and the Ogaden War, 1978-79*, New York: International Peace Academy. On the UK's role in the colonial background, see Estelle Sylvia Pankhurst (1946) *British Policy in Eastern Ethiopia: The Ogaden and the Reserved Area*, Newcastle: Richard Mayne's Press.

[56] India's annexation of Kashmir in 2019 is a violation of UNSCR 38 (1948), which obliges Indian and Pakistani governments "to refrain from making any statements and from doing or causing to be done or permitting any act which might aggravate the situation" (https://undocs.org/S/RES/38(1948)). On the history, including pre-colonial, but especially for Britain's role, see Chitralekha Zutshi (2017) *Kashmir: History, Politics, Representation*, Cambridge: Cambridge university Press. For the arguments on both sides, see Alastair Lamb (1991) *Kashmir: A Disputed Legacy, 1846-1990*, Oxford: Oxford University Press. For an overview of grassroots resistance, sometimes terrorism, see Haley Duschinski, Mona Bhan, Ather Zia and Cynthia Mahmood (eds.) (2018) *Resisting Occupation in Kashmir*, Philadelphia: University of Pennsylvania Press.

[57] Since 1999, US "aid" to Israel has been packaged in 10-year periods via Memoranda of Understanding. By 2019, post-WWII "aid" to Israel totalled $142.3bn. Jeremy M. Sharp, "U.S. Foreign Aid to Israel," Congressional Research Service, 7 August 2019, RL33222, Washington, DC: Government Printing Office, p. 5. "Aid" is actually hi-tech military investment, the results of R&D being potential applications for commercial or health products. See Reich, from whom those who believe that Israel controls US foreign policy could learn much, writes: "The bulk of U.S. military aid to Israel is used to purchase military items produced in the United States. This is a clear case in which foreign aid creates jobs in the donor country ... [O]nly a small percentage of U.S. military grants is spent in Israel itself, and most of the economic grant aid is devoted to servicing loans

used to finance past weapon sales" (Bernard Reich (1995) *Securing the Covenant: United States-Israel Relations After the Cold War*, Santa Barbara: Praeger, pp. 93-98). For a different perspective, see Konstantin Yanovskiy (2014) "US Aid for Israel - A Historical Overview," *SSRN*: http://dx.doi.org/10.2139/ssrn.2403748.

[58] This seems to be interpreted today as meaning that positive outcomes arising from mass participation can only be realised if *a priori* structures are in place; which is anti-anarchistic, if those *a priori* structures have not been mutually and reciprocally developed. Recall that Aristotle advocated for democracy as form of social control to prevent peasant revolution. Ober, for instance, writes: "one way that the promise of epistemic democracy might be fulfilled [is] through appropriate institutional design." Here is where the wisdom of crowds analogy is most appropriate for Wikipedia in that the structures are organized by dominant hierarchies and creative work is realized within those limitations. (Josiah Ober (2013) "Democracy's Wisdom: An Aristotelian Middle Way for Collective Judgment," *American Political Science Review*, 107(1): 104-22.)

[59] (2004) *The Wisdom of Crowds: Why the Many are Smarter Than the Few and how Collective Wisdom Shapes Business, Economies, Societies and Nations*, Boston: Little, Brown.

[60] Anarchism is a broad spectrum consisting of many types and factions. Anarchists oppose institutions that inhibit personal and societal development. To give a small and inadequate sketch of anarchist thinking on important matters such as the state, law, money and representational democracy vs. direct participation and autonomy:

Mikhail Bakunin (1814-76) is credited with establishing collectivist anarchism. He opposed Karl Marx's statism, arguing that the state is another factor in the control and exploitation of humans. "Marxists say that this minority [of rulers] will consist of workers. Yes, possibly of former workers, who, as soon as they become the rulers of the representatives of the people, will cease to be workers and will look down at the plain working masses from the governing heights of the State; they will no longer represent the people, but only themselves and their claims to rulership over the people. Those who doubt this know very little about human nature" ((1873) *Statism and Anarchy*, London: The Anarchist Library, p. 5).

Emma Goldman (1869-1940), for example, felt that state-law was among the many constraints placed on human freedom. Laws that derived from religion and the state turn individuals into "bloodhound[s]" who waste the social and personal potential of criminals by locking them up, rather than attempting to rehabilitate them. The law has little practical utility and it tends to make crime flourish underground ((1911 2nd) *Anarchism and Other Essays*, New York: Mother Earth Publishing Association, pp. 127, 180, 209).

In a critique of the classical capitalist David Ricardo (1772-1823), Rosa Luxemburg (1871-1919) cites money as an "agent" that places an obstacle between non-elite individuals and control over their environment: "money, in a simple circulation of commodities ... separates the two transactions of circulation, sale and purchase, and them independent of one another in respect of both time and place" ((1953 [1913]) *The Accumulation of Capital*, Agnes Schwarzchild (trans.), London: Routledge and Kegan Paul, pp. 193).

Using the most benign example of voting in an association of lifeboat search and rescuers, Pyotr Kropotkin (1842-1921) criticizes majoritarian representative voting (the system on which our Western so-called democracies are allegedly based): "these brave men do not allow those who have never faced a storm to legislate for them about saving life." Other committees and groups consist of non-hierarchically arranged associations of volunteers. Kropotkin asks why the broader political and social system cannot be based on such a model ((1913 [1892]) *The Conquest of Bread*, London: Chapman and Hall, p. 198).

In more recent years, the Curious George Brigade say that: "Most mass structures are a result of habit, inertia, and the lack of creative critique. Desire for mass is accepted as common sense in the same way it is 'common sense' that groups must have leaders, or that they must make decisions by voting. Even anarchists have been tricked into accepting the necessity of superstructures and large organizations for the sake of efficiency, mass, and unity" ((2003) *Anarchy in the Age of*

Dinosaurs, p. 95,
https://ia802304.us.archive.org/5/items/AnarchyInTheAgeOfDin
osaurs/Anarchy.pdf).

[61] Individualism and collectivism are crude designations that are
nuanced in reality (Vladimir D. Mamontov, Tatiana M.
Kozhevnikova and Yana Y. Radyukova (2014) "Collectivism
and Individualism in Modern Russia ," *Asian Social Science*,
10(23): 199-207). Krylova repudiates the notion of a continuum
in the Soviet system, arguing that the notion of "collectivism"
barely survived beyond the 1930s (Anna Krylova (2017)
"Imagining socialism in the Soviet century," *Social History*,
42(3): 315-41). Willimott notes non-elite collectivists in the
Soviet Union were marginalized, while the state premised
housing, urban and architectural designs on the notion of
"collectivism" (Andy Willmott (2011) "The Kommuna Impulse:
Collective Mechanisms and Commune-ists in the Early Soviet
State," *Revolutionary Russia*, 24(1): 59-78).

[62] Russell writes: "Anaxagoras maintained that snow is black,
but no one believed him. The social psychologists of the future
will have a number of classes of school children on whom they
will try different methods of producing an unshakable conviction
that snow is black ... [T]he opinion that snow is white must be
held to show a morbid taste for eccentricity" (Bertrand Russell
(1968 [1953]) *The Impact of Science on Society*, New York:
AMS Press, p. 30).

[63] In the so-called *Confession* (1865), Marx wrote that his motto
was *de omnibus dubitandum* ("we should doubt everything" or
"doubt everything"). Whether Marx was able to do this in
practice any more than other people is an open question. Ray
and Wilkinson write that the *Confession* "should make us
cautious about attributing to Marx firm or dogmatic ideas about
the nature and trajectory of capitalism and especially the
timescale for any socialist transformation" (Larry Ray and Iain
Wilkinson (2019) "Introduction -- Bicentennial

Marx," *Journal of Classical Sociology*, 19(1): 3-9).

[64] Interviewed by Patrick Wood, "Wikipedia aims for 'consensus
and trust' as fake news spreads, boss Katherine Maher says,"
ABC (Australia), 2 May 2017,

https://www.abc.net.au/news/2017-05-02/wikipedia-aims-for-consensus-and-trust-as-fake-news-spreads/8489744.

[65] Wikipedia (no date) "Wikipedia: The Free Encyclopedia," https://en.wikipedia.org/wiki/Wikipedia:The_Free_Encyclopedia

[66] Wikipedia (no date) "Wikipedia: Five pillars," https://en.wikipedia.org/wiki/Wikipedia:Five_pillars.

[67] Wikipedia (no date) "Arbitration Committee," https://en.wikipedia.org/wiki/Arbitration_Committee.

[68] Wikipedia (no date) "Wikipedia: Banning policy," https://en.wikipedia.org/wiki/Wikipedia:Banning_policy.

[69] Wikipedia (no date) "Wikipedia: Protection policy," https://en.wikipedia.org/wiki/Wikipedia:Protection_policy.

[70] Some anarchists argue that Do-It-Yourself should be Do-It-Together (DIT); one of whom is Randall Amster. He writes that groups such as the Curious George Brigade argue for DIT actions, in which they and Amster include Wikipedia, which he describes as "a manifestation of decentralized, do-it-yourself anarchism" ((2012) *Anarchism Today*, Santa Barbara: Praeger, p. 38).

[71] Fourteen percent of Americans cite busyness as a reason for not voting, let alone deeper political engagement; the same percentage who cite health issues and disability for non-engagement. See Barry C. Burden, Jason M. Fletcher, Pamela Herd, Bradley M. Jones and Donald P. Moynihan (2016) "How Different Forms of Health Matter to Political Participation," *Journal of Politics*, 79(1): 166-78. On so-called civic engagement, Price and Simpson write that both in the US and Britain, "[t]he growth of two-career families mean people are too busy to give time to anything else." This results in part from the expansion of city-work, requiring long commutes (Vicky Price and Graeme (2007) *Transforming Society? Social Work and Sociology*, Bristol: Policy Press, p. 129). In the UK 60 percent agreed that political engagement "would take time away from one's family"; 69 percent that "it can be tiring after a hard day's work"; and that 18 percent are "too busy to vote" (Charles Pattie, Patrick Seyd and Paul Whiteley (2003) "Citizenship and Civic Engagement: Attitudes and Behaviour in Britain," *Political Studies*, 51: 451).

[72] For an overview with plenty of evidence, see Broido who writes: "Lenin lost no time in acquiring complete control over the inner life of the country. The muzzling of the press and of public opinion, the suppression of political parties and the penetration by Bolsheviks of all independent organisations of workers and peasants were virtually completed within the first year of Bolshevik rule. It was never done openly; the pretence that Russia was a 'workers' and peasants' democracy' was never dropped, and elections -- to soviets, trade unions and so on -- were held publicly. But the results were rigged when the vote went against the Bolsheviks. The destruction of elected bodies was carried out from within in various underhand ways" (Vera Briodo (2018 [1987]) *Lenin and the Mensheviks: The Persecution of Socialists Under Bolshevism*, London: Routledge, p. 67).

Lenin himself denounced the "infantile" leftism of anarchists and others ((1974 [1966] *V.I. Lenin: Collected Works: Volume 31, April-December 1920*, Julius Katzer (trans.), Moscow: Progress Publishers, pp. 17-104).

[73] Peter Jebsen (2017) *Bolshevik for Capitalism: Ayn Rand and Soviet Socialist Realism*, Claremont McKenna College, http://scholarship.claremont.edu/cgi/viewcontent.cgi?article=1172&context=cmc_theses.

[74] Susan Meyer (2013) *Jimmy Wales and Wikipedia*, New York: Rosen Publishing, pp. 30-35.

[75] (2009) *Goddess of the Market: Ayn Rand and the American Right*, Oxford: Oxford University Press.

[76] Quoted in Chozick, op. cit.

[77] Cade Metz, "Ex-Wikipedia staffer harpoons Wales over expenses," *The Register*, 5 March 2008, https://www.theregister.co.uk/Print/2008/03/05/jimmy_wales_and_danny_wool/.

[78] Chozick, op. cit.

[79] WEF, Forum of Young Global Leaders, "Accelerating Entrepreneurship in the Arab World," October 2011, http://www3.weforum.org/docs/WEF_YGL_AcceleratingEntrepreneurshipArabWorld_Report_2011.pdf.

[80] Atlas Society, "Wikipedia founder Jimmy Wales on Ayn Rand, art, and making money,"
YouTube, 31 October 2014,
https://www.youtube.com/watch?v=43-wvNbXVxY.

[81] Rebecca Greenfield, "Jimmy Wales Is Only Worth $1 Million," *The Atlantic*, 7 June 2013,
https://www.theatlantic.com/technology/archive/2013/06/jimmy-wales-net-worth/313851/.

[82] Amy Chozick, "Jimmy Wales Is Not an Internet Billionaire," *NYT Magazine*, 27 June 2013,
https://www.nytimes.com/2013/06/30/magazine/jimmy-wales-is-not-an-internet-billionaire.html.

[83] Evan Hansen, "Wikipedia Founder Edits Own Bio," *Wired*, 19 December 2005, https://www.wired.com/2005/12/wikipedia-founder-edits-own-bio/.

[84] Interviewed by Sophie Foggin, "'Wikipedia is a broken system,' says co-founder Larry Sanger," 150sec.com, 23 May 2019, https://150sec.com/wikipedia-is-a-broken-system-says-co-founder-larry-sanger/11453/.

[85] Orlowski, op. cit. and Hansen, op. cit.

[86] ProMedical (no date) "Fury over Virgin Care pay out," https://promedical.co.uk/fury-over-virgin-care-pay-out/.

[87] Andrew Ross Sorkin, "Thinking Green While Sifting Through the Sand," *New York Times*,
22 March 2008,
https://www.nytimes.com/2008/03/22/business/worldbusiness/22deal.html.

[88] Chozick, op. cit. The author does not refer to Blair or Cameron as war criminals. Blair's record on Iraq alone is proof enough, other war crimes include Serbia (1999) and Afghanistan (2001). Cameron's war crimes include escalation of war in Iraq, the use of proxies in Syria and the bombing of Libya in 2011.

[89] Christopher Williams, "Wikipedia co-founder Jimmy Wales restricts discussion of Tony Blair friendship," *The Telegraph*, 24 December 2012,
https://www.telegraph.co.uk/technology/wikipedia/9764719/Wikipedia-co-founder-Jimmy-Wales-restricts-discussion-of-Tony-Blair-friendship.html.

[90] Ibid.

[91] Wikimedia Foundation (no date), "Profile: Katherine Maher," https://wikimediafoundation.org/profile/katherine-maher/.

[92] Truman National Security Project (no date), "About," http://trumanproject.org/home/about/.

[93] Katherine Maher (no date), "Cybersecurity: The New Westphalian Web," Truman National Security Project, http://trumanproject.org/home/doctrine-blog/cybersecurity-the-new-westphalian-web/.

[94] WEF (2019) "Meet the 2019 class of Young Global Leaders," https://www.weforum.org/agenda/2019/03/meet-the-2019-class-of-young-global-leaders/.

[95] World Economic Forum (no date), "About: Klaus Schwab," https://www.weforum.org/about/klaus-schwab.

[96] Associated Press, "Wiki founder wins $1m Israeli prize," 10 February 2015, https://www.timesofisrael.com/wikipedia-founder-wins-1m-israeli-prize/.

[97] WEF (2014) *Reports: The Forum of Young Global Leaders*, http://reports.weforum.org/the-forum-of-young-global-leaders-2014/ygl-stories/crowdsourced/.

[98] Quoted in Tina Eshleman, "Steven Pruitt '06: Wikipedia's most prolific editor," *William and Mary Alumni Magazine*, 29 October 2018, https://www.wm.edu/news/stories/2018/the-wikiman.php.

[99] Ibid.

[100] CBS This Morning, "Meet the man behind a third of what's on Wikipedia," 26 January 2019, https://www.youtube.com/watch?v=JhNczOuhxeg.

[101] In addition to the internet and computers in general many of the technologies and industries in use today originated in the publicly-funded US military sector: Container shipping from naval designs; passenger jets from bombers; telecoms from satellites; nuclear power from nuclear weapons; climate science from the ILLIAC IV federal computer and military weather research; the Global Positioning System; touchscreen technology from Air Force designs; and so on. Mowrey and Rosenberg write: "World War II transformed the U.S. R&D system. Federal government support for industrial and academic research

expanded dramatically, although in contrast to other nations, nongovernmental institutions retain primary responsibility for the performance of much of this R&D" (David C. Mowrey and Nathan Rosenberg, "The U.S. National Innovation System" in Richard R. Nelson (ed.) *National Innovation Systems: A Comparative Analysis*, Oxford: Oxford University Press, p. 39). For a contemporary analysis, see Mariana Mazzucato (2018) *The Entrepreneurial State: Debunking Public vs. Private Sector Myths*, London: Penguin.

[102] Name redacted (2004) "The Wiki and the Blog" in Director of Central Intelligence, *The DCI's Galileo Awards: Winning and Honorable Mention Papers for 2004*, https://www.cia.gov/library/readingroom/docs/DOC_0001241738.pdf.

[103] Wilson said: "When properly directed ... there is no people not fitted to self-government" (quoted in Stephen Kinzer (2013) *The Brothers: John Foster Dulles, Allen Dulles, and Their Secret World War*, New York: Times Books, p. 32.)

[104] Name redacted (2004) op. cit.

[105] Ibid.

[106] Jonathan Fildes, "Wikipedia 'shows CIA page edits'," BBC News Online, 15 August 2007, http://news.bbc.co.uk/1/hi/technology/6947532.stm.

[107] For extensive details and sources, see my (2018) *Manufacturing Terrorism: When Governments Use Fear to Justify Foreign Wars and Control Society*, West Hoathley: Clairview Books, pp. 90-92.

[108] Stratfor (2009), emails,16 February 2009, https://wikileaks.org/gifiles/docs/12/1259371_re-wikipedia-.html.

[109] L. Gordon Crovitz, "Julian Assange, Information Anarchist," *Wall Street Journal*, 6 December 2010, https://web.archive.org/web/20101215002714/http://topics.wsj.com/article/SB10001424052748703989004576653113548361870.html.

[110] Central Intelligence Agency (no date), "(U) Project MK-ULTRA." Released under John Greenewald's FOIA request, F-2013-00620/DNI#DF-2009-00110.

[111] US Army (no date), "Wikified Army Field Guide," Obama White House, Archives, https://obamawhitehouse.archives.gov/open/innovations/wikifiedArmy.

[112] Open Government Initiative, "Open Energy Information," https://obamawhitehouse.archives.gov/open/innovations/OpenEnergyInformation.

[113] Adam Segal, "Cyber Week in Review," Council on Foreign Relations, 13 March 2015, https://www.cfr.org/blog/cyber-week-review-march-13-2015.

[114] Spencer Ackerman and James Ball, "Optic Nerve: millions of Yahoo webcam images intercepted by GCHQ," *Guardian*, 28 February 2014, https://www.theguardian.com/world/2014/feb/27/gchq-nsa-webcam-images-internet-yahoo.

[115] Nate Cardozo, Kurt Opsahl and Rainey Reitman (2015) *Who has your back? The Electronic Frontier Foundation's Fifth Annual Report on Online Service Providers' Privacy and Transparency Practices Regarding Government Access to User Data*, The Electronic Frontier Foundation, June 17.

[116] In 1992, NATO and Ukraine agreed a High Level Working Group of the North Atlantic Cooperation Council. IBP (2013) *Ukraine Country Study Guide Volume 1 Strategic Information and Developments*, Washington, DC: International Business Publications, p. 106. In 1997, NATO and Ukraine signed the Charter on a Distinctive Partnership, which included the possibility of NATO enlargement. Text available at: https://www.nato.int/cps/en/natohq/official_texts_25457.htm?.

[117] A US Congressional Research Service report notes: "An estimated 15%-20% of the population identifies as ethnic Russian, mostly concentrated in the south (Crimea) and east, where ties to Russia are stronger than in the rest of the country." Cory Welt, "Ukraine: Background, Conflict with Russia, and U.S. Policy," CRS, R45008, 19 September 2019, Washington, DC: Government Printing Office, p. 8.

[118] For the background details, see Hew Strachan (1978) "Soldiers, Strategy and Sebastopol," *The Historical Journal*, 21(2): 303-25.

[119] Russia's efforts to build pipelines that bypass Ukraine stem "from the removal of the Yanukovich government in Ukraine in February 2014 and includes: Russian annexation of Crimea in March 2014; the military conflict in eastern Ukraine, which has resulted in 10,000 deaths, the internal displacement of 1.8 million people in Ukraine and the migration of 430,000 refugees to Russia; Russian economic, political and (in a manner and on a scale that are disputed) military support for the separatist 'republics' in eastern Ukraine; and the collapse of Russian-Ukrainian trade." Simon Pirani (2018) "Russian gas transit through Ukraine after 2019: the options," *Oxford Energy Insight*, 41: 3, https://www.oxfordenergy.org/wpcms/wp-content/uploads/2018/11/Russian-gas-transit-through-Ukraine-after-2019-Insight-41.pdf.

[120] Balázs Jarábik, Gwendolyn Sasse, Natalia Shapovalova and Thomas de Waal present a mixed picture: "Ukraine and the EU are closer than ever before. But events over the last four years have also shown how far apart they still are in economic capacity, governance, and their visions for the future" ("The EU and Ukraine: Taking a Breath," Carnegie Endowment for International Peace, 27 February 2018, https://carnegieendowment.org/2018/02/27/eu-and-ukraine-taking-breath-pub-75648).

[121] Pre-2014 coup "reforms," says USAID: "have been developed without consultation with the opposition or with citizens, and often are not particularly designed to benefit Ukrainian society as a whole. Thus, USAID programs will continue to be needed to support the engagement of civil society organizations, the independent media, and citizens in the policy development process, as well as to provide technical assistance to ensure that the reforms developed reflect international best practices" (USAID, *Ukraine: Country Development Cooperation Strategy, 2012-2016*, https://2012-2017.usaid.gov/sites/default/files/documents/1863/USAID_Ukraine_CDCS_2012-2016.pdf, p. 21). One of the donors to the Wikimedia Foundation, Pierre Omidyar (owner of *The Intercept* website), funded the New Citizen initiative in Ukraine in 2010. "New Citizen coordinates the efforts of concerned members of society, reinforcing their ability to shape public policy"

(Omidyar Network (no date), "New Citizen (Centre UA),"
https://web.archive.org/web/20120310103804/http://www.omid
yar.com/portfolio/new-citizen-centre-ua. Another billionaire
interfering in Ukraine on behalf of elite US interests is George
Soros. "After Ukraine became fully independent in 1991,
[Soros's Open Society foundation] gradually expanded its
support for Ukraine's often-painful transition to democracy and
a market economy" (The Open Society Foundation, "The Open
Society Foundations in Ukraine," 30 September 2019,
https://www.opensocietyfoundations.org/newsroom/the-open-
society-foundations-in-ukraine). Reuters and others have
reported that the transition to a market economy includes the use
of neo-Nazis by elements within the Ukrainian armed forces as
part of their anti-Russia operations (Josh Cohen, "Commentary:
Ukraine's neo-Nazi problem," Reuters, 19 March 2018,
https://www.reuters.com/article/us-cohen-ukraine-
commentary/commentary-ukraines-neo-nazi-problem-
idUSKBN1GV2TY). Married to the neocon Robert Kagan, US
State Department Assistant Secretary for European and Eurasian
Affairs, Victoria Nuland, told the Senate Foreign Relations
Committee in 2015 of "U.S. support" for the opposition,
"including a $1 billion loan guarantee last year and $355 million
in foreign assistance and technical advisors" (Nuland,
"Testimony on Ukraine Before the Senate Foreign Relations
Committee," Statement Before the Senate Foreign Relations
Committee, 10 March 2015, US Department of State,
https://2009-2017.state.gov/p/eur/rls/rm/2015/mar/238722.htm).

[122] Even CBS reported in December 2013, when the protests
were intensifying, that Obama officials were meeting opposition
leaders. CBS, "Top U.S. official visits protesters in Kiev as
Obama admin. ups pressure on Ukraine president Yanukovich,"
11 December 2013, https://www.cbsnews.com/news/us-victoria-
nuland-wades-into-ukraine-turmoil-over-yanukovich/.

[123] YES (no date) "Board," https://yes-ukraine.org/en/about/yes-
board.

[124] YES (2014) "Ukrainian and Russian Wikipedia must work
together, - Jimmy Wales," 12 September, https://yes-
ukraine.org/en/news/ukrayinska-ta-rosiyska-vikipediya-mayut-
pratsyuvati-v-yednosti-dzhimmi-veylz.

[125] Jon Roozenbeek and Mariia Terentieva (2017) "Attention Please! Exploring Attention Management on Wikipedia in the Context of the Ukrainian Crisis" in Giovanni Luca Ciampaglia, Afra Mashhadi and Taha Yasseri (eds.), *Social Informatics: 9th International Conference, SocInfo 2017, Oxford, September 13-15, 2017, Proceedings, Part II*, Cham: Springer, pp. 169-91.

[126] Martin Körner, Tatiana Sennikova, Florian Windhäuser, Claudia Wagner and Fabian Flöck (2016) "Wikiwhere: An Interactive Tool for Studying the Geographical Provenance of Wikipedia References," arXiv, https://arxiv.org/pdf/1612.00985.pdf.

[127] Wikimedia Foundation (no date), "Profile: Nataliia Tymkiv," https://wikimediafoundation.org/profile/nataliia-tymkiv/.

[128] CEDEM (no date), "Who we are," https://cedem.org.ua/en/who-we-are/.

[129] CEDEM (no date), "Partners," https://cedem.org.ua/who-we-are/partners/.

[130] CIA (2007) "A Look Back ... The National Committee for Free Europe, 1949," https://www.cia.gov/news-information/featured-story-archive/2007-featured-story-archive/a-look-back.html.

[131] Wikimedia Foundation (no date), website homepage, https://wikimediafoundation.org/.

[132] Wikimedia Foundation (no date), "Profile: Raju Narisetti," https://wikimediafoundation.org/profile/raju-narisetti/.

[133] Wikimedia Foundation (no date), "Profile: Dr Dariusz Jemielniak," https://wikimediafoundation.org/profile/dr-dariusz-jemielniak/.

[134] Wikimedia Foundation (no date), "Profile: Shani Evenstein Sigalov," https://wikimediafoundation.org/profile/shani-evenstein-sigalov/

[135] Azriel Foundation (no date), "Our priorities: Holocaust education and legacy," https://azrielifoundation.org/our-priorities/holocaust-education-and-legacy/.

[136] Wikidata (no date), "User:Esh77," https://www.wikidata.org/wiki/User:Esh77.

[137] Wikimedia Foundation (no date), "Profile: Tanya Capuano," https://wikimediafoundation.org/profile/tanya-capuano/.

[138] G5, "G5 Announces New Chief Financial Officer – Veteran Silicon Valley Financial Executive Tanya Capuano Joins G5," 5 October 2017, https://www.getg5.com/g5-announces-new-chief-financial-officer-veteran-silicon-valley-financial-executive-tanya-capuano-joins-g5/.

[139] Wikimedia Foundation (no date), "Profile: Lisa Lewin," https://wikimediafoundation.org/profile/lisa-lewin/.

[140] The Ready (no date), website, https://theready.com/.

[141] Wikimedia Foundation (no date), "Profile: Valerie D'Costa," https://wikimediafoundation.org/profile/valerie-dcosta/.

[142] Wikimedia Foundation (no date), "Profile: Lisa Seitz-Gruwell," https://wikimediafoundation.org/profile/lisa-seitz-gruwell/.

[143] WEF (no date), "People: Lila Tretikov," https://www.weforum.org/people/lila-tretikov.

[144] Samuel P. Huntington (1996) *The Clash of Civilizations and the Remarking of World Order*, London: Simon & Schuster, p. 57.

[145] WEF (no date), "People: Trevor Neilson," https://www.weforum.org/people/trevor-neilson.

[146] WEF (2008) "List of technology pioneers 2008," https://www.weforum.org/about/list-of-technology-pioneers-2008.

[147] WEF (2017) "Annual meeting of the global future councils," https://www.weforum.org/events/annual-meeting-of-the-global-future-councils-2017/?tab=LiveBlogs.

[148] Patrick Wood, "Wikipedia aims for 'consensus and trust' as fake news spreads, boss Katherine Maher says," ABC (Australia), 2 May 2017, https://www.abc.net.au/news/2017-05-02/wikipedia-aims-for-consensus-and-trust-as-fake-news-spreads/8489744.

[149] WEF (2016) "Who are the Technology Pioneers?", http://widgets.weforum.org/techpioneers-2016/.

[150] For at least eight examples, see Unpopular Truths, "Should you use Airbnb?," *Invisible Tourist*, 12 March 2019, https://www.theinvisibletourist.com/why-you-shouldnt-use-airbnb-issues-you-didnt-know/.

[151] Peter Waldman, Lizette Chapman and Jordan Robertson, "Palantir Knows Everything About You," *Bloomberg*

Businessweek, 19 April 2018,
https://www.bloomberg.com/features/2018-palantir-peter-thiel/.
Noah Feldman, "The Future of Policing Is Being Hashed Out in
Secret," *Bloomberg*, 28 February 2018,
https://www.bloomberg.com/opinion/articles/2018-02-
28/artificial-intelligence-in-policing-advice-for-new-orleans-
and-palantir. Ken Dilanian, "US special operations forces are
clamoring to use software from Silicon Valley company
Palantir," Associated Press,

26 March 2015.

[152] The Knight Foundation researching for George Washington
University found that Twitter had what it describes as a fake
news "ecosystem" that enabled over 6 million, mainly pro-
Trump tweets to spread in the months before the US Presidential
election 2016. "More than 80% of accounts that repeatedly
spread misinformation during the 2016 election campaign are
still active" (quoted in Don Reisinger, "Twitter Had a 'Fake
News Ecosystem' Around the 2016 Election, Study Says,"
Fortune, 10 April 2018,
https://web.archive.org/web/20181004154849/https://fortune.co
m/2018/10/04/twitter-2016-election-fake-news/). In 2018, the
UK Parliament's Digital, Media, Sports and Culture Committee
considered fining Facebook and Twitter over its Brexit-related
handling of fake news (Alice Tozer, "The U.K.'s 'Fake News'
Report Suggests Fining Tech Companies for Misinformation,"
Fortune, 30 July 2018,
https://web.archive.org/web/20180907115945/https://fortune.co
m/2018/07/30/uk-fake-news-brexit-facebook-twitter/). Prior to
the EU elections in 2019, Twitter introduced counter-fake news
software (Reuters, "Twitter launching tool to report fake news
ahead of EU elections," 24 April, 2019). The tables turned in
October 2019 during the UK general election, when Twitter
accused the right-wing Conservative government of using it to
spread fake news (Lizzy Buchan, "Brexit: Conservatives
accused of 'fake news' over tweets about Boris Johnson's deal,"
Independent, 24 October 2019,
https://www.independent.co.uk/news/uk/politics/boris-johnson-
brexit-deal-mps-approve-conservative-twitter-post-tweet-latest-
a9169626.html).

[153] CFR, "Moderating Online Content With the Help of Artificial Intelligence," 14 November 2018, https://www.cfr.org/event/moderating-online-content-help-artificial-intelligence.

[154] Sharone Tobias, "Internet and Press Freedom in Taiwan," CRF (*Net Politics*), 27 June 2013, https://www.cfr.org/blog/sharone-tobias-internet-and-press-freedom-taiwan.

[155] Youngwhan Lee and Heuiju Chun (2016) "Nation image and its dynamic changes in Wikipedia," *Asia Pacific Journal of Innovation*, 11(1): 38-49.

[156] Martin Dittus and Mark Graham, "To reduce inequality, Wikipedia should consider paying editors," *Wired*, 11 September 2018, https://www.wired.co.uk/article/wikipedia-inequality-pay-editors.

[157] Quoted in Chozick, op. cit.

[158] Wikipedia (no date), "Wikipedia Zero," https://en.wikipedia.org/wiki/Wikipedia_Zero.

[159] M.V. Lee Badgett, Sheila Nezhad, Kees Waaldijk and Yana van der Meulen Rodgers (2014) "The Relationship between LGBT Inclusion and Economic Development: An Analysis of Emerging Economies," November, USAID and Williams Institute, https://williamsinstitute.law.ucla.edu/wp-content/uploads/lgbt-inclusion-and-development-november-2014.pdf.

[160] Wikimedia Foundation (no date), "Profile: Esraa Al Shafei," https://wikimediafoundation.org/profile/esraa-al-shafei/

[161] Majal (no date), "About us," https://majal.org/about-us.

[162] Mideast Youth (no date), "About us," https://web.archive.org/web/20110104101455/http://www.mideastyouth.com/about-us.

[163] WEF (no date), "People: Esra Al Shafei," https://www.weforum.org/people/esra-a-shafei.

[164] Randall Livingstone (2014) "Immaterial Editors: Bots and Bot Policies across Global Wikipedia" in Pnina Fichman and Noriko Hara (eds.), *Global Wikipedia: International and Cross-Cultural Issues in Online Collaboration*, Lanham: Rowman & Littlefield, pp. 7-24.

[165] Sanna Ojanperä, Mark Graham and Matthew Zook, "The Digital Knowledge Economy Index: Mapping Content Production," 9 November 2017, https://www.imf.org/~/media/Files/Conferences/2017-stats-forum/session-3-ojanpera.ashx.

[166] Sanna Ojanperä, Mark Graham and Matthew Zook (2017) "The digital Knowledge Economy Index: Mapping Content Production," Fifth IMF Statistical Forum - Measuring the Digital Economy, 16 November 16, https://www.imf.org/~/media/Files/Conferences/2017-stats-forum/session-3-sanna-ojanpera-presentation.ashx.

[167] Stephen Armstrong, "Inside Wikipedia's volunteer-run battle against fake news," *Wired*, 21 August 2018, https://www.wired.co.uk/article/fake-news-wikipedia-arbitration-committee.

[168] Monica Anderson, Paul Hitlin and Michelle Atkinson, "Wikipedia at 15: Millions of readers in scores of languages," Pew Research Center, 14 January 2016, https://www.pewresearch.org/fact-tank/2016/01/14/wikipedia-at-15/.

[169] Michael Blanding, "Is Wikipedia More Biased Than Encyclopædia Britannica?," *Harvard Business School*, 19 January 2015, https://hbswk.hbs.edu/item/is-wikipedia-more-biased-than-encyclopdia-britannica.

[170] George Gao, "Most visited Wikipedia articles by language in 2015," Pew Research Center, 14 January 2016, https://www.pewresearch.org/2016/01/14/wikipedia-top-10/.

[171] Jürgen Lerner and Alessandro Lomi (2017) "The Third Man: hierarchy formation in Wikipedia," *Applied Network Science*, 2(24): DOI 10.1007/s41109-017-0043-2.

[172] Srijan Kumar and Neil Shah (2018) "False Information on Web and Social Media: A Survey," arXiv:1804.08559v1, 23 April, https://arxiv.org/abs/1804.08559.

[173] Katherine Q. Seelye, "Snared in the web of a Wikipedian liar," *New York Times*, 4 December 2005, https://www.nytimes.com/2005/12/04/weekinreview/snared-in-the-web-of-a-wikipedia-liar.html.

[174] Marc Miquel-Ribé and David Laniado (2018) "Wikipedia Culture Gap: Quantifying Content Imbalances Across 40

Language Editions," *Frontiers in Physics*, 6(54): doi: 10.3389/fphy.2018.00054.

[175] M. Zeeshan Jhandir, Ali Tenvir, Byung-Won On, Ingyu Lee and Gyu Sang Choi (2017) "Controversy detection in Wikipedia using semantic dissimilarity," *Information Sciences*, 418(419): 581-600.

[176] Quoted in van Dijck, op. cit., p. 145.

[177] Ibid, p. 135.

[178] Wikipedia (no date) 'Template: Five pillars', https://en.wikipedia.org/wiki/Template:Five_pillars.

[179] Van Dijck, op. cit., p. 132.

[180] Ibid, p. 136.

[181] Ibid, p. 138.

[182] Ibid, p. 139.

[183] Ibid, p. 137.

[184] Ibid, p. 138.

[185] Ibid, p. 139.

[186] Ibid, pp. 137-38.

[187] Quoted in ibid, pp. 136-37.

[188] Cited in Randall Livingstone (2014) "Immaterial Editors: Bots and Bot Policies across Global Wikipedia" in Pnina Fichman and Noriko Hara (eds.) *Global Wikipedia: International and Cross-Cultural Issues in Online*, Lanham: Rowman & Littlefield, p. 10.

[189] Nicole Torres, "Why Do So Few Women Edit Wikipedia?," *Harvard Business Review*, 2 June 2016, https://hbr.org/2016/06/why-do-so-few-women-edit-wikipedia.

[190] Lin Taylor, "New board game asks 'Who's She?' to spotlight famous women in history," Reuters, 9 January 2019, https://www.weforum.org/agenda/2019/01/new-board-game-asks-whos-she-to-spotlight-famous-women-in-history.

[191] To give some examples of female pioneers in the sciences alone, whose work and results were hijacked by men who took the credit: Lise Meitner's (1878-1968) work on nuclear fission led to a Nobel Prize for Otto Hahn in 1944; Inge Lehmann's (1888-1993) seismology work led to the discovery of the Earth's inner core; Rosalind Franklin's (1920-58) chemistry led to the

discovery of the molecular structures of DNA; Chien-Shiung (1912-97) used cobalt-60 to disprove the 'law' of parity in quantum physics; Jocelyn Bell Burnell (born 1943) discovered the pulses of the neutron star PSR B1919+21 in the Vulpecula constellation. For these and many more, see Rachel Swaby (2015) *Headstrong: 52 Women Who Changed Science—and the World*, New York: Broadway Books.

[192] There is little or no evidence to suggest that this is a result of brain structure of innateness, but rather, as a result of early-years environmental conditioning, learning and adaptation that presupposes boys and young men should and thus will be better skilled at technical tasks.

[193] Christina Shane-Simpson and Kristen Gillespie-Lynch (2017) "Examining potential mechanisms underlying the Wikipedia gender gap through a collaborative editing task," *Computers in Human Behavior*, 66: 312-28.

[194] Ibid.

[195] Quoted in Maude Gauthier and Kim Sawchuk (2017) "Not notable enough: feminism and expertise in Wikipedia," *Communication and Critical/Cultural Studies*, 14(4): 387.

[196] Gauthier and Sawchuk, op. cit.

[197] Ibid.

[198] T. Yasseri, A. Spoerri, M. Graham and J. Kertész (2014) "The most controversial topics in Wikipedia: A multilingual and geographical analysis" in Pnina Fichman and Noriko Hara (eds.), *Global Wikipedia: International and Cross-cultural Issues in Online Collaboration*, Lanham: Rowman & Littlefield pp. 25-48.

[199] Ibid.

[200] Ibid.

[201] Milena Tsvetkova, Ruth Garcia-Gavilanes, Luciano Floridi and Taha Yasseri (2017) "Even good bots fight: The case of Wikipedia," *PLoS ONE*, 12(2): e0171774.

[202] Thomas Halleck, "Wikipedia and Paid Editors," *IBT*, 8 August 2013.

[203] Debra Cassens Weiss, "DC lawyer pursues suit to unmask authors who changed her Wikipedia page," *ABA Journal*, 16 September 2013,

http://www.abajournal.com/news/article/dc_lawyer_pursues_suit
_to_unmask_authors_who_changed_her_wikipedia_page.

[204] Center for Individual Rights, 'Burke v. Doe: Free speech protections bolstered in District of Columbia', 15 March 2016.

[205] Daniel Terdiman, "Is Wikipedia safe from libel liability?", CNET, 7 Decemer 2005, https://www.cnet.com/news/is-wikipedia-safe-from-libel-liability/.

[206] Claudine Beaumonet, "Wikipedia fights defamation lawsuit," *The Telegraph*, 11 May 2008, https://www.telegraph.co.uk/news/1946275/Wikipedia-fights-defamation-lawsuit.html.

[207] ITProPortal, "Wikipedia not liable for libel, rules French court," 13 November 2007, https://www.itproportal.com/2007/11/13/wikipedia-not-liable-for-libel-rules-french-court/.

[208] Andrew Orlowski, "Jimbo Wales: Wikipedia servers in UK? No way, not with YOUR libel law," *The Register*, 8 August 2012, https://www.theregister.co.uk/2012/08/08/jimmy_wales_wikipedia_listen_up_london_and_learn/.

[209] Louise Matsakis, "The 'Guerrilla' Wikipedia Editors Who Combat Conspiracy Theories," *Wired*, 25 July 2018, https://www.wired.com/story/guerrilla-wikipedia-editors-who-combat-conspiracy-theories/.

[210] Oliver Kamm, "How credulous cranks made me the subject of their baseless conspiracy theory," CAPX, 23 November 2018.

[211] Cross's father told journalist Neil Clark: 'He's grossly overweight and he can't walk'. Neil Clark, 'Andrew Philip Cross: Wikipedia Editing Scandal Continues (But For How Much Longer?)', *Sputnik*, https://sputniknews.com/columnists/201910131077038943-andrew-philip-cross-wikipedia-editing-scandal-continues-but-for-how-much-longer/.

[212] BBC Trending, "Galloway's war of words with a mystery Wikipedia editor," 18 June 2018, https://www.bbc.co.uk/news/blogs-trending-44495696.

[213] Media Lens, "Caught In The Cross Hairs – Media Lens And The Mystery Of The Wikipedia Editor," 17 October 2018,

https://www.medialens.org/2018/caught-in-the-cross-hairs-media-lens-and-the-mystery-of-the-wikipedia-editor/.

[214] Kim Osman, "Paid editors on Wikipedia--should we be worried?" *The Conversation*, 22 August 2014.

[215] Joe Pinsker, "The Covert World of People Trying to Edit Wikipedia for Pay," *The Atlantic*, 11 August 2015.

[216] Martin Robbins, "Is Wikipedia for Sale?", Vice.com, 19 October 2013.

[217] Julie Bort, "PR Company Says It Was Demonized By The World's Biggest Internet Encyclopedia," 25 January 2014, https://www.businessinsider.com/wiki-pr-ceo-says-wikipedia-ban-was-unfair-2014-1?r=US&IR=T.

[218] Chartered Institute of Public Relations (2012) *Wikipedia: Best Practice Guidance for Public Relations Professionals (Version 2.1)*, https://www.cipr.co.uk/sites/default/files/CIPR_Wikipedia_Best_Practice_Guidance_v2.1.pdf.

[219] Ibid.

[220] Ibid.

[221] Ibid.

[222] Ibid.

[223] US Department of State, "U.S. Relations with Russia," Bureau of European and Eurasian Affairs, 23 April 2018, https://www.state.gov/r/pa/ei/bgn/3183.htm.

[224] US Department of Defense (2018) *Summary of the National Defense Strategy 2018 of The United States of America: Sharpening the American Military's Competitive Edge*, Washington, DC: Government Printing Office, https://dod.defense.gov/Portals/1/Documents/pubs/2018-National-Defense-Strategy-Summary.pdf.

[225] Congressional Research Service, "U.S. Sanctions and Russia's Economy," 17 February 2017, https://www.everycrsreport.com/files/20170217_R43895_74248c7fee69a5c1e9575f399d6b6cba27ab61e9.pdf.

[226] Wikipedia, "Foreign relations," *United States*, https://en.wikipedia.org/wiki/United_States#Foreign_relations. Accessed 9 January 2018. All references to Wikipedia's entry on

US foreign relations refer to this link. Given that each entry is subject to change at any time, the original entry from which we are working can also be found here: https://web.archive.org/web/20181231013609/https://en.wikiped ia.org/wiki/United_States#Foreign_relations.

[227] Wikipedia, "Foreign relations," Russia, https://en.wikipedia.org/wiki/Russia#Foreign_relations. Accessed 9 January 2018. All references to Wikipedia's entry on Russian foreign relations refer to this link. Given that each entry is subject to change at any time, the original entry from which we are working can also be found here: https://web.archive.org/web/20190109041336/https://en.wikiped ia.org/wiki/Russia#Foreign_relations.

[228] Foreign and Commonwealth Office (UK), Country profile: Russia, 27 July, 2009, https://web.archive.org/web/20091106134129/http://www.fco.go v.uk/en/travel-and-living-abroad/travel-advice-by-country/country-profile/europe/russia.

[229] Foreign and Commonwealth Office (UK), Country profile: Russia, 27 July, 2009, https://web.archive.org/web/20091107062805/http://www.fco.go v.uk/en/travel-and-living-abroad/travel-advice-by-country/country-profile/europe/russia?profile=all.

[230] Ibid.

[231] Kathleen Burk, "Old world, new world" in John Dumbrell and Axel Schäfer (eds.) *America's 'Special Relationships'*, London and New York: Routledge, eBook.

[232] For example: Joanna Dawson and Samantha Godec, 'Oversight of the intelligence agencies: a comparison of the "Five Eyes" nations', House of Commons Library Briefing Paper, Number 7921, 15 December 2017. Andrew O'Neil (2017) 'Australia and the "Five Eyes" intelligence network: the perils of an asymmetric alliance', *Australian Journal of International Affairs*, 71(5): 529-43.

[233] Thomas Lum (2012) "The Republic of the Philippines and U.S. Interests," *Congressional Research Service*, 5 April, Washington, DC: Government Printing Office, https://fas.org/sgp/crs/row/RL33233.pdf.

[234] Emma Chanlett-Avery et al. (2017) "Japan-U.S. Relations: Issues for Congress," *Congressional Research Service*, 16 February, Washington, DC: Government Printing Office, https://fas.org/sgp/crs/row/RL33436.pdf.

[235] For extensive details and sources, see T.J. Coles (2017) *Fire and Fury: How the US Isolates North Korea, Encircles China and Risks Nuclear War in Asia*, West Sussex: Clairview Books.

[236] Mark E. Manyin (2017) "U.S.-South Korea Relations," *Congressional Research Service*, 23 May, Washington, DC: Government Printing Office, https://fas.org/sgp/crs/row/R41481.pdf.

[237] Space Command, "Vision for 2020," February, Colorado: Peterson AFB, https://ia802705.us.archive.org/10/items/pdfy-j6U3MFw1cGmC-yob/U.S.%20Space%20Command%20Vision%20For%202020.pdf.

[238] Megan K. Stack, "Venezuela's Hugo Chavez recognizes independence of breakaway Georgia republics," *LA Times*, 11 September 2009, https://web.archive.org/web/20181119132602/http://articles.latimes.com/2009/sep/11/world/fg-russia-chavez11.

[239] RT, "Russia is a superpower in every sense of the word – Netanyahu," 15 February 2010, https://web.archive.org/web/20110430182020/http://freevideo.rt.com/video/1759.

[240] Ronald Steel, "A Superpower Is Reborn," *New York Times*, 24 August 2008, https://web.archive.org/web/20110427085654/https://georgiandaily.com/index.php?option=com_content&task=view&id=6527.

[241] Mark Armstrong, "NATO contributions country-by-country," *Euronews*, 11 July 2018, https://www.euronews.com/2018/07/10/nato-contributions-country-by-country. See also NATO's data: NATO, 'Defence Expenditure of NATO Countries (2011-2018)', Press Release, PR/CP(2018)091, https://www.nato.int/nato_static_fl2014/assets/pdf/pdf_2018_07/20180709_180710-pr2018-91-en.pdf.

[242] Richard L. Kugler (1991) *The Great Strategy Debate: NATO's Evolution In the 1960s*, CA: RAND Corporation, https://apps.dtic.mil/dtic/tr/fulltext/u2/a256882.pdf.

[243] Col. Patrick T. Warren, "Alliance History and the Future NATO: What the Last 500 Years of Alliance Behavior Tells Us about NATO's Path Forward," Brookings Institution, 30 June 2010, https://www.brookings.edu/wp-content/uploads/2016/06/0630_nato_alliance_warren.pdf.

[244] For a sample of the wealth of literature on the Pink Tide, see: Mike Gonzalez (2018) *The Ebb of the Pink Tide: The Decline of the Left in Latin-America*, London: Pluto Press. Lee Artz (2017) *The Pink Tide: Media Access and Political Power in Latin America*, New York: Rowman & Littlefield International. Tom Chodor (2015 2nd) *Neoliberal Hegemony and the Pink Tide in Latin America: Breaking Up With TINA?*, Basingstoke: Palgrave Macmillan. María del Rosario Queirolo (2013) *The Success of the Left in Latin America: Untainted Parties, Market Reforms, and Voting Behavior*, Paris: University of Notre Dame Press.

[245] M. Angeles Villarreal and Ian F. Fergusson, "NAFTA Renegotiation and Modernization," Congressional Research Service, 26 July 2018, https://fas.org/sgp/crs/row/R44981.pdf.

[246] US Chamber of Commerce (2014) *NAFTA Triumphant: Assessing Two Decades of Gains in Trade, Growth, and Jobs*, Washington, DC: US Chamber of Commerce, https://www.uschamber.com/sites/default/files/legacy/reports/11 12_INTL_NAFTA_20Years.pdf.

[247] Anup Shah, "Foreign Aid for Development Assistance," *Global Issues*, 25 April 2010, https://web.archive.org/web/20100504115905/http://www.global issues.org/article/35/foreign-aid-development-assistance.

[248] Ibid.

[249] Ibid.

[250] Konstantin Kosachev, "Russian Foreign Policy Vertical," *Russia in Global Affairs*, 10 August 2004, https://eng.globalaffairs.ru/number/n_3372.

[251] Andrew Monaghan (2014) "The Ukraine crisis and NATO-Russia relations," *NATO Review*,

https://www.nato.int/docu/review/2014/russia-ukraine-nato-crisis/Ukraine-crisis-NATO-Russia-relations/EN/index.htm.

[252] *Daily Beast*, "Trump: Russia—U.S. Relations at Worst Level in History," 11 April 2018, https://www.thedailybeast.com/trump-russiaus-relations-at-worst-level-in-history.

[253] NATO, "NATO-Russia relations," 19 March 2007, https://web.archive.org/web/20070411124719/http://www.nato.int/issues/nato-russia/topic.html.

[254] Amnesty International (2009) *Russian Federation: Human Rights in Russian Federation*, https://web.archive.org/web/20100713010532/http://www.amnesty.org/en/region/russia/report-2009.

[255] Amnesty International (2009) *Amnesty International Report 2009: The State of the World's Human Rights*, POL 10/001/2009, London: Amnesty International Publications, pp. 348-49, https://www.amnesty.org/download/Documents/48000/pol100012009en.pdf.

[256] Human Rights Watch, "Russia on trial" (video), 6 April 2008, https://www.hrw.org/video-photos/video/2008/04/06/russia-trial.

[257] Human Rights Watch (2008) *Human Rights Watch: World Report 2008: Events of 2007*, pp. 545-48, https://www.hrw.org/legacy/wr2k8/pdfs/wr2k8_web.pdf.

[258] Freedom House (2004) "Russia," https://freedomhouse.org/report/freedom-world/2004/russia.

[259] Freedom House (2009) "Russia," https://freedomhouse.org/report/freedomworld/2009/russia?page=22&year=2009&country=7689#.VT7KCuH9ycw.

[260] In a nuclear war, "The targeted regions would lie in ruins. For a large enough nuclear war, the rest of the world could struggle to feed itself due to the global environmental phenomenon known as nuclear winter. Avoiding nuclear war is thus an important priority for the international community." Seth D. Baum, Robert de Neufville, and Anthony M. Barrett (2018) "A Model For The Probability Of Nuclear War," Global Catastrophic Risk Institute, Working Paper, 8 March, https://papers.ssrn.com/sol3/papers.cfm?abstract_id=3137081.

Another study notes: "A limited, regional nuclear war between India and Pakistan in which each side detonates 50 15 kt weapons could produce about 5 Tg of black carbon." The many consequences include: "combined cooling and enhanced UV [which] would put significant pressures on global food supplies and could trigger a global nuclear famine." Michael J. Mills, Owen B. Toon, Julia Lee-Taylor and Alan Robock (2014) "Multidecadal global cooling and unprecedented ozone loss following a regional nuclear conflict," *Earth's Future*, 2(4): 161-76.

Finally, another notes: "Each U.S. Trident submarine can carry 96 warheads, each of which is 10 to 30 times more powerful than the weapons that were considered in the South Asia study," updated by Mills et al. above. "That means that each of these submarines can cause this nuclear famine scenario many times over." Ira Helfand (2013) "The Humanitarian Consequences of Nuclear War," *Arms Control Today*, November, pp. 22-26.

[261] One US Strategic Command document from the mid-1990s explains: "Fear is not the possession of the rational mind alone. Deterrence is thus a form of bargaining which exploits a capability for inflicting damage at such a level as to truly cause hurt far greater than military defeat ... [D]eterrence must create fear in the mind of the adversary ... It should ultimately create the fear of extinction." Nukes are the best weapons with which to achieve fear-inducement because, unlike other WMDs, "the extreme destruction from a nuclear explosion is immediate, with few if any palliatives available to reduce its effects." STRATCOM (1995) *Essentials of Post-Cold War Deterrence*, http://www.nukestrat.com/us/stratcom/SAGessentials.PDF.

[262] Wikipedia, "Nuclear weapon," https://en.wikipedia.org/wiki/Nuclear_weapon.

[263] Wikipedia, "Nuclear strategy," https://en.wikipedia.org/wiki/Nuclear_strategy.

[264] Wikipedia, "Nuclear disarmament," https://en.wikipedia.org/wiki/Nuclear_disarmament.

[265] Wikipedia, "Nuclear explosion," https://en.wikipedia.org/wiki/Nuclear_explosion.

[266] See note 5 above.

[267] Wikipedia, "Nuclear Warfare," https://web.archive.org/web/20181209040049/https://en.wikipedia.org/wiki/Nuclear_warfare.

[268] British Admiral Sir Raymond Lygo explains: "Having a nuclear deterrent does give us the freedom to operate at lower levels of conventional military capability should we be required to do so politically." This undermines the notion of "deterrence." Likewise, future Defence Secretary, Liam Fox, asks readers to consider: "the position in which we would have been if the Argentines had possessed even a few mass-destruction weapons and we had renounced ours before the Falklands were invaded. Whether we would then have dared to re-take the Islands with our conventional forces is very much open to doubt." In other words, having nuclear weapons allowed the UK to retake the Falklands Islands, safe in the know that it could threaten the non-nuclear Argentina. Lygo and Fox writing in Ken Booth and Dr. Frank Barnaby (eds.) (2006) *The Future of Britain's Nuclear Weapons*, Oxford Research Group, https://www.nuclearinfo.org/sites/default/files/The%20future%20of%20Britain%27s%20nuclear%20weapons.pdf.

[269] For instance, in the context of Russia escalation, but not actual Russian use of nuclear weapons, the US Congressional Research Service states: "The deployment of a low-yield D-5 warhead would ... bolster deterrence by convincing Russia that the United States could respond with a proportional, limited attack." Amy F. Wolf, "A Low-Yield, Submarine-Launched Nuclear Warhead: Overview of the Expert Debate," Congressional Research Service, 21 March 2019, RL33640, https://fas.org/sgp/crs/nuke/IF11143.pdf.

[270] "Almost immediately after the Japanese surrender, teams of scientists from various American military agencies raced to Hiroshima and Nagasaki to assess the effects of the bombings ... [T]he Atomic Energy Commission agreed to provide most of the finance for the study, the U.S. National Academy of Sciences agreed to provide most of the financing for the study, the U.S. National Academy of Sciences agreed to supervise the design and operation of the research program, and Japanese National Institutes of Health became a formal participant." Philip M.

Boffey (1970) "Atomic Bomb Casualty Commission," *Science*, 168(3932): 679.

[271] For instance, Pugwash (2018) "Statement on the United States 2018 Nuclear Posture Review," https://pugwash.org/2018/02/06/statement-on-the-united-states-2018-nuclear-posture-review/.

[272] John W. Birks and S.L. Stephens (1986) "Possible Toxic Environments Following a Nuclear War" in Fred Solomon and Robert Q. Marston (eds.), *The Medical Implications of Nuclear War*, Washington, DC: National Academies Press, pp. 155-66.

[273] Editors (no date) "Nuclear winter," https://www.britannica.com/science/nuclear-winter.

[274] More recent research factors in ozone damage and UV radiation, for instance. See Mills et al. at note 1 above.

[275] Brian Martin (1982) "The global health effects of nuclear war," *Current Affairs Bulletin*, 59(7): 14-26.

[276] Brian Martin (1982) "Critique of nuclear extinction," *Journal of Peace Research*, 19(4): 287-300.

[277] Robert Johnston (1988, updated August 2003) "The effects of a global thermonuclear war," *Robert Johnston Archives*, http://www.johnstonsarchive.net/nuclear/nuclearwar1.html.

[278] Philip Handler, "Letter," (1975) *Long-term worldwide effects of multiple nuclear-weapons detonations/Committee to Study the Long-Term Worldwide Effects of Multiple Nuclear-Weapons Detonations*, National Research Council, Washington, DC: Academy of Sciences.

[279] Joshua M. Pearce and David C. Denkenberger (2018) "A National Pragmatic Safety Limit for Nuclear Weapon Quantities," *Safety*, 4(2): doi.org/10.3390/safety4020025. This madcap article claims that detonating more than 100 nukes would be "irrational." Alan Robock (2011) "Nuclear winter is a real and present danger," *Nature*, 473: 275-276. Michael J. Mills, Owen B. Toon, Richard P. Turco, Douglas E. Kinnison and Rolando R. Garcia (2008) "Massive global ozone loss predicted following regional nuclear conflict," *PNAS*, 105(14): 5307-12. Rutgers and State University of New Jersey (2006) "Regional Nuclear War Could Devastate Global Climate," *ScienceDaily*, 11 December, www.sciencedaily.com/releases/2006/12/061211090729.htm.

For opinions to the contrary, see Russell Seitz (2011) "Nuclear winter was and is debatable," *Nature*, 475: https://www.nature.com/articles/475037b. For a nuanced approach factoring in particle differentiation, Francesco S. R. Pausata, Jenny Lindvall, Annica M.L. Ekman and Gunilla Svensson (2016) "Climate effects of a hypothetical regional nuclear war: Sensitivity to emission duration and particle composition," *Earth's Future*, 4(11): 498-511.

[280] US Department of Energy (no date), "The Atomic Bombing of Hiroshima," The Manhattan Project: An Interactive History, https://www.osti.gov/opennet/manhattan-project-history/Events/1945/hiroshima.htm.

[281] John Mecklin (2017) "It is two and a half minutes to midnight 2017 Doomsday Clock Statement," *Bulletin of the Atomic Scientists*, https://thebulletin.org/sites/default/files/Final%202017%20Clock%20Statement.pdf.

[282] ICAN (2017) "Catastrophic harm," The Facts, http://www.icanw.org/the-facts/catastrophic-harm/.

[283] Nikolai N. Sokov, "Why Russia calls a limited nuclear strike 'de-escalation'," *Bulletin of the Atomic Scientists*, 13 March 2014, https://thebulletin.org/2014/03/why-russia-calls-a-limited-nuclear-strike-de-escalation/.

[284] Alan F. Philips (no date) "20 mishaps that might have started accidental nuclear war," Project of the Nuclear Age Peace Foundation, http://www.nuclearfiles.org/menu/key-issues/nuclear-weapons/issues/accidents/20-mishaps-maybe-caused-nuclear-war.htm.

[285] Jaya Tiwari and Cleve J. Gray (no date) "U.S. nuclear weapons accidents," Center for Defense Information, https://web.archive.org/web/20001118115400/http://www.cdi.org/issues/nukeaccidents/accidents.htm.

[286] Robert P. Newman (1995) *Truman and the Hiroshima Cult*, East Lansing: Michigan State University Press, pp. 65-66.

[287] Robert Higgs, "How U.S. Economic Warfare Provoked Japan's Attack on Pearl Harbor," 7 December 2012, Mises Institute, http://mises.org/library/how-us-economic-warfare-provoked-japans-attack-pearl-harbor.

[288] Mark Weber (1997) "Was Hiroshima Necessary? Why the Atomic Bombings Could Have Been Avoided," *The Journal of Historical Review*, 16(3): 4-11.

[289] Available at: http://afe.easia.columbia.edu/ps/japan/potsdam.pdf.

[290] Maj. Gen. Curtis LeMay quoted in C.V. Glines, "The bomb that ended the war," *Air Force Times*, 8 August 2018, https://www.airforcetimes.com/news/your-air-force/2018/08/09/the-bomb-that-ended-the-war/.

[291] Quoted in Jonathan Glover (1991) *Humanity: A Moral History of the 20th Century*, London: Pimlico.

[292] Memorandum Discussed with the President, 25 April 1945, https://nsarchive2.gwu.edu/nukevault/ebb525-The-Atomic-Bomb-and-the-End-of-World-War-II/documents/006b.pdf.

[293] Harry S. Truman (1955) *Year of Decisions: Volume One*, New York: Signet Books, pp. 457-458, 104.

[294] Col. Phillip S. Meilinger (Ret.), "How LeMay Transformed Strategic Air Command," *Air and Space Power Journal*, March-April, 2014, pp. 77-86.

[295] Frank Dikötter (2011) *Mao's Great Famine: The History of China's Most Devastating Catastrophe, 1958-62*, London: Bloomsbury, p. 13.

[296] Keir A. Lieber and Daryl G. Press (2013) "The New Era of Nuclear Weapons, Deterrence, and Conflict," *Strategic Studies Quarterly*, 7(1): 41n3.

[297] Forrest E. Morgan (2010) *Deterrence and First-Strike Stability in Space: A Preliminary Assessment*, Santa Monica: RAND Corporation, p. 9.

[298] Wikipedia, "Climate change," https://web.archive.org/web/20181230123406/https://en.wikipedia.org/wiki/Climate_change.

[299] Jim Giles, "Internet encyclopaedias go head to head," *Nature*, 438: 900-01.

[300] Ibid.

[301] Lawrence Solomon, "Wikipropaganda On Global Warming," CBS News, https://www.cbsnews.com/news/wikipropaganda-on-global-warming/.

[302] Wikipedia (no date), "Wikipedia:Arbitration/Requests/Case/Cold fusion 2,"

https://en.wikipedia.org/wiki/Wikipedia:Arbitration/Requests/Case/Cold_fusion_2.

[303] Quoted by Tea Party, "Donald Trump Scoffs at 'Climate Change': 'It's Called Weather',"
1 September 2014, https://www.teaparty.org/donald-trump-scoffs-climate-change-called-weather-53577/.

[304] Donald Trump, "Remarks by President Trump in Briefing on Hurricane Michael,"
White House, 15 October 2018,
https://www.whitehouse.gov/briefings-statements/remarks-president-trump-briefing-hurricane-michael/.

[305] Tim Ball (no date), "The Sun Can Cause Climate Change," Friends of Science,
https://friendsofscience.org/assets/documents/The%20Sun%20Can%20Cause%20Climate%20Change.pdf.

[306] Richard Lindzen, "Global warming and irrelevance of science," Global Warmning Policy Foundation, Essayv4, p. 10, https://www.thegwpf.org/content/uploads/2016/04/Lindzen.pdf.

[307] Jane Hsiung (1985) "Estimates of Global Oceanic Meridional Heat Transport," *Journal of Physical Oceanography*, 15: 1405-13.

[308] Geoffrey K. Vallis and Riccardo Farneti (2009) "Meridional energy transport in the coupled atmosphere–ocean system: scaling and numerical experiments," *Quarterly Journal of the Royal MeteorologicalSociety*, 135: 1643-1660.

[309] National Research Council (2010) *Advancing the Science of Climate Change*, Washington, DC: The National Academies Press, p. 1.

[310] J.R. Petit et al. (1999) "Climate and atmospheric history of the past 420,000 years from the Vostok ice core, Antarctica," *Nature*, 399: 429-436.

[311] T. Tesi et al. (2016) "Massive remobilization of permafrost carbon during post-glacial warming," *Nature Communications*, 7(13653): https://www.nature.com/articles/ncomms13653.

[312] Robert M. DeConto, Simone Galeotti, Mark Pagani, David Tracy, Kevin Schaefer, Tingjun Zhang, David Pollard and David J. Beerling (2012) "Past extreme warming events linked to massive carbon release from thawing permafrost," *Nature*, 484: 87-91.

[313] IPCC (2007) "Climate Change 2007: Working Group I: The Physical Science Basis" in IPCC Fourth Assessment Report: Climate Change 2007, https://web.archive.org/web/20100430143742/https://www.ipcc.ch/publications_and_data/ar4/wg1/en/ch9s9-1.html.

[314] UN Framework Convention on Climate Change (1994) "Article 1: Definitions," http://unfccc.int/resource/ccsites/zimbab/conven/text/art01.htm.

[315] NASA, "What's in a Name? Global Warming vs. Climate Change," 12May 2008, https://www.nasa.gov/topics/earth/features/climate_by_any_other_name.html.

[316] Mike Hulme (2017) "Climate change, concept of," in Douglas Richardson, Noel Castree, Michael F. Goodchild, Audrey Kobayashi, Weidong Liu and Richard A. Marston (eds.) *The International Encyclopedia of Geography*, London: John Wiley & Sons.

[317] NHTSA (2018) *Draft Environmental Impact Statement*, Docket No. Docket No. NHTSA-2017-0069, https://www.nhtsa.gov/sites/nhtsa.dot.gov/files/documents/ld_cafe_my2021-26_deis_0.pdf.

[318] Juliet Eilperin, Brady Dennis and Chris Mooney, "Trump administration sees a 7-degree rise in global temperatures by 2100," *Washington Post*, 28 September 2018, https://www.washingtonpost.com/national/health-science/trump-administration-sees-a-7-degree-rise-in-global-temperatures-by-2100/2018/09/27/b9c6fada-bb45-11e8-bdc0-90f81cc58c5d_story.html?noredirect=on&utm_term=.5cb916af62e9.

[319] Susan Solomon, Gian-Kasper Plattner, Reto Knutti and Pierre Friedlingstein (2009) "Irreversible climate change due to carbon dioxide emissions," *PNAS* 106(6): 1704-1709.

[320] Australian Academy of Sciences (2015) *The Science of Climate Change: Questions and Answers*, https://www.science.org.au/learning/general-audience/science-booklets-0/science-climate-change/3-are-human-activities-causing.

[321] Wikipedia (2003) "Climate Change,"
https://web.archive.org/web/20031229012430/https://en.wikipedia.org/wiki/Climate_change.

[322] Editorial Board, "What the Paris Climate Meeting Must Do," *New York Times*, 28 November 2015,
https://www.nytimes.com/2015/11/29/opinion/sunday/what-the-paris-climate-meeting-must-do.html.

[323] Benjamin I Cook, Jason E Smerdon, Richard Seager and Sloan Coats (2014) "Global Warming and Drought in the 21st Century," *Climate Dynamics*, 43(9-10): DOI: 10.1007/s00382-014-2075-y.

[324] Andrew Beardy and Mikhail V. Chester (2017) "Climate change vulnerability in the food, energy, and water nexus: concerns for agricultural production in Arizona and its urban export supply," *Environmental Research Letters*, 12: 035004.

[325] Chaoqing Yu (2018) "Assessing the Impacts of Extreme Agricultural Droughts in China Under Climate and Socioeconomic Changes," *Earth's Future*, 6: 689-703.

[326] UNFCCC (no date) *Climate Change and Freshwater Resources*, UN: Nairobi, p. 13,
https://unfccc.int/resource/docs/publications/11_nwp_clim_freshwater_en.pdf.

[327] FAO (2018) "Water stress and human migration: a global, georeferenced review of empirical research," Land and Water Discussion Paper 11,
http://www.fao.org/3/I8867EN/i8867en.pdf.

[328] Climate Council (no date) "Intense Rainfall and Flooding: The Influence of Climate Change,"
https://www.climatecouncil.org.au/uploads/5dafe61d7b3f68d156abd97603d67075.pdf.

[329] Svetlana Jevrejeva, Luke P. Jackson, Riccardo E. M. Riva, Aslak Grinsted and John C. Moore (2016) "Coastal sea level rise with warming above 2 °C," *PNAS*, 113(47): 13342-47.

[330] Sarah Opitz Stapleton, Rebecca Nadin, Charlene Watson and Jan Kellett (2017) *Climate change, migration and displacement*, London: ODI and UNDP,
https://www.odi.org/sites/odi.org.uk/files/resource-documents/11874.pdf.

[331] European Environment Agency, "Climate change and water — Warmer oceans, flooding and droughts," 30 August 2018, https://www.eea.europa.eu/signals/signals-2018-content-list/articles/climate-change-and-water-2014.

[332] Exxon Research and Engineering Company (1982) "Summary," *CO2 Greenhouse Effect: A Technical Review*, Coordination and Planning Division, EC-11-5/A2, https://insideclimatenews.org/sites/default/files/documents/1982%20Exxon%20Primer%20on%20CO2%20Greenhouse%20Effect.pdf.

[333] Quoted in Lesly Curwen, "Science climate conflict warms up," BBC, 26 April 2007, http://news.bbc.co.uk/1/hi/business/6595369.stm. Exxon Secrets (2004) "Factsheet: Richard Lindzen," https://web.archive.org/web/20041013201729/http://www.exxonsecrets.org/html/personfactsheet.php?id=17.

[334] CACC (no date), "The funders of climate disinformation," https://www.campaigncc.org/climate_change/sceptics/funders.

[335] The US National Defense Strategy (NDS) states that terrorism has been relegated below interstate cooperation as a national security threat to the US. That said, it also notes that terrorists "continue to pursue WMD, while the spread of nuclear weapon technology and advanced manufacturing technology remains a persistent problem". Department of Defense (2018) The National Defense Strategy: Summary, https://dod.defense.gov/Portals/1/Documents/pubs/2018-National-Defense-Strategy-Summary.pdf. Likewise, the British Ministry of Defence writes: "The likelihood of violent extremist organisations acquiring and using a nuclear weapon remains low but plausible, particularly for groups with sufficient funds to suborn those with legitimate access to technology. All known instances of planned or actual theft of nuclear radiological material have been facilitated by insider who stated their motivation was financial gain." Ministry of Defence (2018 (6th ed.)) *Global Strategic Trends: The Future Starts Today*, p. 138, https://assets.publishing.service.gov.uk/government/uploads/system/uploads/attachment_data/file/771309/Global_Strategic_Trends_-_The_Future_Starts_Today.pdf. An article in a major arms control journal notes: "Even as nuclear terrorism remains a

credible and urgent threat, the challenge of securing global supplies of nuclear material and nuclear facilities is growing. This stems from the projected growth globally of nuclear power plants in response to increasing needs for energy and the desire of a number of states to generate that energy without producing the pollution and carbon emissions associated with fossil fuel plants." Kenneth C. Brill and John H. Bernhard, "Preventing Nuclear Terrorism: Next Steps in Building a Better Nuclear Security Regime," Arms Control Today, October 2017, p. 7, https://www.armscontrol.org/system/files/ACT%20October17%20Digital%20Reduced%20%281%29.pdf.

[336] Wikipedia (no date) "History," https://en.wikipedia.org/wiki/Al-Qaeda#History.

[337] Wikipedia (no date), "Alleged CIA involvement," https://en.wikipedia.org/wiki/Al-Qaeda#Alleged_CIA_involvement.

[338] Wikipedia (no date) "Al-Qaeda," https://en.wikipedia.org/wiki/Al-Qaeda.

[339] US District Court, Southern District of NY, *USA v. Usama bin Laden* et al., S(7)98 Cr. 1023, 6 February 2001, http://cryptome.org/usa-v-ubl-02.htm.

[340] Jason Burke (2003) Al-Qaeda, London: Penguin.

[341] Peter L. Bergen (2006) *The Osama bin Laden I Know: An Oral History of al Qaeda's Leader*, NY: Free Press, pp. 77-80.

[342] BBC, "Al-Qaeda's origins and links," 20 July 2004, http://news.bbc.co.uk/1/hi/world/middle_east/1670089.stm.

[343] History Commons (no date) "Context of '1986-1992: CIA and British Recruit and Train Militants Worldwide to Help Fight Afghan War'," https://web.archive.org/web/20130818210324/http://www.cooperativeresearch.org/context.jsp?item=a86operationcyclone.

[344] History Commons (no date) "About this site," https://web.archive.org/web/20130825093010/http://www.cooperativeresearch.org/aboutsite.jsp.

[345] "Telegram from the Embassy in Afghanistan to the Department of State" (1978), Kabul, April 10, 1025Z. Reproduced in David Zierler and Adam M. Howard (eds.) (no date) *Foreign Relations of the United States, 1977–1980,*

Volume XII: Afghanistan, US Department of State, Office of the Historian, Washington, DC: Government Printing Office, p. 15, https://static.history.state.gov/frus/frus1977-80v12/pdf/frus1977-80v12.pdf.

[346] "Intelligence Memorandum Prepared in the Central Intelligence Agency" (1978), RPM–78–10208 Washington, May 5. Reproduced in Zierler and Howard, op. cit., p. 26.

[347] "Telegram from the Embassy in Afghanistan to the Department of State" (1979), Kabul, September 18, 1149Z. Reproduced in ibid, p. 184.

[348] Wikipedia (no date), "Soviet-Afghan War," https://en.wikipedia.org/wiki/Soviet%E2%80%93Afghan_War.

[349] Alexander Cockburn and Jeffrey St. Clair, "How Jimmy Carter and I Started the Mujahideen," *CounterPunch*, 15 January, https://www.counterpunch.org/1998/01/15/how-jimmy-carter-and-i-started-the-mujahideen/.

[350] John K. Cooley (2002) *Unholy Wars*, London: Pluto Press.

[351] See T.J. Coles (2018) *Manufacturing Terrorism*, West Sussex: Clairview Books, p. 45.

[352] Cockburn and St. Clair, op. cit.

[353] Wikipedia (no date), "Gulbuddin Hekmatyar," https://en.wikipedia.org/wiki/Gulbuddin_Hekmatyar.

[354] Global Security, "

[355] Afzal Khan, "The War on Terror and the Politics of Violence in Pakistan," *Jamestown Terrorism Monitor*, 7 February 2004, https://web.archive.org/web/20061208102951/http://www.jamestown.org/news_details.php?news_id=54.

[356] Paul Klebnikov, "Who Is Osama Bin Laden?," *Forbes*, 14 September 2001, https://www.forbes.com/2001/09/14/0914whoisobl.html#61c867264d27.

[357] Burke, op. cit.

[358] Steve Coll (2004) *Ghost Wars*, London: Penguin.

[359] Robin Cook, "The struggle against terrorism cannot be won by military means," *Guardian*, 7 July 2005, https://www.theguardian.com/uk/2005/jul/08/july7.development.

[360] John Rollins (2011) *Al Qaeda and Affiliates: Historical Perspective, Global Presence, and Implications for U.S. Policy*, Congressional Research Service, R41070, Washington, DC: Government Printing Office, pp. 5-6, https://fas.org/sgp/crs/terror/R41070.pdf.

[361] Sean N. Kalic, "Combating a Modern Hydra Al Qaeda and the Global War on Terrorism," Global War on Terrorism Occasional Paper 8, Fort Leavenworth, Kansas: Combat Studies Institute Press, pp. 20, 22.

[362] National Security Council (2004) *The Rise of UBL and Al-Qaida and the Intelligence Community Response* (Draft), https://www.documentcloud.org/documents/368992-2004-03-19-dci-report-the-rise-of-ubl-and-al.html.

[363] Quoted in Coles, op. cit.

[364] The poster was published in June 1999 and even after 9/11 stated: "Usama Bin Laden is wanted in connection with the August 7, 1998, bombings of the United States Embassies in Dar es Salaam, Tanzania, and Nairobi, Kenya. These attacks killed over 200 people. In addition, Bin Laden is a suspect in other terrorist attacks throughout the world." FBI (1999, revised 2001) "FBI Ten Most Wanted Fugitive: Usama Bin Laden," https://nsarchive2.gwu.edu/NSAEBB/NSAEBB410/docs/UBLDocument2.pdf.

[365] Ibid:

[366] Wikipedia (2018) "Sanctions against Iraq," https://web.archive.org/web/20181229032946/https://en.wikipedia.org/wiki/Sanctions_against_Iraq.

[367] R.E. Cheeseman (1923) "A History of Steamboat Navigation on the Upper Tigris" *The Geographical Journal* 61(1): 27-34.

[368] Declassified documents quoted in Mark Curtis (2004) *Unpeople* London: Vintage, p. 127.

[369] CIA (1950) *The Importance of Iranian and Middle East Oil to Western Europe* https://www.cia.gov/library/readingroom/docs/CIA-RDP79R01012A000300070011-8.pdf.

[370] CIA (1984) *International Oil Supplies: Availability of Capacity and Oil Stocks to Offset a Disruption* GI 84-10129

https://www.cia.gov/library/readingroom/docs/CIA-RDP85S00315R000100090003-0.pdf.

[371] CIA (1987) *Iraq's Tikritis: Power Base of Saddam Husayn* NESA 87-10006
https://www.cia.gov/library/readingroom/docs/CIA-RDP88T00096R000400540002-8.pdf.

[372] Seymour M. Hersh (1992) "U.S. Secretly Gave Aid to Iraq Early in Its War Against Iran" *New York Times* 26 January
https://www.nytimes.com/1992/01/26/world/us-secretly-gave-aid-to-iraq-early-in-its-war-against-iran.html.

[373] Shane Harris and Matthew M. Aid (2013) "The U.S. knew Hussein was launching some of the worst chemical attacks in history -- and still gave him a hand" *Foreign Policy* 26 August
https://foreignpolicy.com/2013/08/26/exclusive-cia-files-prove-america-helped-saddam-as-he-gassed-iran/.

[374] Mark Phythian (1997) *Arming Iraq: How the U.S. and Britain Secretly Built Saddam's War Machine* Northeastern University Press.

[375] CIA (1975) *Past and Present Problems of Iraq's Boundaries with Kuwait and Saudi Arabia* CIA/OGCR/RP 75-28
https://www.cia.gov/library/readingroom/docs/CIA-RDP86T00608R000600140013-8.pdf.

[376] Nigel Ashton (1998) "Britain and the Kuwaiti crisis, 1961" *Diplomacy and Statecraft* 9(1): 163-81.

[377] Quoted in Richard N. Haass (2009) *War of Necessity, War of Choice: A Memoir of Two Iraq Wars* London: Simon and Schuster.

[378] Michael R. Gordon (1992) "Pentagon Objected to Bush's Message to Iraq" *New York Times* 25 October
https://www.nytimes.com/1992/10/25/world/pentagon-objected-to-bush-s-message-to-iraq.html.

[379] Commander David M. Armitage (1998) *Economic Sanctions on Iraq: Going Nowhere Fast* 17013-5050 PA: US Army War College, Carlisle Barracks.

[380] Robert E. Morabito (1991) *Maritime Interdiction: The Evolution of a Strategy*, Naval War College, AD-A236 449, Newport: NWC,
https://apps.dtic.mil/dtic/tr/fulltext/u2/a236449.pdf.

[381] Quoted in Human Rights Watch (1992) *World Report 1992: Events of 1991*, NY and Washington, DC: HRW, pp. 707-08.

[382] George H.W. Bush "Statement on the Anniversary of Operation Desert Story," 16 January 1992 in Public Papers of the Presidents of the United States: George Bush 1992-93: January 1 to July 31, 1992, Washington, DC: Government Printing Office, p. 116.

[383] Quoted in Armitage, op. cit.

[384] A full and devastating list appears in Geoff Simons (1998) *The Scourging of Iraq: Sanctions, Law and Natural Justice*, London: Palgrave Macmillan.

[385] John Mueller and Karl Mueller (1999) "Sanctions of Mass Destruction," *Foreign Affairs*, 78(3): 43.

[386] Ahmed Shehabaldin and William M. Laughlin (1998) "Economic sanctions against Iraq: Human and economic costs," *The International Journal of Human Rights*, 3(4): 1-18.

[387] Ibid.

[388] Abbas Alnasrawi (2001) "Iraq: economic sanctions and consequences, 1990–2000," *Third World Quarterly*, 22(2): 205-218.

[389] Shehabaldin and Laughlin, op. cit.

[390] Alnasrawi, op. cit.

[391] Will D. Swearingen (1988) "Geopolitical Origins of the Iran-Iraq War," *Geographical Review*, 78(4): 405-16.

[392] On the effects of Saddam's reliance on privatization and military spending, see Jochen Hippler (1991) "Iraq's Military Power: The German Connection," *Middle East Report*, 168: 27-31. On the UK's role, see Mark Phythian (1997) *Arming Iraq: How the US and Britain Secretly Built Saddam's War Machine*, Boston: Northeastern University Press.

[393] Consider: "... sanctions are believed to have been very effective in limiting Iraq's ability to rebuild conventional forces that were essentially cut by 50% as a result of the Gulf War." Col. William J. Bender (2002) "Strategic Implications for U.S. Policy in Iraq: What Now?," Strategy Research Project, Pennsylvania: US Army War College, p. 12,

https://www.bits.de/public/documents/iraq/reports-docs/Bender.pdf.

[394] Quoted in *The New York Times*, "After the War," 23 March 1991, https://www.nytimes.com/1991/03/23/world/after-war-excerpts-un-report-need-for-humanitarian-assistance-iraq.html.

[395] Ibid.

[396] Shehabaldin and Laughlin, op. cit.

[397] Alnaswari, op. cit.

[398] Shehabaldin and Laughlin, op. cit.

[399] Ibid.

[400] Alnaswari, op. cit.

[401] Shehabaldin and Laughlin, op. cit.

[402] Alnaswari, op. cit.

[403] Shehabaldin and Laughlin, op. cit.

[404] Alnaswari, op. cit.

[405] The source is, however, more denialism. The sections not quoted by Wikipedia include outright lies, that Saddam Hussein "prevented humanitarian organizations to conduct their own fieldwork to verify the claims." Michael Rubin (2001) "Sanctions on Iraq: A Valid Anti-American Grievance?," *Middle East Review of International Affairs Journal*, 5(4), https://www.washingtoninstitute.org/policy-analysis/view/sanctions-on-iraq-a-valid-anti-american-grievance.

[406] Michael Spagat (2010) "Truth and death in Iraq under sanctions," *Significance: The Royal Statistical Society*, September, pp. 116-20.

[407] Farrokh Habibzadeh (2018) "Economic sanction: a weapon of mass destruction," *The Lancet*, 392(10150): 816-17.

[408] Tim Dyson and Valeria Cetorelli (2017) "Changing views on child mortality and economic sanctions in Iraq: a history of lies, damned lies and statistics," *BMJ Global Health*, 2(2): e000311.

[409] Harvard Study Team (1991) "The Effect of the Gulf Crisis on the Children of Iraq," *New England Journal of Medicine*, 325: 977-80.

[410] Alberto Ascherio et al. (1992) "Effect of the Gulf War on Infant and Child Mortality in Iraq," *New England Journal of Medicine*, 327: 931-36.

[411] Sarah Zaidi and Mary C. Smith Fawzi (1995) "Letters to the Editor: Health of Baghdad's Children," *The Lancet*, 346: 1485.

[412] Claudia Court (1995) "Iraq sanctions lead to half a million child deaths," *BMJ*, 311: 1523.

[413] Mary C. Smith Fawzi and Sarah Zaidi (1996) "Letter's Sanctions against Iraq: Author's reply (sic)," *The Lancet*, 347: 198.

[414] Omar A. Obeid and Abdul-Hussein Al-Hadi (1996) "Sanctions against Iraq," *Lancet*, 347(8995): 198–9.

[415] Sarah Zaidi (1997) "Child mortality in Iraq," *The Lancet*, 350(9084): 1105.

[416] UNICEF (1999) "Iraq surveys show 'humanitarian emergency'," https://www.unicef.org/newsline/99pr29.htm

[417] M.M. Ali and I.H. Shah (2000) "Sanctions and childhood mortality in Iraq," *The Lancet*, 355(9218): 1851-57.

[418] UN (2007) "World population prospects: The 2006 Revision," https://web.archive.org/web/20080615205838/http://www.un.or g/esa/population/publications/wpp2006/English.pdf.

[419] Felicity Barringer (2003) "After the war: Population puzzle," *New York Times*, 8 August, https://www.nytimes.com/2003/08/08/world/after-the-war-population-puzzle-fewer-iraqi-men-dead-or-undercounted.html.

[420] Ibid.

[421] Working Group (2005) "The impact of the oil-for-food programme on the Iraqi people," Independent Inquiry Committee, p. 133, https://reliefweb.int/sites/reliefweb.int/files/resources/E6E4556C C93A3747492570AC001D4705-iic-irq-7sep.pdf.

[422] Ministry of Planning and Development Cooperation (2004) Living Conditions Survey, Volume II: Analytical Report, p. 50, https://web.archive.org/web/20050520014940/http://www.iq.und p.org/ILCS/PDF/Analytical%20Report%20-%20English.pdf.

[423] Dyson and Cetorelli, op. cit.

[424] For example, the RAND Corporation talks about the "centrality of the Israeli-Palestinian conflict" in broader Middle

Eastern politics, which recently started "receding" due to the rise of Daesh. The Costs-of-Conflict Studies Team (2015) *The Costs of the Israeli-Palestinian Conflict: Executive Summary*, Santa Monica: RAND Corporation, p. 36, https://www.rand.org/content/dam/rand/pubs/research_reports/R R700/RR740z1-1/RAND_RR740z1-1.pdf.

A report by Chatham House in the UK, to give another example, states: "If Arab leaders see regional stability as being in their countries' interests, they should be trying to shape any eventual peace plan advanced by the administration of US President Donald Trump in such a way that it forms a framework for negotiations that both Israeli and Palestinian leaderships can accept." Yossi Mekelberg and Greg Shapland (2019) "Israeli–Palestinian Peacemaking: The Role of the Arab States," Chatham House, Briefing Paper, January, front matter, https://www.chathamhouse.org/sites/default/files/publications/re search/2019-01-24-MekelbergShapland.pdf.

[425] A partly-declassified National Intelligence Estimate (NIE) report from 2006 states: "Greater pluralism and more responsive political systems in Muslim majority nations would alleviate some of the grievances jihadists exploit." It goes on to note that "Jihadists point to the US military presence in Iraq and Afghanistan, policies vis-à-vis Israel and the Palestinians, and perceptions that the US-led war on terror is a campaign against Islam." It adds that: "Jihadists are re-branding terrorism as justified resistance by exploiting in their propaganda emotions of revenge, anger, fear, and humiliation with images, of Muslims under attack, particularly in the Palestinian territories and Iraq." NIE (2006*) Trends in Global Terrorism: Implications for the United States*, NIE 2006-02R, https://www.dni.gov/files/documents/FOIA/DF-2016-00118%20(Knapp)%20Final%20Response.pdf.

Another, infamous report, from the Defense Science Board of the Pentagon states: "U.S. policies on Israeli-Palestinian issues and Iraq in 2003-2004 have damaged America's credibility and power to persuade." It goes on to note that "Muslims do not 'hate our freedom,' but rather, they hate our policies. The overwhelming majority voice their objections to what they see as one-sided support in favor of Israel and against Palestinian rights, and the longstanding, even increasing support for what Muslims collectively see as tyrannies, most notably Egypt, Saudi Arabia, Jordan, Pakistan, and the Gulf states." William Schneider (2004) *Report of the Defense Science Board Task Force on Strategic Communication*, Office of the Under Secretary of Defense For Acquisition, Technology, and Logistics, Washington, DC: Government Printing Office, pp. 18, 40, https://fas.org/irp/agency/dod/dsb/commun.pdf.

[426] Reuters reports that US "aid" to Egypt was suspended, allegedly because of its human rights violations and, more realistically, its ties to North Korea. Between 1948 and 2011, the US government has invested $71.6bn in its military interests in Egypt, second only to US government investment in Israel. Bruce Clingan, "Commentary: The U.S. is right to restore aid to Egypt," Reuters, 30 July 2018, https://www.reuters.com/article/us-clingan-egypt-commentary/commentary-the-u-s-is-right-to-restore-aid-to-egypt-idUSKBN1KK1YE.

[427] Khaled Elgindy, "Egypt, Israel, Palestine," Brookings Institution, 25 August 2012, https://www.brookings.edu/articles/egypt-israel-palestine/.

[428] Regional media report that Palestinian activists have been arrested for supporting Hamas, for example. Qods News Agency, "Saudi activist charged for supporting Palestinian resistance," 10 September 2018, http://qodsna.com/en/317507/Saudi-activist-charged-for-supporting-Palestinian-resistance.

[429] For example, the United Nations' special Rapporteur on the Situation of Human Rights in the Palestine Territories Occupied Since 1967 states: "The Special Rapporteur recommends that the Government of Israel comply with international law and bring a complete end to its 50 years of occupation of the Palestinian territories occupied since 1967." Special Rapporteur (2018) "Report of the Special Rapporteur on the situation of human rights in the Palestinian territories occupied since 1967," Human Rights Council, 37th Session, General Assembly of the United Nations, A/HRC/37/75, 14 June, https://documents-dds-ny.un.org/doc/UNDOC/GEN/G18/183/28/PDF/G1818328.pdf?OpenElement.

[430] For example, in 2013 61% of US Jews (including religious and regardless of party affiliation) said that a two-state solution was viable. Interestingly, 38% said that Israeli should make a "sincere" effort, compared to 12% who said the Palestinians should make a "sincere" effort. Pew (2013) "Connection with and attitudes toward Israel," *Religion and Public Life*, https://www.pewforum.org/2013/10/01/chapter-5-connection-with-and-attitudes-towards-israel/.

[431] A plurality of Israelis and Palestinians (43%) support a two-state solution, according to a survey: notwithstanding Israeli media euphoria, that support for a two-state solution is at its lowest in 20 years. "Still, fewer people on both sides support three possible alternatives to a two-state solution: one state with equal rights, one state without rights, and expulsion or 'transfer,'" the report says. Policy and Survey Research and Tami Steinmetz Center for Peace Research (2018) "Palestinian-Israeli Pulse: A Joint Poll," 13 August, https://www.pcpsr.org/sites/default/files/Summary_%20English_Joint%20PAL-ISR%20Poll%205_Jun2018.pdf.

[432] In late-2018, a General Assembly draft resolution on The Palestine Question (73/19) was brought to the house. It calls on states to recognize inalienable Palestinian rights and accept UN Resolution 242 (among others). It notes "that it has been over 70 years since the adoption of its resolution 181 (II) of 29 November 1947 and 51 years since the occupation of Palestinian territory, including East Jerusalem, in 1967, and that a just, lasting and comprehensive solution to the question of Palestine has yet to be achieved." General Assembly, "Resolution adopted by the General Assembly on 30 November 2018," 73rd session, 5 December 2018, A/RES/73/19, https://www.un.org/unispal/document/peaceful-settlement-of-the-question-of-palestine-ga-resolution-ares7319/.

The draft resolution was adopted by 156 votes to 8, with 12 abstentions. The eight that voted against it were: "Australia, Canada, Israel, Kiribati, Marshall Islands, Micronesia (Federated States of), Nauru, [and the] United States of America." General Assembly, Agenda Item 39, 43rd plenary meeting, 30 November 2018, A/73/PV.43, https://www.un.org/unispal/document/ga-

73rd-session-43rd-plenary-meeting-question-of-palestine-verbatim-record/.

This voting record, sometimes with only the US and Israel voting against it, has been US policy at the UN General Assembly since 1989, following the Palestinian government's acceptance of the provisions of UN Security Council Resolution 242.

[433] In 2004, the International Court of Justice issued an advisory opinion on the construction of Israel's wall in and around Palestinian territory. It references the Green Line as a *de facto* boundary delineating Israel and Palestine: "the commencement and continuation of construction by Israel, the occupying Power, of a wall in the Occupied Palestinian Territory, including in and around East Jerusalem, ... is in departure from the Armistice Line of 1949 (Green Line) and which has involved the confiscation and destruction of Palestinian land and resources." ICJ (2004) *Legal Consequences of the construction of a Wall in the Occupied Palestinian Territory*, Advisory Opinion, 9 July, https://www.icj-cij.org/files/case-related/131/131-20040709-ADV-01-00-EN.pdf, p. 8.

[434] Wikipedia (no date) "Israeli-Palestinian conflict," https://web.archive.org/web/20181219134511/https://en.wikipedia.org/wiki/Israeli%E2%80%93Palestinian_conflict.

[435] BBC (no date) "A History of Conflict," http://news.bbc.co.uk/1/shared/spl/hi/middle_east/03/v3_ip_timeline/html/history.stm.

[436] BBC (no date) "UN partition of Palestine," http://news.bbc.co.uk/1/shared/spl/hi/middle_east/03/v3_ip_timeline/html/1947.stm.

[437] Lorena S. Neal (1995) "The Roots of the Israeli-Palestinian Conflict: 1882-1914," *Honors Projects*, Paper 27, http://digitalcommons.iwu.edu/history_honproj/27.

[438] Salim Munayer and Lisa Loden (2014) *Through My Enemy's Eyes: Envisioning Reconciliation in Israel-Palestine*, Milton Keynes: Paternoster Books.

[439] Virginia Page Fortna (2004) *Peace Time: Cease-fire Agreements and the Durability of Peace*, NJ: Princeton University Press, p. 144.

[440] Avner Falk (2004) *Fratricide in the Holy Land: A Psychoanalytic View of the Arab-Israeli Conflict*, Madison: Wisconsin University Press, pp. 8, 76.

[441] Amnon Cohen (1982) *Political parties in the West Bank under the Jordanian regime, 1949-1967*, NY: Cornell University Press.

[442] On Britain, see Noel Joseph Guckian (1985) *British Relations with Trans-Jordan, 1920-1930* (doctoral thesis), Department of International Politics, Aberystwyth University. See also Nigel J. Ashton, "A 'Special Relationship' sometimes in spite of ourselves: Britain and Jordan, 1957–73," *The Journal of Imperial and Commonwealth History*, 33(2): 221-44.

[443] Foreign Affairs and International Trade Canada (no date) "Canadian Policy on Key Issues in the Israeli-Palestinian Conflict," http://web.archive.org/web/20110811030300/http://www.interna tional.gc.ca/name-anmo/peace_process-processus_paix/canadian_policy-politique_canadienne.aspx?lang=eng&view=d.

[444] World Bank Technical Team (2007) "Movement and access restrictions in the West Bank: Uncertainty and Inefficiency in the Palestinian Economy," 9 May, http://siteresources.worldbank.org/INTWESTBANKGAZA/Res ources/WestBankrestrictions9Mayfinal.pdf.

[445] Edward Wright, "Tourism Curbed in Palestinians Areas," *Los Angeles Times*, 28 May 2000, https://web.archive.org/web/20140715165856/http://articles.lati mes.com/2000/may/28/travel/tr-34813.

[446] The Likud Party: Original Party Platform (1977), which has been modified but not withdrawn, says: "…between the Sea and the Jordan there will only be Israeli sovereignty ... A plan which relinquishes parts of western Eretz Israel, undermines our right to the country, unavoidably leads to the establishment of a 'Palestinian State,' jeopardizes the security of the Jewish population, endangers the existence of the State of Israel, and frustrates any prospect of peace." Available at https://www.jewishvirtuallibrary.org/original-party-platform-of-the-likud-party.

[447] The original Hamas Charter states: "Israel will exist and will continue to exist until Islam will obliterate it, just as it obliterated others before it." The Charter of Allah: The Platform of the Islamic Resistance Movement (Hamas). It should be noted that the translation is by Raphael Israeli at the Harry Truman Institute, Hebrew University, Jerusalem. Available at https://fas.org/irp/world/para/docs/880818.htm.

[448] Ephraim Yaar, "Just Another Forgotten Peace Summit," *Haaretz*, 11 December 2007, https://www.haaretz.com/1.4964833.

[449] Lev Luis Grinberg (2010) *Politics and Violence in Israel/Palestine: Democracy Verses Military Rule*, London: Routledge, p. 214.

[450] On support for Cast Lead (2008-09) in Israel, see Hassan Abdul Halim, "War on Gaza, fuel for the Israeli elections," *Menassat*, 21 January 2009, https://web.archive.org/web/20090125023715/http://www.mena ssat.com/?q=en/news-articles/5820-war-gaza-fuel-israeli-elections. On Protective Edge (2014), see 92% of Israeli Jews (as opposed to Israeli Arabs) thought Protective Edge was justified, including 67% of left-wing Israeli Jews. Forty-eight percent thought that the operation didn't go far enough. Mirren Gidda, "Poll: 92% of Israeli Jews Say Operation Protection Edge Was Justified," *TIME*, August 2014, https://web.archive.org/web/20140819210054/http://time.com/3 144232/israeli-jews-poll-gaza-protective-edge/.

[451] On 30 March 2018, the imprisoned people of Gaza began a sustained demonstration. By late-April, Amnesty International was reporting that: "The Israeli military has killed 35 Palestinians and injured more than 5,500 others – some with what appear to be deliberately inflicted life-changing injuries – during the weekly Friday protests." Amnesty International, "Israel: Arms embargo needed as military unlawfully kills and maims Gaza protesters," 27 April 2018, https://www.amnesty.org/en/latest/news/2018/04/israel-arms-embargo-needed-as-military-unlawfully-kills-and-maims-gaza-protesters/. See also B'Tselem (2018) *If the heart be not callous: On the unlawful shooting of unarmed demonstrators in Gaza*, https://www.btselem.org/sites/default/files/publications/201804_

if_the_heart_be_not_callous_eng.pdf. For deliberate targeting of civilians in the West Bank and Gaza by snipers, dating back years, see Derek Summerfield (2004) "Palestine: the assault on health and other war crimes," *BMJ*, 329: doi: https://doi.org/10.1136/bmj.329.7471.924.

[452] *YNet News* describes the phrase as "a common metaphor used in reference to stopping attacks on Israel from the Hamas-ruled strip." Roi Rubinstein, "Bennett implies IDF should 'mow the lawn' in Gaza," *YNet News*, 4 September 2018, https://www.ynetnews.com/articles/0,7340,L-5341225,00.html. See also Daniel Byman, "Mowing the Grass and Taking Out the Trash," *Foreign Policy*, 25 August 2014, https://foreignpolicy.com/2014/08/25/mowing-the-grass-and-taking-out-the-trash/. The author claims that Gaza rocketing, as opposed to ongoing Israeli occupation, started the latter's Operation Cast Lead. And see Efraim Inbar and Eitan Shamilr (2013) " 'Mowing the Grass': Israel's Strategy for Protracted Intractable Conflict," *Journal of Strategic Studies* 37(1): 1-26. The authors claim that Israel shows general "restraint" until its launches periodic massacres. The reality is that massacre is an inevitable consequence of foreign occupation.

[453] United Nations Office for the Coordination of Humanitarian Affairs (no date) "Israeli-Palestinian Fatalities Since 2000 – Key Trends," https://www.un.org/unispal/document/israeli-palestinian-fatalities-since-2000-ocha-special-focus/. The 2009 ratio can be worked out from B'Tselem's figures: "Fatalities during Operation Cast Lead," https://www.btselem.org/statistics/fatalities/during-cast-lead/by-date-of-event.

[454] Linah Alsaafin, "Palestinians see Abbas as sell out in peace talks," *Al-Monitor*, 5 March 2014, https://www.al-monitor.com/pulse/originals/2014/03/palestine-abbas-israel-peace-sham.html#ixzz5k3t9iIXF.

[455] Middle East Quartet (2016) "Report of the Middle East Quartet," https://www.un.org/News/dh/infocus/middle_east/Report-of-the-Middle-East-Quartet.pdf.

[456] Following the Palestinian government's acceptance of the provisions of UNSCR 242 in 1988, the General Assembly's annual efforts to bring a solution to the so-called conflict have been voted down by Israel and the US. GA Resolution 44/48 states that members are: "Deeply concerned at the alarming situation in the Palestinian territory occupied since 1967, including Jerusalem, as well as in the other occupied Arab territories, as a result of the continued occupation by Israel, the occupying Power, and of its persistent policies against the Palestinian people." General Assembly (1989) "Report of the Special Committee to Investigate Israeli Practices Affecting the Human Rights of the Population of the Occupied Territories," 78th plenary meeting, 8 December, A/RES/44/48, https://www.un.org/documents/ga/res/44/a44r048.htm. The US and Israel were the sole opponents. See *Year Book of the United Nations: Volume 43* (1989), Department of Public Information, NY: United Nations, https://unispal.un.org/DPA/DPR/unispal.nsf/0/DF0BB291D1E5 5CF4052565B80063E183.

[457] European Parliament (2014) "Recognition of Palestine statehood," P8_TA(2014)0103, http://www.europarl.europa.eu/cmsdata/121961/Resolution%20 of%2017%20December%202014%20(EN).pdf.

[458] European Commission (no date) "Israel," http://ec.europa.eu/trade/policy/countries-and-regions/countries/israel/index_en.htm.

[459] For example, the Saudi-proposed Arab Peace Initiative was adopted by the Arab League (whose members include Palestine) in 2005. But the US Congressional Research Service states that the Plan was "reaffirmed by the Arab League at its Doha, Qatar summit in 2009, but King Abdullah of Saudi Arabia and other Arab leaders have warned that the offer will not last indefinitely." Jim Zanotti (2010) "Israel and the Palestinians: Prospects for a Two-State Solution," Congressional Research Service, 7-5700, Washington, DC: Government Printing Office, p. 2n6, https://fas.org/sgp/crs/mideast/R40092.pdf.

[460] Jeremy M. Sharp and Christopher M. Blanchard (2006) "U.S. Foreign Aid to the Palestinians," Congressional Research

Archive, RS22370, 27 June, Washington, DC: Government Printing Office, https://web.archive.org/web/20060728003756/https://fpc.state.gov/documents/organization/68794.pdf.

[461] Eve Spangler (2015) *Understanding Israel/Palestine: Race, Nation, and Human Rights in the Conflict*, Rotterdam: Sense Publishers.

[462] Jimmy Carter, "Palestinian Elections: Trip Report by Former U.S. President Jimmy Carter," The Carter Center, 29 January 2006, https://www.cartercenter.org/news/documents/doc2287.html.

[463] B'Tselem, "50 Days: More than 500 Children: Facts and figures on fatalities in Gaza, Summer 2014," 20 July 2016, https://www.btselem.org/press_releases/20160720_fatalities_in_gaza_conflict_2014.

[464] United Nations Security Council, Resolution 242 (1967), S/RES/242 (1967), 22 November, https://unispal.un.org/DPA/DPR/unispal.nsf/0/7D35E1F729DF491C85256EE700686136.

[465] Hamas Chater (2017). Available at https://www.middleeasteye.net/news/hamas-2017-document-full.

[466] Quoted in Robert A. Pape (2006) *Dying to Win: Why Suicide Terrorists Do It*, London: Gibson Square, p. 69.

[467] Quoted in Chris McGreal, "Israel on the road to ruin, warn former Shin Bet chiefs," *Guardian*, 15 November 2003, http://www.theguardian.com/world/2003/nov/15/israel.

[468] Breaking the Silence, "Organization," no date, http://www.breakingthesilence.org.il/about/organization.

[469] *Guardian*, "Israeli intelligence veterans' letter to Netanyahu and military chiefs – in full," 12 September 2014, http://www.theguardian.com/world/2014/sep/12/israeli-intelligence-veterans-letter-netanyahu-military-chiefs.

Index